Music in Middle-earth

Music in Middle-earth

edited by
Heidi Steimel & Friedhelm Schneidewind

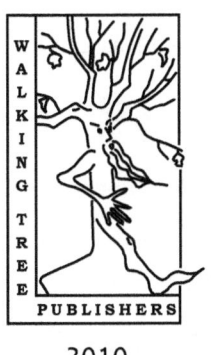

2010

Cormarë Series No. 20

Series Editors: Peter Buchs • Thomas Honegger • Andrew Moglestue • Johanna Schön

Editors responsible for this volume: Andrew Moglestue and Johanna Schön

Library of Congress Cataloging-in-Publication Data

Steimel, Heidi and Friedhelm Schneidewind:
Music in Middle-earth
ISBN 978-3-905703-14-6

Subject headings:
Tolkien, J.R.R. (John Ronald Reuel), 1892-1973 – Music
Middle-earth (Imaginary place)
Literature, Comparative

Cormarë Series No. 20

© Walking Tree Publishers, Zurich and Jena, 2010

All rights reserved. No portion of this book may be reproduced, by any process or technique, without the express written consent of the publisher

Cover illustration: "Daeron and Lúthien", Anke Eißmann 2008

Set in Adobe Garamond Pro and Shannon by Friedhelm Schneidewind
Printed by Lightning Source in the United Kingdom and United States

The book is simultaneously released in German as *Musik in Mittelerde* by "Stein und Baum Edition", an imprint of the Villa Fledermaus Publishers.

Contents

Foreword   7

Part A: Creation and Music

"Behold Your Music!": The Themes of Ilúvatar,   11
the Song of Aslan, and the Real Music of the Spheres
   Kristine Larsen

Tonality, Atonality and the *Ainulindalë*   29
   Reuven Naveh

Ainulindalë: Tolkien, St. Thomas, and the Metaphysics   53
of the Music
   Jonathan McIntosh

Part B: Music in Tolkien's World

A Speculative History of the Music of Arda   75
   Steven Linden

"Bring Out the Instruments!": Instrumental Music in   91
Middle-earth
   Heidi Steimel

The Harp in Middle-earth   107
   Norbert Maier (translated from German by Heidi Steimel)

Part C: Influences of Our World on Tolkien's Music

Music, Myth, and Literary Depth in the "Land ohne Musik"   127
   Gregory Martin

Strains of Elvish Song and Voices: Victorian Medievalism,   149
Music, and Tolkien
   Bradford Lee Eden

Sleeps a Song in Things Abounding: J.R.R. Tolkien and the German Romantic Tradition *Julian Eilmann (translated from German by Heidi Steimel)*	167
"They Began to Hum Softly": Some Soldiers' Songs of World Wars I and II and of Middle-earth Compared and Contrasted *Murray Smith*	185

Part D: Interpretations of Tolkien's Music in Our World

An Impenetrable Darkness: An Examination of the Influence of J.R.R. Tolkien on Black Metal Music *Michael Cunningham*	215
Microphones in Middle-earth: Music in the BBC Radio Play *Paul Smith*	241
Elven Music in Our Times *Mira Sommer (translated from German by Marie-Noëlle Biemer)*	255
Making Texts Audible: A Workshop Report on Setting Tolkien to Music *Fabian Geier (translated from German by Heidi Steimel)*	283

Appendix

Embodying the Voices: Documentation of a Failure *Friedhelm Schneidewind* *(translated from German by Heidi Steimel)*	303
Afterword: Greater Music Still Shall be Made	309

Foreword

Music plays an important role in Tolkien's mythology, and his stories include many songs as well as references to musicians and instruments. Though numerous melodies for his poems have been composed, sung, played and recorded, secondary literature on Middle-earth has hardly mentioned the subject of music in the past. This work would like to fill that gap and offers a number of viewpoints on various topics concerning music in Tolkien's works.

Appropriately, the book begins with the creation of Tolkien's secondary world, Arda. How it relates to our universe and to another musical creation tale, that of Narnia, is examined by physicist and astronomist Kristine Larsen, who brings her unique point of view to the topic. Reuven Naveh then considers Tolkien's narrative under the aspect of music theory, finding interesting parallels between form and content. The metaphysical side of music is the focus of Jonathan McIntosh's essay; he points out connections to St. Thomas' teachings.

The next chapters deal with the development of music in Arda. Steven Linden has set up a speculative history of its musical development, contrasting it with the history of music in our own world. The role of instruments and their usage in Middle-earth are considered in Heidi Steimel's article; which ones are played by whom and for what purpose? A harp player and builder, Norbert Maier, then concentrates on the harp as it is played by Tolkien's characters and provides ideas and illustrations of possible harps for different races of Middle-earth.

Tolkien's songs and poems were shaped by numerous factors in the literature that he knew; the next section of the book deals with comparisons of literary influences, thereby focusing on vocal music in Middle-earth. Gregory Martin points out known musical factors in Tolkien's biography and connects his wish to provide a mythology for England with that of Ralph Vaughan Williams to compose music that is English in nature. The influence of English Victorian fiction on Tolkien's style is examined by Bradford Lee Eden, who shows its relation to musical-literary symbolism by comparison with a number of other poems. Julian Eilmann provides a view of parallels between Tolkien and German Romantic literature, exploring the music that is so important to the works of both. An unusual comparison rounds up this subject, that of soldiers' songs during the world wars which Tolkien experienced and the songs sung by characters in his works, written by Murray Smith.

Finally there are several articles which examine today's interpretations of Tolkien's lyrics. The least expected connection is that to heavy metal music. Michael Cunningham shares insights obtained in part by personal contacts with Black Metal musicians who feel an affinity for the dark side of Middle-earth. The BBC radio plays of *The Lord of the Rings* are the subject of Paul Smith's paper; as a musician and speaker, he has participated in live performances of the play and can compare its score to other specifically English music. Another score, that of the movies, written by Howard Shore, is the focus of Mira Sommer's essay; she concentrates on Elvish songs as interpreted in the films. The final chapter is a report of Fabian Geier's personal experiences in setting Tolkien's poems to music; he explains the thoughts that motivated his project.

The Appendix gives an account of Friedhelm Schneidewind's failed attempt to write a chapter for this book, which however still manages to contribute valuable information despite that failure. The second section provides additional information for those wishing to pursue the topic of music in Middle-earth in more detail.

We hope that readers of this book will enjoy the diversity of its articles, contributed by authors of several different nationalities. We have endeavoured to retain the individual styles in translating and editing to reflect the richness of their various viewpoints.

The book is simultaneously released in German as *Musik in Mittelerde* by "Stein und Baum Edition", a branch of the Villa Fledermaus Publishers. Those who wish to read the chapters initially written in German in their original language may do so there.

Heidi Steimel and Friedhelm Schneidewind

Part A

Creation and Music

Kristine Larsen

"Behold Your Music!": The Themes of Ilúvatar, the Song of Aslan, and the Real Music of the Spheres

In his 1993 popular-level book, *The Music of the Spheres: Music, Science, and the Natural Order of the Universe*, Jamie James reminds us that "every scholar of the history of science or of music can attest to the intimate connection between the two. In the classical view it was not really a connection but an identity" (James 10). For example, Aristotle wrote in his *Metaphysics* how the Pythagoreans ascribed numerical values to the musical scales, which could then be related to the universe at large, especially the motions of the planets. This "music of the spheres" was considered a natural outgrowth of the posited harmony and perfection of the heavens, and reportedly could not be heard by any but the especially gifted (allegedly including Pythagoras himself). This was just as well, according to Philo of Alexandria, as "like the song of the Sirens, it would induce frenzied longings" (Chadwick 79). Plato's *Republic* (Book X) contained within the myth of Er the idea that each of the seven classical planets (Sun, Moon, Mercury, Venus, Mars, Jupiter, and Saturn) emits a unique note, which combines with that of the fixed stars to create a heavenly melody. Aristotle himself believed the idea to be "beautiful and poetical but absurd, since a principal feature of the heavenly bodies is their silence." (ibid.)

Several centuries later, Boethius, the early medieval philosopher, described three discrete types of music: that of the universe, human music, and music created by instruments. He believed that the first

> is especially to be studied in the combining of the elements and the variety of the seasons which are observed in the heavens. How indeed could the swift mechanism of the sky move silently in its course? And although this sound does not reach our ears [...]. the extremely rapid motion of such great bodies could not be altogether without sound, especially since the courses of the stars are joined together by such mutual adaptation that nothing more equally compacted or united could be imagined. (Strunk 84)

In the early 17th century, Johannes Kepler gave the idea serious consideration (one might say obsessively so), in his *Harmonices Mundi* (Harmony of the

Worlds). He discovered that the ratio of certain properties of planetary and lunar motions were approximately the same numerical value as that between the notes in chords. For example, he calculated the ratio of the extreme values of the "hourly motions in arc" (apparent angular distance traveled in the sky per hour) of the moon at its closest and farthest approach to earth to be nearly 3:4, or a musical fourth (Field 148). On the basis of the observational relationships he found, he constructed musical scales composed of notes representing each of the planets. Interestingly, in order to do so, he had to ignore the octave of the notes (for example, lowering the "sound" of Mercury at its farthest orbital point from the sun by six octaves in order to fit it into the scale) (Field 150).

However, the connection between music and the universe is far older and more widespread than classical Western Culture, dating back to ancient creation myths from across the world. In many such myths, the earth and/or entire universe comes into being through the utterance of sacred words or songs of power. For example, according to the Netsilik of Greenland, in the beginning "words were the most powerful things [...]. It was the hare who created day by saying, 'Day'" (Leeming and Leeming 209). In the Mayan *Popol Vuh*, it is said of the two creator gods that "whatever they thought and whatever they said came into being. They thought the emptiness of the void should become something and it did. 'Let there be earth', they said, and there was earth" (Leeming and Leeming 186). According to the Hopi, Spider Woman and Tawa possessed the "Sacred Thought" which "became the first song" and was utilized to create and breathe life into all creatures (Leeming and Leeming 124). In the Judeo-Christian tradition, the *Book of Genesis* describes how God said, "Let there be light, and there was light."

Despite the universality and poetic qualities of the music of the spheres, the concept became little more than a historical footnote in the minds of scientists for nearly four centuries. It was only in literature and the arts that the idea remained. For example, Gustav Holst created his famous The Planets Suite (1914-16) based on his personal meditation "on the nature of the planets ('my' planets as he called them, in other words his [astrological] chart)" and through that process discovered "new worlds of sound" (Head 17). Likewise, the music of the spheres and its creative powers found prominence in the subcreations of writers like J.R.R. Tolkien and C.S. Lewis, Middle-earth and Narnia, respectively.

Although he is sometimes portrayed as being "antiscience," Tolkien clearly embraced the scientific mode of thinking, instead rejecting the corruption of science into technology. For example, in a letter to Michael Straight, Tolkien explained that

> The Elves represent, as it were, the artistic, aesthetic, and purely scientific aspects of the Humane nature raised to a higher level than is actually seen in Men. That is: they have a devoted love of the physical world, and a desire to observe and understand it for its own sake and as 'other' – sc. as a reality derived from God in the same degree as themselves – not as a material for use or as a power-platform. (Carpenter 236)

Likewise, in several letters Tom Bombadil is said to embody this pure nature of science as a wish to understand the natural world rather than to apply that knowledge to practical uses (Carpenter 179, 192). Tolkien approached his own academic career as a self-described "scientific philologist," and his main interest in the topic was, as he noted, "largely scientific" (Carpenter 345). As a child, his interests were varied, and included "history, astronomy, botany, grammar, and etymology" (Flieger and Anderson 56). All these were to later play a vital role in making Middle-earth such a lush playground for the casual reader and the academic alike. Chief among the sciences, astronomy played a pivotal role in the fleshing out of Middle-earth. Quiñonez and Raggett report that Priscilla Tolkien affirmed that her father "had a general interest in astronomy" and that "Tolkien had enough interest in and knowledge of astronomy to use it convincingly and to lend believability to his stories" (Quiñonez and Raggett 5). Tolkien himself noted in a letter to Naomi Mitchinson concerning the transition of a "flat earth" to a "round earth" after the great changing of the world that "so deep was the impression made by 'astronomy' on me that I do not think I could deal with or imaginatively conceive a flat world, though a world of static Earth with a Sun going round it seems easy (to fancy if not to reason)" (Carpenter 197). In recent decades, several authors[1] have summarized the remarkable breadth of astronomical allusions contained in Tolkien's work.

---

1 E.g. Larsen, "Rose-Stained"; Larsen, "Borgil"; Larsen, "Burning Briar"; Manning; Quiñonez and Raggett.

As Eden argues, the medieval concept of the music of the spheres would have been a natural part of Tolkien's education, as it was a historical perspective on the geocentric (earth-centered) cosmology noted above (Eden 183). This is reflected in Tolkien's grand creation myth, the *Ainulindalë* (Music of the Ainur). Despite the infamous tinkering and revisions which prevented Tolkien from completing his *legendarium* in an internally consistent and self-satisfactory form, the concept of the Music of the Ainur endures largely intact over the decades of his writings. In its published form in *The Silmarillion*, we read that Ilúvatar, the Creator, charged the Ainur, the offspring of his thought, with a great theme of music, which they then sang as a heavenly symphony and chorus and filled the Void. The perfection of this initial theme was marred by the self-serving thoughts of Melkor, the Satanic character, who interwove discord into the harmony. Unfazed, Ilúvatar began a second theme, which was again ruined by the discord of Melkor. Finally, Ilúvatar began, without the accompaniment of the Ainur, a third theme,

> At first soft and sweet, a mere rippling of gentle sounds in delicate melodies; but it could not be quenched, and it took to itself power and profundity. And it seemed at last that there were two musics progressing at one time before the seat of Ilúvatar, and they were utterly at variance…. Ilúvatar arose a third time… he raised up both his hands, and in one chord, deeper than the Abyss, higher than the Firmament, piercing as the light of the eye of Ilúvatar, the Music ceased. (S 16-17)

Ilúvatar then proclaimed "those things that ye have sung, I will show them forth, that ye may see what ye have done…" With this preamble, like the creator gods of the *Popol Vuh*, Ilúvatar proclaimed "Behold your Music!" and afterwards "showed to them a vision, giving to them sight where before was only hearing; and they saw a new World made visible before them" (*S* 17). At the wonder and beauty of the vision, the Ainur wished for it to become manifest, and Ilúvatar granted their wish, in an obviously Biblical scene: "Therefore I say: *Eä!* Let these things Be! And I will send forth into the Void the Flame Imperishable, and it shall be at the heart of the World, and the World shall Be; and those of you that will may go down into it" (*S* 20). With that charge, some of the Ainur went into the world and became known as the Valar, and became bound to both the world and its fate. Melkor followed suit, and hence evil is interwoven into the universe and our world from the beginning, and therefore the creatures of Middle-earth inhabit an imperfect world, Arda Marred. However, since the Children of Ilúvatar (Humans and Elves) were part of the third theme, which the Ainur had no direct part in, much of what is to befall them – including their ultimate fate – is unknown, both to the Valar and Melkor.

As noted by numerous scholars, C.S. Lewis likewise demonstrated his profound knowledge of and respect for medieval cosmology in his own writings, including the concepts of astrology and the music of the spheres.[2] In *Planet Narnia*, Michael Ward argues that medieval concepts of the universe, such as the music of the spheres, permeates the *Chronicles of Narnia* and forms a basic framework for interpreting the series. A key example is found in the creation myth of Narnia, a central portion of *The Magician's Nephew*. Here, Digory, Polly, and their companions witness the creation of a new world from emptiness and darkness through the song of power sung by Aslan the lion. With its first theme, Aslan's wordless song created the stars, who joined in Aslan's song "in harmony with it, but far higher up the scale: cold, tingly, silvery voices" (Lewis, *Narnia* 61). A change in Aslan's song, "the mightiest and most glorious sound it had yet produced," brought about the first sunrise (ibid. 62). The music changed again, becoming "softer and more lilting than the song by which he had called up the stars and the sun; a gentle rippling music" (ibid. 64). This heralded the creation of grass, trees, and other vegetation. A final theme brought about the birth of creatures, which burst forth from the ground, rivers, and trees. If we take literally the comment that the stars and sun were called up by one song, this leads us to a count of three themes, mirroring the three themes of Ilúvatar in *The Silmarillion*. Upon the completion of Aslan's great song, the stars – sentient beings, some of whom become characters in the Narnia Chronicles – commenced singing again, "a pure, cold, difficult music," before Aslan awakens the beings of Narnia with words of power: "Narnia, Narnia, Narnia, awake. Love. Think. Speak." (ibid. 70) Scholars have drawn obvious connections between Aslan's Song and the Music of the Ainur,[3] but in an interesting twist to Tolkien's creation myth, Jadis the evil Witch, and Uncle Andrew, who had fallen under her spell, loathed the song of Aslan, but unlike Melkor were powerless to affect or stop it. Jadis "would have smashed

---

2 E.g. Duriez; Ward; Zambreno.
3 E.g. Duriez; Ford; Pearce.

that whole world, or all worlds, to pieces, if it would only stop the singing," but when she finally threw an iron bar at Aslan, it merely bounced off of him and the song continued unabated (ibid. 62, 66).

This idea of the stars as sentient beings is a medieval one, as Lewis explained in *The Discarded Image*. There he elaborates on the concept that the motions of the heavenly bodies are governed by "Intelligences" who are moved "by 'intellectual love' of God" (Lewis, *Discarded Image* 115). Lewis noted in a speech entitled "Imagination and Thought in the Middle Ages" that the music of the spheres "is the only sound which has never for one split second ceased in any part of the universe; with this positive we have no negative to contest [...]. The music which is too familiar to be heard enfolds us day and night and in all ages" (Ward 21).

While the concept of a heavenly music which bathes the universe is at the same time curious and comforting, does it have any connection to the primary creation, the universe we truly inhabit? Interestingly, it does. Sound is created by the propagation of pressure waves through a medium. Since the word "sound" is usually thought of in connection with the sense of hearing, a more generic term is acoustic wave, which encompasses frequencies both too high and too low for the human ear to register.

A modern convenience commonly misunderstood by the general public is the radio. Sound waves are converted into an electromagnetic signal (light waves), travel through the air as light to an antenna where they are received, and are converted back into sound waves via an electromagnetic circuit (which explains why you cannot directly hear a radio station's broadcast with your ears alone). However, for several decades astronomers and science writers have capitalized on this common misconception in order to help the general public understand astronomical objects that emit light waves in radio frequencies. For example, rapidly rotating neutron stars emit characteristic beams of radio light at their poles, creating a phenomenon known as a pulsar. The exceedingly regular ticks of radio signals have been likened to "a bongo player in the sky" (Boyle and Grimes 40). Pulsar radio signals have also been converted into audible signals of the same frequency as pedagogical aids.[4] Researchers searching for evidence of extraterrestrial intelligence (so-called SETI surveys) have largely focused on "listening" for artificially generated radio waves, as depicted in the movie *Contact*. Interestingly, in that film, the character of Kent Clark, the blind radio astronomer, was based on real-life SETI radio astronomer Kent Cullers, who has been blind since infancy (Stephans). Cullers approaches his research as an attempt to "ride those waves, extend my senses into a realm they've never been, hear songs from a cloud of gas" (Richards 63).

Closer to home, a number of atmospheric phenomenon are created when charged particles such as electrons interact with the Earth's magnetic field and generate radio waves, which scientists can translate into audible sounds using radio technology. These include lightning, meteors, and aurora. In fact, these can be "heard" through their affect on AM or shortwave radio signals (as crackles, whistles, or a general hum). (ibid.)

As the trailers for the film *Alien* correctly warned, "in space, no one can hear you scream." In general, interstellar space is currently so close to a perfect vacuum that sound waves cannot propagate through it. However, in astronomical locations where the gas density is high enough, acoustic waves can and do occur. For example, sound waves can travel through the atmospheres of Venus, Mars, and Saturn's moon Titan. Stars, as hot spheres of dense gas, are also laboratories for the detection of acoustic waves. In 1962 it was discovered that the visible surface of the sun is bubbling with a period of about five minutes. This "five minute oscillation" was found to be a global rather than local phenomenon caused by sound waves traveling through the sun (Demarque and Guenther 5356). This "solar symphony" is commonly likened to a vibrating gong, pipe-organ, or bell in popular-level articles, as the sun is now known to have millions of different overtones. Helioseismologists have monitored these oscillations for a number of years, most notably using the ground-based Global Oscillation Network Group (GONG) and sun-orbiting SOHO spacecraft (Solar and Heliospheric Observatory), allowing astronomers to map the sun's interior. Similar observations have been made of a number of stars, including Alpha Centauri, Procyon, Xi Hydrae, and Beta Hydri. The action of black

---

4 E.g. Jodrell Banks Observatory.

holes interacting with their environment has also been associated with sound. For example, NASA's Chandra x-ray satellite has detected evidence of acoustic waves in the extremely hot, gaseous regions surrounding super-massive black holes in distant galaxies.[5]

Perhaps the most important celestial "song" is that leftover from the early universe, a prediction of the Big Bang model, which posits the universe as having been created from a small, dense state. Unknown to most people is the fact that the earliest version of this theory was published by Belgian priest and cosmologist Georges Lemaître in the late 1920s. The current model, which owes its genesis to George Gamow and his collaborators in the late 1940s, has as one of its core predictions that there should be an energy in the form of electromagnetic radiation pervading the universe, a relic energy of the first few 100,000 years of the universe's history. Over the intervening 13.7 billion years, this energy has cooled from the temperature of the surface of the sun down to 3 degrees above absolute zero, and is faintly visible as microwaves. In fact, when one tunes their tv to a channel which is all static, a few percent of that static is primordial photons from this cosmic microwave background.

In Britain, the Big Bang model was challenged for a time by a rival theory called the Steady State model. Developed by physicists Fred Hoyle, Hermann Bondi, and Thomas Gold, the Steady State posited an eternal, unchanging universe, thereby requiring neither a primary creation nor creator. However, in order to explain how the universe could remain unchanging despite the observed expansion independently discovered by Lemaître and the American Edwin Hubble in the 1920s, Hoyle developed a theory of a slow spontaneous creation of matter in the form of protons which would keep the density of the universe constant over time. Despite the lack of experimental observation of this creation (and its apparent violation of fundamental conservation laws of physics), Hoyle remained a staunch and vocal supporter of the Steady State until his death in 2001. During the 1950s and 1960s, the debate between proponents of the two models was very public and occasionally bitter, the flames fueled by the intrusion of religion into the scientific sphere. Most notably, in a 1951 address to the Pontifical Academy of Science, Pope Pius XII proclaimed that

---

5 E.g. Fabian et al.

the Big Bang model "has succeeded in bearing witness to that primordial 'Fiat lux' uttered at the moment when, along with matter, there burst forth from nothing a sea of light and radiation" (Pope Pius XII).

To his credit. Lemaître clearly separated his science from his religion and explained at the XIth Solvay Conference in Physics "As far as I can see, such a theory remains entirely outside any metaphysical or religious question… when Pascal tries to infer the existence of God from the supposed infinitude of Nature, we may think that he is looking in the wrong direction" (Kragh 60). However, it appears that Tolkien may have agreed with Pope Pius XII in his interpretation of the Big Bang cosmology, explaining in a 1969 letter that although believers in the Christian God do not worship the universe itself, "devoted study of it may be one of the ways of honouring Him" (Carpenter 400). A possible echo of this sentiment may also be found in Tolkien's epilogue of his famed speech and essay "On Fairy-Stories" where he related how

> It is not difficult to imagine the peculiar excitement and joy that one would feel, if any specially beautiful fairy-story were found to be 'primarily' true, its narrative to be history, without thereby necessarily losing the mythical or allegorical significance that it had possessed.... The Christian joy, the Gloria, is of the same kind; but it is pre-eminently… high and joyous. (Flieger and Anderson 78)

Confirmed atheist Fred Hoyle used his popular BBC radio program and the resulting book as a platform to criticize both Gamow's theory (which he dubbed a "Big Bang" as a form of insult) (e.g. Hoyle 102) and religion in general,[6] while at the same time offering his model of an eternal, unchanging universe as a more scientifically palatable alternative. Hoyle compared the Big Bang to "'the outlook of primitive peoples' who postulate the existence of gods to explain the physical world" (Kragh 253). As one might expect, fellow Brit and astronomy aficionado (Wood 247, 311). C. S. Lewis took issue with many of Hoyle's ideas, some of which he addressed in the essays "Will We Lose God in Outer Space" (1958) and "The Seeing Eye" (1963). In a May 15, 1952 letter to Genia Goelz, he dismissed Hoyle as follows: "He is not a great philosopher (and none of my scientific colleagues think much of him as a scientist) but he

---

6 E.g., "It seems to me that religion is but a blind attempt to find an escape from the truly dreadful situation in which we find ourselves," Hoyle, p. 115.

is strong enough to do some harm" (Ward 312; Lewis, *Letters* 241). Likewise, shortly after Hoyle's original 1950 radio broadcasts, the BBC aired a rebuttal by Dorothy L. Sayers, a woman with strong connections to the Inklings (*Sayers*; Frederick and McBride 20).

When Gamow's predicted "echo" was accidentally discovered by engineers Arno Penzias and Robert Wilson in 1965, the Steady State model was relegated to simply becoming a curious chapter in the history of cosmology (except in the mind of Fred Hoyle and a handful of colleagues). In the intervening decades, improvements and refinements to the original Big Bang model have successfully aligned it with all major observations of the early universe, including its overall chemical composition, age, and the evolution of structures such as galaxies. While the Big Bang theory makes unequivocal predictions for the early state of the universe, it is more ambivalent about its ultimate fate. Depending on the balance between the self-gravitation of all matter and energy of the universe and the initial energy of expansion associated with the universe's creation, the universe may well expand forever (although with a decreasing rate), only to die in utter icy-cold darkness after all possible generations of stars die out – the often-cited "heat death" of the universe – or recollapse in a fiery cataclysm dubbed the Big Crunch, itself perhaps the initial stage in a rebirth analogous to the legendary phoenix.

A violent end of the world is posited in many mythologies, such as the Ragnarok, "Doom of the Gods", in Norse tradition. The Gods are doomed to lose a final battle against an army of monsters, but from this battle a new world, or *Gimle*, will be born, and ruled by Balder and other children of the old Gods. Just as the ultimate fate of the world was pondered in ancient creation myths and modern cosmological theories, so too do we find the end of all things within the subcreations of Middle-earth and Narnia. Like the Norse gods, Tolkien's Valar are bound to the world, and presumably have an end in its end (although perhaps not a true death, as in the case of the Norse gods). Tolkien himself even acknowledged the parallels which might be drawn between Ragnarok and the Last Battle between Morgoth and the Valar briefly mentioned in various places throughout the published form of *The Silmarillion* (Carpenter 148-9). Several versions of this Great End appear in the early incarnations of his *legendarium*,[7] taking its most complete form in the Second Prophecy of Mandos in the "Quenta Silmarillion" (circa 1937). Here it is said that "When the world is old, and the Powers grow weary," Morgoth will once again reenter the world and destroy the sun and moon. However, he will suffer a final defeat at the hands of Eärendel, Tulkas, Fionwë, and Túrin Turambar, and afterwards the Earth will "be broken and re-made, and the Silmarils shall be recovered out of Air and Earth and Sea…." Aided by the Silmarils, Yavanna will revive the Two Trees, and in their light "the Gods will grow young again, and the Elves awake and all their dead arise, and the purpose of Ilúvatar be fulfilled concerning them" (*LR* 333).

A detailed description of the end of the world was largely expunged from Tolkien's revisions of *The Silmarillion* proper by the 1950s, except for the occasional offhanded references to the Last Battle and the tantalizing philosophical discussions later published in *Morgoth's Ring*, such as the *Athrabeth Finrod ah Andreth*. In the published version of the *Ainulindalë*, we find a reference to a future Music of the Ainur (sometimes called the Second Music in other writings[8]) in which the Ainur, humans, and elves will take part and the "themes of Ilúvatar shall be played aright" (*S* 15). In this way the initial marring of the world by Melkor will be corrected. What is unclear (and Tolkien himself seemed to debate both internally and in his later writings) are the details of this Arda Remade, a new stage of creation beyond the finite lifespan of this world. For example, was this to be considered as an afterlife, or as some new physical existence in another "dimension"?[9] In these later writings Tolkien was also vague about the ultimate fate of the Eä, the entire universe, as opposed to the presumed catastrophic fate of Arda (which he identified with our solar system). What is plainly said (in Tolkien's notes to the Athrabeth) is that the Elves "held that the physical universe, Eä, had a beginning and would have an end: that it was limited and finite in all dimensions" (*MR* 338). Finrod echoes this sentiment in the Athrabeth itself, when he explains

> None of us know, though the Valar may know, the future of Arda, or how long it is ordained to endure. But it will not endure for ever. It was made by

---

7 E.g. Tolkien, *The Book of Lost Tales, Part Two*, p. 281-82; Tolkien, *The Shaping of Middle-earth*, p. 40f.
8 E.g. Tolkien, *The Book of Lost Tales, Part One*, p. 59-60.
9 E.g. Tolkien, *Morgoth's Ring*, p. 405; Carpenter, p. 325.

Eru, but He is not in it. The One only has no limits. Arda, and Eä itself, must therefore be bounded. (*MR* 311-12)

This again suggests that if asked his opinions about the Big Bang vs Steady State debate, Tolkien would not surprisingly fall completely on the side of the Big Bang, and more specifically the recollapsing or so-called "closed" model. This is possibly bolstered by a line in the same commentary that the Elves did not think that "Arda ... would just run down into lifeless inanition" (*MR* 339), although this could also refer to the death of the sun only and not the universe at large.

The deaths of two worlds, considered to be parallel universes in a sense, are also described in *The Chronicles of Narnia*. In both the world of Charn and Narnia, the end is heralded by their suns' evolution into a swollen red giant. In *The Magician's Nephew* we read of Charn that "Low down and near the horizon hung a great, red sun, far bigger than our sun. Digory felt at once that it was also older than ours: a sun near the end of its life, weary of looking down upon that world" (Lewis, *Narnia* 40). Lewis's descriptions are scientifically reasonable, and ironically are consistent with descriptions of the sun's eventual death described by Fred Hoyle in his radio addresses and popular-level articles and books. In fact, Hoyle played a pivotal role in the first detailed theoretical explorations of stellar death and red giants. In the case of Narnia, the imminent death of the world was heralded by a horn blast from the giant formerly known as Father Time, which called the stars home from the sky in the form of meteors. This closely parallels aspects of Ragnarok, in which the beginning of the battle would be heralded by Heimdell blowing a terrible blast on the trumpet Giallar-horn, and the stars subsequently falling from the sky (Guerber 14). At the final end of Narnia, the giant crushes the red giant sun into darkness with his hand, an interesting metaphor for the collapse of a red giant into the corpse of a white dwarf, neutron star, or black hole. Aslan and his companions leave the dead world through a doorway and enter a paradise world, a parallel world which becomes an afterlife for the children (as we learn that they were killed in a train accident in our own world).

Returning to our own universe, what can we learn about its fate through the cosmic microwave background (CMB)? This background energy is not perfectly smooth, but has been found to contain miniscule variations in temperature (a few parts per 100,000 from one location to another) which provide vital clues as to the conditions in the early universe, during the first million years of its history. For during that period, the universe was a hot, dense sea of plasma, and acoustic waves – sound – travelled between places of slightly higher and lower density, planting the seeds for structures we see today, including galaxies. Detailed observations by the COBE and WMAP satellites of these temperature fluctuations – the fingerprints of these one-time sound waves now forever frozen in time – have provided confirmation of the age of the universe (13.8 billion years) as well as provided clues about the ultimate fate of the universe. Like the creation songs of Middle-earth and Narnia, the "music" of the Big Bang has three themes, each corresponding to one of the three major components of the universe: radiation or light, matter (including unseen dark matter) and a mysterious force which is currently accelerating the expansion of our universe, termed dark energy. Each of these components ruled a separate epoch in the history of our universe in turn, with the radiation-dominated phase consisting of the first few 100,000 years, and the transition from the matter-dominated phase to dark energy-dominated phase having occurred a few billion years ago. This transition is reflected in the surprising acceleration in the expansion rate of the universe discovered in the late 1990s. All three components have left their mark on the cosmic microwave background, in the form of those temperature fluctuations and other details, and recent observations of the CMB by the WMAP satellite and other experiments have allowed scientists to hone their understanding about the early universe as well as its possible mode of demise.

Since the variations in the cosmic microwave background were generated by acoustic waves, it was not surprising when Mark Whittle of the University of Virginia electronically represented these important variations in the cosmic microwave background in audible sound, covering the first million years of the cosmos in ten seconds (Whittle, "Big Bang Acoustics"). In contrast to the popular misconception fostered by the term "Big Bang", Whittle's work dramatically demonstrated that the universe began in silence, because there were no initial acoustic waves (due to the fact that the expansion of the infant universe was the same in all directions). However, inherent inhomogeneities in the density of matter and energy are predicted by cosmological models. These eventually gave rise to acoustic waves of increasing wavelength (or deeper tone) once enough time had elapsed for pressure waves to complete an oscillation. An overall drop in pitch was also caused by the expansion of the universe, which stretched the wavelengths. The largest pressure variations correspond to approximately 110 dB, commensurate with the volume of the average rock concert. In order to make the acoustic waves "hearable" by the human ear, he had to shift them upward approximately fifty octaves. He described the results as "a descending scream, building into a deep rasping roar, and ending in a deafening hiss" (Whittle, "Primordial").

Turning our attention specifically to the end of our "primary" universe, we are faced with less certainty than the citizens of Middle-earth or Narnia. The ultimate fate of the universe appears to be inextricably linked with the basic properties of the mysterious dark energy, which makes up approximately 70% of the total mass and energy of the universe. Currently there are several competing theoretical models for dark energy, and WMAP and other observations cannot rule any of them out at this time. In the most widely accepted models, the universe will continue to expand forever, perhaps accelerating so rapidly as to eventually rip apart all matter, and even the very fabric of space and time, in the sensational yet psychologically disturbing "Big Rip" scenario (Frieman et al.). Therefore, with all apologies to Tolkien and Lewis, unless the universe rips itself to shreds, it will indeed run down in a rather unpoetic heat death as it expands forever unbounded.

Science historian Helge Kragh reflects that

> For most of its history, cosmology has been part of mankind's religious rather than scientific world view. With the progression of astronomy and the advent of cosmological models based on the laws of physics, the association between cosmology and religion has loosened, but it never disappeared. It probably never will. (Kragh 251)

In the cosmological works of Tolkien and Lewis we also see the twin threads of theology and science intertwined. Like Music of the Ainur and the song of Aslan, our universe owes much of its early history to the force of acoustic waves, also containing three movements or themes. Just as Narnia and Middle-earth were ultimately marred by the dark hand of evil, so too is the fate of our universe bound up in the unseen force of dark energy. Therefore, like Tolkien's Elves, astronomers appear to have "a Shadow before them" (*MR* 331). But our world will not live to witness the eventual victory of dark energy trillions of years from now, as our earth will be swallowed up by our sun when it becomes a red giant in approximately 6 billion years. There is, perhaps, little comfort in that knowledge. Aslan sagely warned that all worlds end. But before then, we should take the advice of C.S. Lewis, his (sub)creator, and walk beneath the stars, and picture ourselves amidst a universe "lighted, warmed, and resonant with music" (Lewis, *Discarded Image* 112).

About the Author

Kristine Larsen is Professor of Physics and Astronomy at Central Connecticut State University. The author of two popular-level books, *Stephen Hawking: A Biography*, and *Cosmology 101*, she draws upon her passion for both astronomy and Tolkien's world for her interdisciplinary teaching and research projects, including papers in Tolkien Studies, Mallorn, Amon Hen, and several book chapters.

Tolkien References

TOLKIEN, J.R.R., *The Book of Lost Tales, Part I*, (ed. by Christopher Tolkien), Boston: Houghton Mifflin, 1984.

The Book of Lost Tales, Part II, (ed. by Christopher Tolkien), Boston: Houghton Mifflin, 1984.

The Letters of J.R.R. Tolkien, (ed. by Humphrey Carpenter with the assistance of Christopher Tolkien), Boston: Houghton Mifflin, 2000.

The Lost Road and Other Writings, (ed. by Christopher Tolkien), Boston: Houghton Mifflin, 1987.

Morgoth's Ring, (ed. by Christopher Tolkien), Boston: Houghton Mifflin, 1993.

The Shaping of Middle-earth, (ed. by Christopher Tolkien), Boston: Houghton Mifflin, 1986.

The Silmarillion, (ed. by Christopher Tolkien), 2nd ed., Boston: Houghton Mifflin, 2001.

References

Boyle, Alison and Ken Grimes, "The Music of the Spheres", In: *Astronomy* (December 2005), 36-41.

Chadwick, Henry, *Boethius*, Oxford: Clarendon Press, 1981.

Demarque, P. and D.B. Guenther, "Helioseismology: Probing the Interior of a Star", In: *PNAS* 96 (1999), 5356-59.

Duriez, Colin, *A Field Guide to Narnia*, Downers Grove, IL: Intervarsity Press, 2004.

Eden, Bradford Lee, "The 'Music of the Spheres': Relationships Between Tolkien's *Silmarillion* and Medieval Cosmological and Religious Theory", In: Jane Chance (ed.), *Tolkien the Medievalist*, London and New York: Routledge, 2003, 183-93.

Fabian, A.C., J.S. Sanders, G.B. Taylor et al., "A Very Deep Chandra Observation of the Perseus Cluster: Shocks, Ripples, and Conduction", In: *MNRAS* 366 (2006), 417-28.

Flieger, Verlyn and Douglas Anderson (eds.), *Tolkien on Fairy-Stories*, London: HarperCollins, 2002.

Fredrick, Candice and Sam McBride, *Women Among the Inklings: Gender, C.S. Lewis, J.R.R. Tolkien, and Charles Williams*, Westport, CT: Greenwood Press, 2001.

Frieman, Joshua A., Michael S. Turner, and Dragan Huteret, "Dark Energy and the Accelerating Universe", In: *Annual Reviews of Astronomy and Astrophysics* 46 (2008), 385-432.

Guerber, H.A., *Myths of the Norsemen*, New York: Dover Publications, 1992.

Head, Raymond, "Holst – Astrology and Modernism in 'The Planets'", In: *Tempo* 187 (1993), 15-22.

Hoyle, Fred, *The Nature of the Universe*, Oxford: Basil Blackwell, 1950.

James, Jamie, *The Music of the Spheres*, New York: Grove Press, 1993.

Jodrell Banks Observatory, *The Sounds of Pulsars*, 2001, 28 Mar. 2009. <http://www.jb.man.ac.uk/~pulsar/Education/Sounds/sounds.html>

Kragh, Helge, *Cosmology and Controversy*, Princeton: Princeton University Press, 1996.

Larsen, Kristine, "A Definitive Identification of Tolkien's 'Borgil': An Astronomical and Literary Approach", In: *Tolkien Studies* 2 (2005), 161-70.

"'Rose-Stained in the Sunset': Elwing and Her Possible Planetary Counterpart", In: *Amon Hen* 209 (2008), 17-20.

"Tolkien's 'Burning Briar' – An Astronomical Explanation", In: *Mallorn* 43 (2005), 49-52.

LEEMING, David and Margaret Leeming, *A Dictionary of Creation Myths*, Oxford: Oxford University Press, 1994.

LEWIS, C.S., *The Chronicles of Narnia*, New York: HarperCollins, 2001.

The Discarded Image, Cambridge: Cambridge University Press, 1964.

LEWIS, W.H. (ed.), *Letters of C.S. Lewis*, New York: Harcourt, Brace, and World, Inc., 1966.

MANNING, Jim, "Elvish Star Lore", In: *Planetarian* (December 2003), 14-22.

PEARCE, Joseph, "Narnia and Middle-earth: When Two Worlds Collide", In: Shanna Caughley (ed.), *Revisiting Narnia,* Dallas: Benbella Books, 2005, 113-27.

POPE PIUS XII, Address to the Pontifical Academy of Sciences, 22 Nov. 1951, 28 Mar. 2009. <http://ewtn.com/library/PAPALDOC/P12EXIST.HTM>

QUIÑONEZ, Jorge and Ned Raggett, "Nólë I Meneldilo: Lore of the Astronomer", In: *Vinyar Tengwar* 12 (1990), 5-15.

RICHARDS, Diane, "Listening to Northern Lights", In: *Astronomy* (December 2001), 63.

SAYERS, Dorothy L., "The Theologian and the Scientist", In: *Listener* 44 (1950), 496-97, 500.

SPERGEL, D.N., R. Bean, O. Doré et. al., "Three-Year Wilkinson Microwave Anisotropy Probe (WMAP) Observations: Implications for Cosmology", In: *Astrophysical Journal Supplemental Series* 170 (2007), 377-408.

STEPHANS, Sally, "Listening for E.T.", In: *Astronomy* (December 2001), 58-63.

STRUNK, Oliver (ed.), *Source Readings in Music History: Antiquity and the Middle Ages*, New York: W.W. Norton and Co., 1965.

WARD, Michael, *Planet Narnia*, New York: Oxford University Press, 2008.

WHITTLE, Mark, *Big Bang Acoustics: Sounds From the Newborn Universe*, 22 Jan. 2008, 28 Mar. 2009. <http://www.astro.virginia.edu/~dmw8f/BBA_web/index_frames.html>

Primordial Sounds: Big Bang Acoustics, Press Release, AAS Meeting, 1 June 2004, 28 Mar. 2009. <http://www.astro.virginia.edu/~dmw8f/sounds/aas/press_release.pdf>

ZAMBRENO, Mary Frances, "A Reconstructed Image: Medieval Time and Space in The Chronicles of Narnia", In: Shanna Caughley (ed.), *Revisiting Narnia*, Dallas: Benbella Books, 2005, 253-66.

Reuven Naveh

Tonality, Atonality and the *Ainulindalë*

Music is prominent in literary works by many authors. E. T. A. Hoffman, who changed one of his names to Amadeus in admiration of Mozart, made a composer (Johannes Kreisler) a hero of several works. One of his stories ("Don Juan") deals with a real musical work, and musical activity is central to another ("Rat Krespel"). In Thomas Mann's works, music is especially salient in the novel *Doctor Faustus*; which combines references to real works of music and imaginary music composed by the protagonist. Music also plays a part in many of Mann's other works, either as a main theme or as a feature of crucial plot events, such as the closing scene in the story "Little Lizzy" or towards the end of the novel *Buddenbrooks*. Music also occupies a significant place in the works of many other authors, including Tolstoy, Proust, Kundera, and Murakami.

At first glance, we might find this interrelationship between music and the written word surprising. Readers cannot hear the music, so the author has to make a special effort to ensure that it is "heard" rather than read. We can propose two main reasons why authors turn to music: first, the use of music is often meant to elicit in the reader feelings that hearing the actual music would have elicited; and second, whereas the organization of prose is relatively free, music frequently adheres to very well-defined formal structures and rules, enabling the author to organize the story clearly and create analogies from the music to the narrative structure that shed light on this structure.

The aim of this paper is to understand, within this context, the use of music in one of the most important texts by Tolkien: the *Ainulindalë*, or "The Music of the Ainur." This is the first stage of Tolkien's mythology in several senses: it grew out of one of Tolkien's earliest texts (the opening chapters of *The Book of Lost Tales*); it forms the opening chapter of *The Silmarillion* as edited and published by Christopher Tolkien;[1] and, of course, it describes the creation of the world and therefore underlies the entire mythology. In addition to depicting the creation of the world, the *Ainulindalë* presents the root conflict of the mythology. The events described in it have to do with not just the creation itself, but what happens afterwards, especially in connection with the coming of the Children of Ilúvatar and the treatment of them, and with the future conflict between Melkor and the rest of the Valar.

The many implications of the *Ainulindalë* almost go without saying; most of them are obvious from the text itself. Particularly noteworthy is the religious content of the text, including the concept of one god who rules and directs the world and the basic conflict between good and evil. This paper discusses these implications by exploring the use of music. The first part of the *Ainulindalë* describes vibrant musical activity that results in the vision of Eä and reflects the relationship between Ilúvatar and the Valar. We will analyze this music with theoretical tools originating in the analysis of Western music, while trying to understand the cultural context in which Tolkien worked and wrote.

This approach views the music as a concrete manifestation of the use of theoretical knowledge pertaining to analysis of Western tonal music. By *tonality* we mean music based on a well defined scale, which has a clear, agreed-upon hierarchy of possible and impossible progressions and revolves around a single center commonly known as the *tonic*. The paper will also discuss the atonal revolution, a significant component of early twentieth-century music. In this sense, the paper complements previous analyses that have looked at aspects of the *Ainulindalë* as an expression of non-earthly music, such as the "music of the spheres" – a medieval concept of celestial music.[2]

What Kind of Music Do the Ainur Sing?

We do not and cannot know what the music sung by the Ainur sounds like. According to *The Silmarillion*, the Valar garbed themselves in bodies only when they came to Arda, and even these bodies do not represent their essence. The

---

[1] Several versions of the *Ainulindalë* were written between the first version and the one that was eventually published. This article will focus only on the first and last, each of which is important in its own way.
[2] See Eden, *The Music of the Spheres;* Flieger, *Splintered Light,* 57–59.

music of the Ainur is clearly supposed to be abstract, celestial music played in the Void and intended for Ilúvatar's ears; thus it certainly does not resemble any music known to humanity today or in any previous era.

But despite its abstract nature, the description of the music is full of much more earthly concepts and images. The first version of the text portrays the Ainur as a genuine orchestra incorporating musical instruments and choirs: "Then the harpists, and the lutanists, the flautists and pipers, the organs and the countless choirs of the Ainur began to fashion the theme of Ilúvatar into great music" (*LT* 53). In the final version (*S* 3), the wording is more cautious, but the orchestral image remains. Melkor's melody also uses very terrestrial images: "It had little harmony, but rather a clamorous unison as of many trumpets braying upon a few notes" (*S* 5).

In other places as well, the music is described using terms from Western theory: chords ("and in one chord [...] the Music ceased", *S* 5); harmony ("and a sound arose of endless interchanging melodies woven in harmony", *S* 3), discord ("and straightway discord arose about him", *S* 4),[3] and themes ("and a new theme began amid the storm, like and yet unlike the former theme", *S* 4). Unlike more general concepts such as melody, these concepts to a large extent reflect Western musical practice, especially homophony, with its harmony and chords.

But the general terminology is not the only clear association with real music; in terms of the overall organization, the music seems to have a clear form and to be divided into sections and themes in a way that closely corresponds to the organization of movements in eighteenth- and nineteenth-century classical music. The development of musical organization from being seen as a continuous process or, alternatively, as a sequence of brief events reached its peak (starting with Mozart, Haydn, and Beethoven) in the structure known as *sonata form*, which is so important that most of the first movements in almost every instrumental genre, as well as many other movements, parts of operas, or even entire works, are structured according to this model. Obviously, the basic principles are developed differently in each movement,

---

3 Although Tolkien uses the term *discord*, we will use the synonym *dissonance*, as it is more widely used today and contrasts with consonance.

and the term *sonata form* may be applied to a very wide range of forms, but it is still customarily described in fairly general terms, and such a description meets the needs of the present paper.

Sonata form can be described schematically as a combination of three main sections: exposition, development, and recapitulation. The exposition presents the basic conflict of the piece, represented by two theme groups in opposing keys linked by what is commonly referred to as a *transition*. This conflict is resolved in the recapitulation, where the themes from the exposition are repeated but in the same key. The development is generally the most dramatic, least stable section, and usually includes a modification of earlier themes, and sometimes new themes as well. There are often additional sections that are not integral parts of the form, such as a slow introduction or a coda that comes at the end of the movement as a conclusion. Sonata form has several overarching principles, especially the idea of creation and resolution of tension, the segmented nature of the structure, symmetry among the sections, and the distinction between relatively stable sections (such as the themes in the exposition) and unstable events such as the transition or the development.

Although the description of the music in the *Ainulindalë* may not fit the schema of sonata form perfectly, it clearly satisfies the formal principles that underlie it. Most importantly, there is a formal structure consisting of several themes with different characters and functions. Altogether, we can discern seven events in the course of the music:

- An introduction, including Ilúvatar's initial music and the response of the Ainur (*S* 3)
- The first theme, which develops under the direction of Ilúvatar (*S* 3–4), and about which it is said: "for a great while it seemed good to him, for in the music there were no flaws" (*S* 4)
- Melkor's entrance, which distorts the melody by introducing dissonance (*S* 4)
- A second, briefly described theme, similar to the first yet different, that emerges in the wake of Ilúvatar's intervention (*S* 4)
- The intensification of Melkor's dissonance, which leads to Melkor's domination of the music and silences many of the Ainur (*S* 4)

- The third theme, heard together with Melkor's melody but clashing with it (*S* 4–5)
- The closing gesture, Ilúvatar's mighty chord with which the music ends (*S* 5)

Aside from the division itself, we can see several parallels between the text and the musical form: the two themes in sonata form parallel those sung by the Valar and by Ilúvatar; Melkor's role parallels the dynamic events in sonata form, such as the transition (his first entrance) and the development (especially his clash with Ilúvatar against the backdrop of the third theme); and the ending of the music on a single chord that creates a strong sense of interruption and corresponds to the way the development often concludes, with the dominant of the scale solidly established and a caesura preceding the recapitulation.[4] This gesture can be seen as an example of the use of the "dramatic" nature of sonata form to shape the narrative drama.

Two main points should be noted:
- Unlike the aforementioned schema of sonata form, our analysis does not include a recapitulation. This can be attributed to the fact that in literature, as opposed to music, the repetition of themes required by a recapitulation is more problematic. As we shall see below, however, the absence of a recapitulation (or perhaps its presence in different garb) may have much broader implications. Even without the musical parallel, the reader is left with a sense of something unresolved, since there has indeed been no resolution yet: the tension between Melkor's melody and the music of the other Ainur remains, even after Ilúvatar's final gesture, which merely preserves the sense of confrontation.
- Tolkien strongly emphasizes the distinction between stable and unstable events. Altogether there are three stable events, which are opposed to Melkor's music. But like the unstable parts of sonata form that bridge the gap between themes, Melkor's music never achieves fruition. Because later in the *Ainulindalë* we find that the music is related to the actual creation

---

4 See, e.g., the end of the development of the first movement of Mozart's Linz Symphony, K. 425 (measures 152–158).

of Arda, this ties in with the assumption that Melkor in particular and Tolkienian evil in general cannot create anything independently.

- Another way of illustrating the concrete nature of the music in the *Ainulindalë* is to try to draw a parallel between it and a musical work from the classical repertoire. In this case there is a natural candidate for such a parallel: the prelude to Wagner's *Das Rheingold*. The comparison begs to be made not only due to Tolkien's familiarity with Wagner's music and the common sources of their work in general, but most importantly because both works describe a world at its inception. Nevertheless, I have no intention of launching a discussion of Wagner's influence in general, and that of *Der Ring des Nibelungen* in particular, on the legendarium, although I believe such a discussion should take place.[5] One obvious parallel (whose importance we are about to see in the present context) is between Tolkien's Valar, the Ainur who came down to Arda, and Erda, the Wagnerian goddess of earth, who is even explicitly called Wala (e.g., at the beginning of the third act of *Siegfried*).

The prelude to *Das Rheingold* does not explicitly depict a creation process, but it does serve as an introduction to the Ring cycle, and as such it presents the mythical world in a pristine, pure state. This purity, embodied by the Rhine and its gold, is violated at the very beginning of the work when the gold is stolen from the Rhine by the Nibelung Alberich. This is expressed in two main ways: first, by the use of leitmotifs, commonly referred to as "Nature" and "Rhein," which form the basis for many motifs in the work; and second, by basing the music entirely on a single chord – the tonic chord in the key of E-flat major – with no other harmonic movement. Thus Wagner also achieves a sense of introduction, but mainly he represents the purity of the world by means of perfect consonance and harmonic stability. In contrast to the static nature imposed by harmony, the prelude is a process of intensification in terms of texture: it starts with an individual note – E-flat in a low orchestral register played by a single tuba – which is then joined by other brass instruments in a layered piece that builds up to the major chord. Afterwards the texture thickens

---

5 Tolkien's famous comment that "both rings were round, and there the resemblance ceases" (Tolkien, *Letters*, 306) has to do not with Wagner, but with the original Nordic ring. In any case, it would be going too far to reject any possible relationship between the works out of hand based on this statement.

as the initial thinness, which may be regarded as a manifestation of the creation process, is replaced by a sense of the constant flow of the Rhine.

Looking at the *Ainulindalë* from the perspective of the Wagnerian connection brings up the following points:

- The intensification process in the prelude to *Das Rheingold* also exists in the organization of the music of the Ainur; moreover, the beginning of the *Ainulindalë* is highly reminiscent of the way Wagner starts his piece. Ilúvatar, the "One," can easily be linked symbolically to Wagner's opening tuba note, and the "offspring of his thought" to the other notes that ensue. Acoustically, these notes belong to the overtone series of the opening note, and thus they are indeed products of it and part of it. Presumably, Wagner was trying to express the idea of unity within multiplicity in this way.

- The significant principle of identifying purity with consonance is also present in the *Ainulindalë*, and the reader experiences it by negation. The first mention of dissonance occurs when Melkor first appears; before that there were no flaws in the music. While "flaws" may be regarded as mistakes, the reference to Melkorian dissonance attests to the consonance that preceded it. To my mind, this is the most important point for understanding the role of music in the *Ainulindalë*, and the next two sections of this paper will focus on it.

- In addition to the aforementioned similarity between Wagner's Erda and Tolkien's Arda, there is a clear connection between them in terms of the content of the passages in question. The goddess Erda is associated with the two aforementioned motifs that appear in the prelude, but she is portrayed as a sad, minor-key version of the nature motif. The idea of the transformation of a motif, which Wagner uses frequently in the Ring, is another expression of the underlying principle that the world becomes imperfect when the gold is stolen. Similarly, Tolkien presents the idea of "Arda Marred" – that Arda was intended to be perfect but was damaged by Melkor's actions. The final paragraph of the *Ainulindalë* describes the damage done to Arda and the fact that the struggle of the Valar against Melkor resulted in the imperfect formation of the earth (*S* 10).

This is not to say that there are not major differences between Wagner's music and Tolkien's text. First of all, as we have already seen, the music in the *Ainulindalë* is organized in a much more complex formal structure than the static prelude, so a direct musical parallel with Wagner's music can only apply to the beginning of the *Ainulindalë*. Second, Tolkien's use of Melkor's dissonance diverges from Wagner's music, which in fact focuses on the absence of such dissonance. Therefore, even insofar as the *Ainulindalë* relates to the prelude to *Das Rheingold*, this is just one aspect of musical organization, and it certainly cannot be argued that the music of the Ainur is an imitation of Wagner.

We could conduct many more analyses of the sort presented here, but there is a limit to the usefulness of such analyses. The *Ainulindalë* is not a work of music, so a "musical" analysis of it, or a comparison with musical works, is obviously limited and problematic, even if information can be derived from it. The aim of this section was first and foremost to illustrate the relevance of the music to works from the Western world and to the principles of composition of tonal music. This relevance is evident both on the surface and in a deep examination of the music. Therefore, in order to better understand the essence of the music and its symbolic function in Tolkien's text, we can and should apply insights taken from analysis of Western music.

From Melkor to Schoenberg

The *Ainulindalë* centers on the conflict between Melkor and Ilúvatar. Melkor is not just the only Ainu mentioned by name (while the music is playing); he is explicitly described as the most gifted and the mightiest. The independent line that he takes determines how the music will develop and forces even Ilúvatar to alter its character and its traits. Musically speaking, Melkor is represented by the dissonance that he introduces into the music, and an exploration of the status of dissonance in music history can tell us a lot about his character.[6] Ever since the use of polyphony began, there has been awareness of dissonance in Western music. The basic definition of dissonance is a combination of notes

---

6 Here we expand on Verlyn Flieger's comment that "the explicitly musical terms *disharmony* and *discord* are thus metaphorically extended to nonmusical concepts where they become expressive of the quarrels and contentions of human interaction" (Flieger, 127).

that clash and, when played together, create a feeling, which might be subjective, of unpleasantness. In contrast, in the case of consonance the notes do not clash. In Western music, there is a basic division into "perfect" consonance, imperfect consonance, and dissonance. The categorization of certain intervals has changed over time; the fourth, for instance, used to be considered consonant and later a dissonant. Most intervals, however, have retained their status even in different styles – the octave and fifth, for example, have always been recognized as perfect consonance, whereas the tritone or seventh have been recognized as dissonant. The tritone deserves special mention as it is especially dissonant: it has even been called "the devil's interval" and was absolutely banned in some medieval styles. This is an illustration of the religious symbolism attributed to musical intervals, where dissonance was attributed to the devil and godliness was associated with perfect consonance.

As attitudes toward consonance and dissonance changed, so did the treatment of them in successive styles, from the polyphonic church style of the Middle Ages to tonal music as it started to develop in the early seventeenth century, and finally to tonal music at its most complex in the late nineteenth century. Whereas the tritone, for instance, was absolutely forbidden at first in Western music, it is frequently used in tonal harmony and forms an integral part of the "dominant seventh chord," one of the cornerstones of any basic harmonic progression. As a rule, as the musical language expanded and became richer, dissonance became common and bolder. Nevertheless, it remains one of the most basic principles of tonal language that on all levels of the musical hierarchy, dissonance must be subordinate to consonance and must be resolved to it. The rules of counterpoint state precisely how to prepare for dissonance and how to resolve it, not only to a consonant interval but in correct voice-leading.

A few examples below illustrate the use of dissonance in tonal music. Obviously, countless other examples could be found, since it is almost impossible to avoid dissonance in musical practice (the prelude to *Das Rheingold* is an exception), even in the most routine harmonic formulas.

- Pergolesi's "Stabat Mater" is an example of a process in which the two main voices create dissonance (seconds) that is immediately resolved properly to consonant intervals.[7] The religious significance of the text is manifested in the way in which the voices cross each other – a clear symbol of Jesus crucified. The musical effect of the dissonance and its proper resolution here functions in a clear religious context.

- The use of dissonance to effect surprise can be found in two pieces by Beethoven that begin with a dissonant chord instead of the tonic chord of the scale.[8] In both cases these are standard chords that are not far removed from the key of the piece, and the deviation is "corrected" within a few measures.

- Mozart's Dissonance Quartet starts in an unusual fashion, with a clash of the notes A and A-flat causing fairly sharp dissonance even though they are not played together.[9] This famous beginning gave the quartet its nickname. Even if the introduction can be regarded as an unusual use of dissonance (and some say it cannot), the introduction itself leads to a clear movement in a major key.

- Haydn makes similar use of dissonance in *The Creation*.[10] The opening of this oratorio describes the chaos that preceded creation. The chaos is manifested not only by amorphousness, but by the immediate establishment of a dissonant chord (a diminished seventh) instead of a clear occurrence of the tonic chord.

- The "Tristan chord" at the start of the prelude to Wagner's *Tristan and Isolde* is one of the best examples of the salience of dissonance;[11] it contains early indications of a violation of the tonal frameworks. Its unusual nature stems from a fierce avoidance of the tonic, and from a chord that is ostensibly not part of the agreed-upon tonal lexicon. However, Wagner presents some sort of resolution to the dissonant chord in the very first phrase, leading it into another dissonant chord, but one familiar from the tonal framework (the dominant seventh chord of the underlying scale).

---

7 Pergolesi, "*Stabat Mater*," 1–5, 12–17.
8 Beethoven, *Symphony no. 1*, I, 1–4; *Piano Sonata op. 31/3*, I, 1–8.
9 Mozart, *String Quartet K. 465*, I, 1–22.
10 Haydn, *The Creation*, Overture ("Representation of Chaos"), 1–59.
11 Wagner, *Tristan and Isolde*, Overture, 1–11.

In the *Ainulindalë*, the dissonance is associated immediately with the character of Melkor and his conflict with Ilúvatar. Just as the tritone was once associated with the devil, it is only natural that the dissonance will be associated with Tolkien's diabolical character. Melkor's attempt to add his own ideas to the melody conflicts with the music played by the rest of the Ainur, thus leading to dissonance. But when Melkor induces many of the Ainur to attune their music to his, the dissonance is reinforced rather than disappearing. Hence the dissonance represented by Melkor is intrinsic and not just a result of incompatibility with the norm. Melkorian dissonance corresponds to its musical parallel, since dissonance can result from the momentary addition of passing notes to more fundamental notes or can be an entity in its own right, resulting from a deliberate combination of notes meant to create momentary tension. Of the examples presented above, the *Dissonance Quartet* and the "Tristan chord" have been described in analyses in the literature as both types, largely depending on the analyst's viewpoint.

Because the character of Melkor has negative traits, we would expect his music to be completely undesirable in the music of the Ainur. The concept of pristine purity, represented in the prelude to *Das Rheingold* as described in the previous section, reflects such an attitude. In Wagner's pure, pristine world there is no room for dissonance. Similarly, the example from Haydn's *Creation* presents dissonance as belonging to the pre-creation world of chaos. But this is not how Tolkien views things. After the music ends, Ilúvatar tells Melkor: "And thou, Melkor, wilt discover all the secret thoughts of thy mind, and wilt perceive that they are but a part of the whole and tributary to its glory" (*S* 5).[12] This is the most significant statement in the entire *Ainulindalë* in terms of the status of evil. Evil is not a deviation from perfection but part of it, and it has a role in the divine activity. As in the case of tonal music, Ilúvatar's comments to Melkor reflect the subordination of dissonance to consonance. However complex the role of dissonance, it is still "part of the whole." It is not entirely ruled out (although in some old styles it was), but it can exist only within a context of rules that ensure its correct resolution.

---

12 In the first version this statement appears in greater detail, explicitly noting that evil deeds "make the theme more worth the hearing, Life more worth the living, and the World so much the more wonderful and marvellous" (*Book of Lost Tales*, 55). Presumably, this explanation was deleted because it was too extreme. It is hard to believe that any of Tolkien's characters would actually find themselves thinking of the deeds of Melkor, Sauron, or their agents in this way.

In this way it can actually illuminate the music with a special light and highlight its perfection. The examples presented above, with the exception of the extreme Wagnerian example, are excellent illustrations of this point.

Thus the music illustrates the religious principle presented by Ilúvatar. Nevertheless, this principle unquestionably makes the reader extremely uncomfortable, especially if the reader knows about the horrors that Melkor and his agents are going to perpetrate. When reading about Melkor's deeds later in *The Silmarillion*, such as the destruction of trees and the darkening of Valinor, the corruption of the Children of Ilúvatar and the disfigurement of Arda in general, one does not get the sense that these actions were carried out in accordance with the will of Ilúvatar, and it is hard to see how they attest to his glory. While the music can symbolize the religious principle in its simple sense, we will try now (and in the next section) to use it to contend with this discomfort.

Whereas Ilúvatar represents the traditional conception of tonality, Melkor himself probably represents the challenge to this conception in the early twentieth century, when some composers abandoned tonality in favor of its diametric opposite, atonality. The leading representative of the atonal revolution was Arnold Schoenberg, head of the "Second Viennese School."[13] The basic components underlying tonality, such as reliance on a stable tonal center and a clear hierarchy of harmonic degrees, were broken down by Schoenberg, and at the inception of atonality his approach seemed to convey the message that everything was possible and that no component reigned supreme.[14] An inherent part of this approach is what is generally termed the "emancipation of dissonance." (Dahlhaus 120-128) As soon as the tonal hierarchy was broken down, the subordination stemming from it, including that of dissonance to consonance, ceased to exist, so there was no longer any reason to view dissonance as something requiring resolution. Moreover, Schoenberg stressed

---

13 Schoenberg receives special mention in this paper, but it should be noted that tonality has been violated or challenged in various ways by many composers, among them Stravinsky, Bartók, Hindemith, and Milhaud. The Second Viennese School is generally said to include Alban Berg and Anton Webern in addition to Schoenberg.

14 Schoenberg worked within the context of "free atonality" in 1908–1921; his works in this style include, for example, the piano pieces Opus 11, the song cycle *Pierrot Lunaire*, and the monodrama *Erwartung*. Later Schoenberg moved in the direction of strict order and created what became known as dodecaphonic music. We will not discuss this style at length because its rules were formulated after the vast majority of the *Ainulindalë* was written.

the legitimacy of many tone clusters, not just chords based on the clusters of thirds standard in the tonal system. Naturally, most of these note combinations are dissonant according to the previous consensus. Although we might have expected the newly liberated dissonance to settle for equal rights, instead twentieth-century music gave dissonance a clearly dominant status, partly as a way of expressing the revolutionary messages that it was trying to convey.[15] Similarly, Melkor tries to break the basic rules of the system by legitimizing dissonance. A victory by Melkor would lead to breakdown and disorder, as characterized in Schoenbergian atonality.

By examining the music we can discover the complexity and dualism embodied by the character of Melkor, which is consistent with the dualism pointed out by scholars who have addressed Tolkien's religious views. (Shippey 112-143) Tolkienian evil maintains the dualism between evil as the absence of good and evil as an entity in its own right. Similarly, dissonance exists as a "shadow" of events, brought into being by the clash of these events, but also as something autonomous. Moreover, the perception of evil as a "shadow" or as the absence of good is consistent with the perception of it as an aspect of the whole, whereas the more independent it becomes, the stronger is its demand for emancipation and independence that diverge from its traditional role. This dualism makes the message of the *Ainulindalë* more complex than it initially appeared: Ilúvatar's words to Melkor may be interpreted as a description of an ideal situation in which Melkor can be part of the overall pattern; this was the situation of the world in which the music functioned for centuries. But there is still a risk that the uprising of evil will exceed expectations and lead to an effect corresponding to overstepping the bounds of tonality and making it collapse.

This interpretation assumes a gap between the music of the Ainur and the actual creation of Arda. The text itself supports this assumption, stating explicitly: "For the Great Music had been but the growth and flowering of thought in the Timeless Halls, and the Vision only a foreshowing" (*S* 8). The first version of the text, however, which appears in *The Book of Lost Tales*, takes the opposite approach, saying that the world was created when the Ainur played the music. As

---

15 These messages are manifested, for instance, in the idea that modern music undermines the existing culture by "shocking" listeners (Adorno, 29).

Christopher Tolkien says in his notes to this chapter, this is the most important difference between the first and last versions of the *Ainulindalë* (*LT1* 62). The fact that in the scenario ultimately chosen the world is not created when the music is played, but rather the Valar have to create it themselves, supports the assumption that the events that follow the descent to Arda are not necessarily as foreseen in the music of the Ainur.

Therefore, we can conclude that while the music of the Ainur described in the *Ainulindalë* is consistent with the basic rules of tonality, in practice, after the Valar descend to Eä and Arda is actually created, it becomes possible for dissonance to breach the boundaries of tonality. This perspective can explain evil in Middle-earth as expressions of Melkor's free will, which, at least ostensibly, is not subject to Ilúvatar's will. However, in the next section – again from a perspective made possible by the study of music theory – we discuss a different explanation of the relationship between the original melody and its realization in Arda that is also consistent with the tonal perspective.

So far we have discussed Tolkien's use of music as a symbol of ethical and religious concepts, and as an image of the relationship between good and evil. But we can also look at the text as relating directly to the music, i.e., as a direct, critical expression of a stance regarding the musical events of the period.[16] From this perspective, Tolkien is, of course, highly critical of atonality and of violations of the frameworks of traditional music. This can be seen both in the association of the new, dissonant, "atonal" music with the diabolical character, but also in the explicit description of this music as "vain." Tolkien is certainly not alone in his opinion, since criticism of modern music and Schoenberg in particular is as old as the atonal movement.[17]

The impact of Schoenberg's revolution is evident not only in the *Ainulindalë* but in at least two other literary examples: Thomas Mann's *Doctor Faustus* and

---

16 Tolkien himself, according to his own statements, loved music but had no talent for it (*L* 173). The fact that his wife Edith was a pianist who had intended to work as a piano teacher is further evidence of his closeness to the world of music.
17 An example of such criticism can be seen in the way in which the five orchestral pieces known as Opus 16 were received. At their premiere in London in 1912, they were described by the *Times* as "an assay in dissonance" and were compared to Tibetan song in terms of their comprehensibility, along with other negative criticisms (Stuckenschmidt, 55). This example also demonstrates that Schoenberg's music was accessible to the English public, so it is not inconceivable that Tolkien had been exposed to it directly and had responded similarly.

Milan Kundera's *Book of Laughter and Forgetting*. These two books, unlike the interpretation presented here, refer mainly to Schoenberg's dodecaphonic system, in which he tried to organize atonal music according to much more stringent rules than the original rules of tonality. Although Mann does not mention Schoenberg explicitly, the musical technique that his protagonist invents is very much like the dodecaphonic technique. Kundera, in contrast, explicitly criticizes Schoenberg and compares the hierarchy in the tonal system to the hierarchical class society, whereas the dodecaphonic system is compared to Communism, with all notes having a uniform, equal status. Interestingly, all these works have a common religious context: the title of Mann's book alludes explicitly to Goethe's protagonist who sells his soul to the devil. In Kundera's book, Schoenberg is associated with the world of the angels, who wipe out every trace of disorder, which comes from the devil. Although Tolkien would certainly not have accepted this interpretation, the principle expressed by Kundera – that a certain degree of disorder or "diabolicalness" is required even in the most just society – is consistent with the religious principle in Ilúvatar's words to Melkor.

It is hardly the main interest of this paper to learn about Tolkien's personal opinion on Schoenberg's music or on modern music in general, interesting as they may be. Modern music has been the subject for criticism or praise by many scholars, and it is very likely that Tolkien himself belonged to the critics. But it is more important to connect between this criticism of modern music, and Tolkien's general opinion about the modern movement, apparent both in his prose and his essays.[18] The fact that we can look at the *Ainulindalë* as a reflection of Tolkien's opinion on modernity, reveals how fundamental this opinion is in his entire work.

From Mandos to Schenker

The previous section highlighted Tolkien's adherence to the tradition of tonal music and his opposition to the atonal revolution of the twentieth century. But the early twentieth century was a significant time not only for music itself but for music theory. The salient figure in this context, Heinrich Schenker,

---

18 For example, the way Tolkien refers to the "the ugliness of our works, and of their evil" (Tolkien, *OFS* 151).

not only expressed theoretical positions that were totally opposed to those of Schoenberg,[19] but also created and developed a theory of tonal music that, as we shall see here, conforms very closely to the viewpoints that emerge from the *Ainulindalë*.

Heinrich Schenker (1868–1935) was a music theorist, pianist, conductor, and composer who lived in Vienna at the same time as Schoenberg. His theoretical works present a new approach to understanding pre-existing theories, such as theories of harmony (*Harmonielehre*, 1906) and counterpoint (*Kontrapunkt*, 1910/1922). His most important and most innovative book is *Der freie Satz* (Free composition, 1935), which develops in full his new theoretical system and includes hundreds of analyses of tonal pieces. Schenker is credited with presenting and reformulating the principles of tonality in a way that relies mainly on the principles of counterpoint and voice-leading as articulated in practice from Palestrina's time forward and as expressed saliently, for example, in the music of Johann Sebastian Bach (Rameau, in contrast, relied mainly on harmonic principles). Like Schoenberg, Schenker had many students who ultimately made his theory dominant today among music theorists and even among performers, such as the pianist Murray Perahia.

Due to space constraints, we can explain here only a few main principles of Schenkerian theory. First and foremost is the idea that tonal music is the result of superstructures shared by all tonal pieces. Schenker termed the superstructure *Ursatz* (the harmonic structure of the piece) and *Urlinie* (its fundamental melodic line). According to this view, tonal music is based on a hierarchy and can be seen as developing out of a transition between stages: the background (the superstructure); the foreground (the surface level of a particular piece); and the middleground, which connects the two.[20] We can describe Schenker's viewpoint as an organicistic one that sees each piece as one whole, all of whose components must be derived from and relate to this whole. The quality of a piece is determined not by the individual events on the musical surface but by the degree to which they relate to su-

---

19 Schenker voiced explicit criticism of Schoenberg's views regarding the legitimacy and autonomy of dissonant chords, especially those that Schenker perceived as passing events in the tonal framework. See Schenker, *Meisterwerk*, 12–17.
20 Schenker, *Der freie Satz*, especially pp. 3–25.

perstructure. Overall, the theory itself reflects Schenker's views on ethics and metaphysics and his perception of the profound connection between music and nature.[21]

A manifestation of similar organicistic thinking can be found in the initial relationship between Ilúvatar and the Ainur. The very first sentence says that the Ainur were not independent entities but the "offspring of his thought." Then, in the final version of the *Ainulindalë*, it says briefly that Ilúvatar propounded musical themes to the Ainur and that they sang before him. In the first version, Ilúvatar tells the Ainur:

> The story that I have laid before you, and that great region of beauty that I have described unto you as the place where all that history might be unfolded and enacted, is related only as it were in outline. I have not filled all the empty spaces, neither have I recounted to you all the adornments and things of loveliness and delicacy whereof my mind is full. It is my desire now that ye make a great and glorious music and a singing of this theme. (*LT1* 53)

Here we see the organicistic approach at its peak, since the music of the Ainur is described as "adornments" and a way of filling in Ilúvatar's basic melody. Beyond the shared principle, this is highly consistent with Schenker's view of processes that lead from deep structures to the surface as expressing expansion or ornamentation of the structural events, since they, too, are present in the final stage of the work. Clearly, although Tolkien demonstrates a high level of musical understanding in writing this, its main function is to present his religious belief that the source of everything is the one God, and everything else is a product of His will.

By coincidence, both Schenker and Tolkien use the term *unfolding* very similarly, to describe the move from a deeper level to the surface. Although clearly Schenkerian theory cannot have influenced Tolkien directly, this is another illustration of their similarity of thought. For Schenker, *unfolding* means changing an interval or chord from a vertical state (in which all the notes are played together) to a horizontal state (in which they are played as a melody); this is one of the most important techniques for moving from one level to another.[22] For Tolkien, the term describes both the way in which the musical theme is

---

21 See Cook, *Ethics*.
22 Schenker, *Der freie Satz*, 50–51, 53–54.

presented to the Ainur by Ilúvatar ("And it came to pass that Ilúvatar called together all the Ainur and declared to them a mighty theme, unfolding to them things greater and more wonderful than he had yet revealed[...]", *S* 3), and the way in which the material world takes shape as a result of the music ("And as they looked and wondered this World began to unfold its history, and it seemed to them that it lived and grew." *S* 5).

The most relevant aspect of Schenkerian theory turns out to be its understanding that concepts such as "preparation" and "resolution," which form the basis for the treatment of dissonance, are not necessarily relevant to the surface level. Thus, part of a piece may appear to be unstable and inconsistent with some of the rules of the tonal system, but an examination on a deeper level may show its internal logic. Specifically, dissonance may not be resolved according to the rules on the surface level, but it may still be subject to consonant events on other levels.[23]

This approach may better explain what we discussed in the previous section: the idea that the dissonance introduced by Melkor into the music of the Ainur serves the overall divine plan. The structural conception of musical organization presents the processes that do not necessarily take place immediately, and as we move farther away from the immediate level of occurrence, they become more and more important. Therefore, dissonance that seems to remain hanging may be resolved later – sometimes even far off in the future – and this may still be a correct resolution. The more unusual and significant the event requiring resolution is, the more its resolution may be delayed, precisely because this resolution takes place on a deep level. In the present context, we can argue that the accentuation of evil deeds and their apparent triumph and accomplishments do not necessarily constitute confirmation of the power of evil, since in the overall understanding of the course of events, the resolution may be significantly delayed.

This explanation will presumably please anyone coming from a religious perspective. But Tolkien does not make do with general statements. He actually

---

23 An extreme expression of Schenker's conception of the secondary nature of dissonance is in his argument that dissonance cannot undergo prolongation, one of the most basic processes in his theory. Today, however, it is customarily maintained that dissonance can indeed be prolonged – while, of course, remaining subordinate to the consonance on deep levels. See Goldenberg.

uses the music to illustrate this point. We have already seen that the musical development in the *Ainulindalë* is cut off at the height of the conflict between Ilúvatar and Melkor. Tolkien makes it clear that the music of the Ainur does not come to an end or achieves its purpose and that an even greater melody will come someday to complete it: "Never since have the Ainur made any music like to this music, though it has been said that a greater still shall be made before Ilúvatar by the choirs of the Ainur and the Children of Ilúvatar after the end of days" [*S* 3]. We can understand this statement by comparing it the events which are about to happen at the "end of days" according to the second prophecy of Mandos. (*LR1* 333) The prophecy describes the ultimate defeat of Melkor, and thus offers a conclusion to the whole *Silmarillion*.

It is no coincidence that the prophecy of Mandos centers on the conflict between Túrin and Melkor. Ostensibly, Melkor is "thrust [...] beyond the Walls of the World" in the War of Wrath, while Túrin meets his end back in the First Age. But Túrin and his fate represent the clearest embodiment of Melkorian dissonance, since Melkor's evil lands in full force on Húrin's family, and this dissonance is never resolved. In addition, the victory over Melkor at the end of the First Age can be perceived as an insufficient resolution that appears to resolve the dissonance but actually leaves it in place. These feelings are manifested in the musical context in the understanding that the resolution has to be on the deepest level, and this level can be reached only at the end – both of the divine creation and of the musical work.

One important model in Schenkerian theory for explaining musical structures is the interruption model.[24] We will use this model to explore additional points raised in the two previous sections, both regarding the formal organization of the music in the *Ainulindalë* (as described in the first part of the paper) and regarding the gap between the music of the Ainur and the actual creation of the world (discussed in the previous section). The interruption model, which is a slight expansion of the abstract superstructures, describes cases in which music is apparently interrupted and starts over. Such structures can be very brief, such as the periodic structures composed of an opening phrase and a closing phrase, but the model is also used to describe complex structures such

---

24 Schenker, *Der freie Satz*, 87.

as sonata form. According to this model, the melodic line presented at the beginning of the structure is not fully realized; instead it is interrupted in the middle, when we reach the dominant of the scale. Afterwards the melody starts over and this time it achieves completion. If we compare it to sonata form, the first part of the model corresponds to the exposition and the development, whereas the recapitulation encompasses the repetition of the superstructure and its final completion.

Looking at the *Ainulindalë* from the standpoint of sonata form, we see that the musical structure is not complete: the music ends at a dramatic peak that corresponds to the end of the development section. Furthermore, as we have seen, in the final version of the *Ainulindalë* what is created by the music is not actually Arda but only a vision of it, and the creation process starts over when the Valar descend to the world. These details, in addition to the fact that the music of the Ainur will be resumed in the future, fits in perfectly with the idea underlying the principle of interruption: both the structural division into two main parts, the first interrupted and the second complete, and the concept of repetition and restarting, where the two parts reflect the same process of creation of the world. However, in contrast to the formal parallel that we drew at the beginning of the paper, here the correspondence relates to much more abstract principles and they can therefore be described and justified much more easily. Clearly, there is no need for a technical analysis of *The Silmarillion* that will find parallels with the parts of the recapitulation. This analysis assumes that the gap between the two stages of the creation of Arda does not diverge from the tonal framework, and that the second stage is the one that ultimately leads to resolution of the tension. Therefore, if in the previous section we suggested that Melkor's deeds after the creation of Arda represent a "breach of tonality", the current view shows this breach is only at the surface level.

In conclusion, the following quotation by Schenker links his musical analyses with his metaphysical beliefs:

> The "chaos" of the foreground belongs with the universal order of the background; it is one with it [...] let us finally learn humbly to love and honor the chaos for the sake of the cosmos, which is God's own. To partake of the cosmos

and its eternal ideas – this alone signifies a life of beauty, true immortality in God.[25]

The relationship that Schenker presents between the chaotic foreground and the orderly background is largely consistent with Tolkien's concept that even Melkor's deeds serve the purpose of divine order. Both Tolkien and Schenker were concerned about the effects of a world represented by Schoenberg's music – as they saw it, an unjustifiable, illogical world of unleashed chaos. This concern, however, did not contradict their basic faith in the order behind things, however hidden it may be.

We can suggest three possible functions for music in prose: it can serve as an organizing factor for the literary material; it can serve as a topic of discussion, whether the focal point or something symbolic; and finally, it can retain its original function – as "music" that the reader tries to hear and sense. The music in the *Ainulindalë*, and perhaps throughout *The Silmarillion*, fulfills all these functions to some degree.

As we have tried to show in this paper, the second function is the most significant. A discussion of the music and an understanding of its overall context make it both the subject of the *Ainulindalë* and the most important vehicle for expressing certain views held by Tolkien. But the other two functions are also present and significant: Tolkien does not organize the text musically; he does not give musical titles to the chapters in *The Silmarillion* (as is done, for instance, in the recent novel *Les Bienveillantes*); and when there is a relatively clear musical formal structure it has to do with the music itself and not the surrounding text. But the view of world history as being subject to the music of the Ainur, with the resolution of all the dissonance due to take place at the end of days according to the Second Prophecy of Mandos, leads to a sense of the interruption model that we discussed in the last part of the paper as a superstructure that dominates the overall organization of *The Silmarillion* and the entire legendarium.

Beyond these analyses, the music in the *Ainulindalë* derives its power mainly from its very existence. The reader is exposed to the divine music and tries to

---

25 Schenker, *Der freie Satz*, 161 (Appendix 4, translated by John Rothgeb).

sense it and understand its intrinsic perfection. Like all good music, it appeals to the reader's emotions and creates the catharsis necessary for accepting the complex, difficult ideas expressed by Tolkien.

About the Author

Reuven Naveh was born in 1970 and studied Mathematics and Musicology in the Hebrew University of Jerusalem, receiving a PhD in Musicology in 2005. He has been a member of the Israeli Tolkien Society since 2003 and a lecturer on its behalf in several SciFi and Fantasy conferences.

I would like to thank the members of the Israeli Tolkien Society for their assistance in preparing this paper; to Prof. Naphtali Wagner for his review of the paper, putting it in the wide context of music and literature; and to my wife Efrat for her thorough reading of the text and her many comments on it.

Tolkien References

TOLKIEN, J.R.R., *The Book of Lost Tales, Part I*, (ed. by Christopher Tolkien), London: George Allen & Unwin, 1983.

The Letters of J.R.R Tolkien, (ed. by Humphrey Carpenter with the assistance of Christopher Tolkien), Boston: Houghton Mifflin, 1981.

The Lost Road and Other Writings, (ed. by Christopher Tolkien), Boston: Houghton Mifflin, 1987.

"On Fairy-Stories", In: *The Monsters and the Critics and Other Essays*, (ed. by Christopher Tolkien), London: George Allen & Unwin, 1983.

The Silmarillion, (ed. by Christopher Tolkien), London: HarperCollins, 1977.

References

ADORNO, Theodor W., *Philosophy of Modern Music*, (transl. by Anne G. Mitchell and Wesley Y. Blomster), New York: Continuum, 1973.

COOK, Nicholas, "Schenker's Theory of Music as Ethics", In: *Journal of Musicology* (1989), 415-39.

DAHLHAUS, Carl, *Schoenberg and the New Music,* (transl. by Derrick Puffet and Alfred Clayton), Cambridge: Cambridge University Press, 1987.

EDEN, Bradford Lee, "The 'Music of the Spheres': Relationships Between Tolkien's *Silmarillion* and Medieval Cosmological and Religious Theory", In: Jane Chance (ed.), *Tolkien the Medievalist*, London and New York: Routledge, 2003, 183-93.

FLIEGER, Verlyn, *Splintered Light: Logos and Language in Tolkien's World*, 2nd ed., Kent, OH: Kent State University Press, 2002.

GOLDENBERG, Yosef, *Prolongation of Seventh Chords in Tonal Music*, Lewiston: The Edwin Mellen Press, 2008.

SHIPPEY, Tom, *J.R.R. Tolkien: Author of the Century*, London: HarperCollins, 2000.

STUCKENSCHMIDT, Hans Heinz, *Twentieth Century Music*, (transl. by Richard Deveson), New York: McGraw-Hill, 1969.

Jonathan McIntosh

Ainulindalë: Tolkien, St. Thomas, and the Metaphysics of the Music

Introduction

At the center of J.R.R. Tolkien's creation-myth, the *Ainulindalë*, is the eponymous "Music of the Ainur", the beautiful, cosmic composition sung by the angelic host and Creator prior to the creation of the physical world, and the pattern according to which the history of the created world later unfolds. The arresting poignancy of Tolkien's music imagery is reflected in part in the considerable attention it has received from his commentators, many of whom have traced its sources to the *musica universalis* tradition of such eminent thinkers as Pythagoras, Plato, Augustine, and Boethius. Yet despite the attention it has received, the precise metaphysical meaning of the Ainur's Music has often been missed, when it has not been outright misunderstood. In addition to the prevalent interpretation of the Ainur and their Music as the true or proximate "creators" of the world, there has been a marked tendency in the Tolkien literature to read his creation-drama and the Music of the Ainur in particular in terms of the emanationist logic of Neoplatonic philosophy. On this understanding, later stages of the creation-process and world-history are seen as metaphysically inferior to, and thus a "tragic" falling away from, the supposedly more authentic and pure reality represented by the primeval Music. In contrast to this prevalent reading of the *Ainulindalë*, I argue that the Ainur's Music – along with the oft neglected, yet not for that reason any less important image from the *Ainulindalë*, the Vision of the Ainur – give mythic expression to the much more positive, comic, or rather "eucatastrophic" metaphysics of creation Tolkien inherited and adapted from his greater Catholic theological forbear, St. Thomas Aquinas. I conclude that through his image of the Music of the Ainur, what Tolkien provides the world is a beautiful yet mythical, ideal pattern that, consistent with his Thomistic existential realism, nevertheless finds itself radically transcended when the world is finally blessed by the Creator with its own, mind-alluring because mind-independent being.

Misreading the Music

While the importance of the *Ainulindalë*'s music imagery – both as an image of the cosmic harmony behind all reality and as an illustration of such central Tolkienian themes as the freedom of creaturely sub-creation – would seem hard to overstate, the metaphysical significance of the Ainur's Music has nevertheless been greatly exaggerated by readers viewing it as a truly creative power and source of the world. One reader, for example, writes that "Tolkien's music of creation actually *creates* the *entire* cosmos" (emphasis original), and that the Ainur's Music represents the "vibratory force in creation, and it is that force which has the power to create and sustain worlds" (Davis 6, 8), while another reader has written that "Middle-earth is created and sustained through the sung words of the 'Great Music'" (Grubbs). Another reader similarly overstates the role of Music in creation when he identifies it by turns as the "creational and cosmological power", "the creative and omnipotent force", "the creational and binding force that sets in motion the entire drama of Middle-earth", "the generational force out of which much of the drama of Middle-earth develops", and "the ultimate power in the cosmological history of Middle-earth" (Eden 185-8). Recognized Tolkien scholars Verlyn Flieger and Brad Birzer are similarly carried away in their accounts of the Music, as when Flieger variously describes the Music as "the initiating force", "creative force", and "ordering force of the universe", (Flieger 57-9), or when Birzer writes that after Eru created the Ainur, "He gave to each of them a piece of his wisdom and knowledge, and together they sang the universe into existence" (Birzer 53). One final writer has claimed that the musical paradigm of Tolkien's creation myth is the "key to" and the "essential nature of" his theory of being (Collins 257, 264). As we shall see, however, the Music of the Ainur is and does none of these things, and understanding this point turns out to be the true key to his theory of being.

Related to this inflated view of the role and power of the Music in creation is a corresponding diminished view some of Tolkien's readers, especially those interpreting him in a Platonic light, have had of the physical world of creation which follows after it. According to the Neoplatonist philosopher Plotinus, the existing universe consists in a cascading hierarchy of "hypostases" or discrete orders of being, in which the supreme, transcendent, and ultimately unknowable first cause of all things, "the One", first "emanates" or "overflows" into the second hypostasis of Divine Mind, which in turn engenders the third hypostasis of World Soul, which in turn overflows into the physical realm of temporal, sensible Nature. Each successive stage of reality, however, as it moves further and further away from its original source in the One, also involves a corresponding corruption or dilution of being, much as it gets darker and colder the further one moves from a source of light and heat. The result is what one writer has aptly described as the "tragic metaphysics" of Neoplatonism, according to which "everything that derives from the One or the forms is necessarily decadent" (Leithart 46).

Not surprisingly, it is this same, tragic metaphysical sensibility that scholars, convinced of the underlying Platonism of Tolkien's mythology, have found in the pages of the *Ainulindalë*. John Cox, for example, argues that, "while Tolkien follows [Plato's creation-myth] the *Timaeus*[…] in creating the Ainur, he follows neo-platonic tradition, beginning with Plotinus, in depicting innumerable series of imitations that radiate outward from a point close to the greatest creative power through stages of gradual diminution" (Cox 58). Cox further compares the way the Ainur mediate between Ilúvatar and the physical world to the way the World Soul of Plato's *Timaeus* functions as a protective "buffer" between the unsullied perfection of the demiurgic creator on the one hand and the "visible, changing, temporal, and only *apparently* real world" (emphasis Cox's) on the other. It is in similarly tragic metaphysical terms that Bradford Lee Eden has likewise understood the relationship between the Ainur's Music and the subsequent phases of creation. According to Eden, the creation and subsequent history of Middle-earth follows a Neoplatonic pattern of progression, or rather *re*gression, paralleling the threefold classification of music (cosmic, human or vocal, and instrumental) which Boethius outlines in his influential treatise *De institutione musica*. As Eden writes,

> The gradations of music's power in Middle-earth from its appearance in the first page of *The Silmarillion* all the way down to the Fourth Age in *The Lord of the Rings* reflects a Neoplatonic hierarchy of being, from the highest form of music, universal or comic [sic] music, down to human/vocal music, and then down to instrumental music. This chain of musical being also embodies the diminution of cosmic love/harmony that ends with the most material and literal, in the instruments of Man. (Eden 192)

A little earlier in his argument, Eden makes the same point in these words:

> There may be an unconscious decay of cosmological theory written into *The Silmarillion* that can only be detected by one who is knowledgeable about the entire mythological reality that is Middle-earth. Each theoretical step taken away from the "Great Music", which set [sic] everything into motion, is a slow descent away from "the divine." This is a strong thread throughout the writings of Plato and Aristotle, that each gradation and division of music away from the "pure" or "universal" results in a type of gradual descent downward in spirit and soul[...]. Elves and Men are farther away in both time and space from the "music of the spheres" and closer to the third and lower type of music in the Third Age. (Eden 190-1)

Verlyn Flieger, finally, has similarly hinted at a tragic dimension to Tolkien's metaphysics in her discussion of the view Tolkien shared with fringe Inkling member Owen Barfield concerning the fragmentation human language, stories, and consciousness inevitably undergo over time, a process to which Tolkien gives mythic embodiment in his recurring image of "splintered light". Of the original source of illumination in the world, for example, the two Lamps established by the Valar on twin mountain-pillars of stone, Flieger observes that the light "is brilliant and constant", but that when the "first light is quenched" by Melkor, it "cannot be renewed", and so in the Two Trees of Valinor "new light is brought into being, but the quality is changed and the brightness is diminished[...] The differences between the Lamps and the Trees are multiple and striking and conform to the pattern of fragmentation and diminution that underlies the whole mythology[...] [T]he Trees give light in waxing and waning cycles of flower and fruit" (Flieger 63). Flieger's study on Tolkien's philosophy of language is excellent, yet unfortunately she seems to read this tragic sensibility back into the metaphysics of his creation-myth, as when in her own comparison of Tolkien's *Ainulindalë* to Plato's *Timaeus* she stresses how the process of creation and sub-creation involves a progressive alienation between the Creator and his ever-more distant effects: the Valar, in short, are "dividing the world from Eru, assisting in a process of separation through which Eru and the world can contemplate each other" (ibid. 55). The theological consequence of this for Flieger is the metaphysically and theologically tragic one in which the Creator emerges as "a strikingly remote and disengaged figure" who has "little or no direct interaction in his world" and who leaves it to his sub-created vassals "to concern themselves specifically with the earth and its inhabitants" (ibid. 53-4).

Against the metaphysically tragic interpretation of Tolkien's creation-myth, the argument in my own analysis of the *Ainulindalë* to follow is that Tolkien's music-imagery in fact presupposes the much more Christian, creational, and therefore positive metaphysics that a number of readers have noted him to share with the thirteenth-century theologian St. Thomas Aquinas. As early as 1972, the year prior to Tolkien's death, Paul H. Kocher, for example, observed how Tolkien's ideas "are best understood when viewed in the context of the natural theology of Thomas Aquinas, whom it is reasonable to suppose that Tolkien, as a medievalist and a Catholic, knows well", and that the "same is true in the area of metaphysics" (Kocher 77). Since that time there have been others who have speculated about the Catholic Doctor's possible influence on the Catholic Don.[1] And while there are many possible points upon which the metaphysics of St. Thomas might be brought to bear on the mythology of Tolkien, the three principal ideas I will be referencing in the discussion to follow concern Thomas's remarks, first, on the abstract and almost mathematical character of music; second, Thomas's metaphysical realism, or his commitment to the irreducibly real, mind-independent, yet for that reason mind-obtruding and seducing character of things; and third, his related doctrine of metaphysical "existentialism", according to which it is the act of existence which constitutes the highest actuality or reality of a thing, including its intelligible essence or form. Corresponding to these three points, respectively, are the three distinct stages of Tolkien's creation-myth around which I will be structuring my own commentary on the *Ainulindalë*: the Ainur's Music, the Ainur's Vision, and "Eä", the "World that Is."

Metaphysics of the Music

The *Ainulindalë* opens with the Creator, Ilúvatar, first making the angelic Ainur and teaching to them "themes of music." Notwithstanding the Creator's evident transcendence over his creatures – and in contrast to the supreme deities of much classical philosophy, whose utter perfection requires that they exist in complete oblivion to every order of being below their own – Ilúvatar not only first teaches the Ainur their Music, but he is also portrayed as an

---

1 See, for example, Milbank (2008) and Candler.

enthusiastic connoisseur of it, one who delights in the new state of affairs the Ainur's Music serves to bring about. As Ilúvatar tells the Ainur, "But I will sit and hearken, and be glad that through you great beauty has been wakened into song" (*S* 15). Yet when Ilúvatar first begins teaching the Ainur their Music, and as the Platonic reading of the *Ainulindalë* might predict, they are unable to grasp completely the theme in its unity or wholeness: "[b]ut for a long while they sang only each alone, or but few together, while the rest hearkened; for each comprehended only that part of the mind of Ilúvatar from which he came, and in the understanding of their brethren they grew but slowly." The Ainur mature, however, in their comprehension and skill over time, so that "as they listened they came to deeper understanding, and increased in unison and harmony." Despite the Ainur's difficulty in learning this first theme, Ilúvatar follows it with a second, "mighty theme, unfolding to them things greater and more wonderful than he had yet revealed; and the glory of its beginning and the splendor of its end amazed the Ainur, so that they bowed before Ilúvatar and were silent." Ilúvatar's own music-making, therefore, turns out to resemble less the Neoplatonic pattern of iterative decay than it does the gradual, eschatological progression described, for example, in the Book of Genesis, where creation's initial status as merely "good" gradually gives way to its later consummation as "very good." More remarkable still is that, notwithstanding the surpassing beauty of Ilúvatar's second theme, this time the Ainur are not told to repeat or imitate (however unsuccessfully) its pattern, but as we have just seen, are instead exhorted to improvise and improve upon it (much as the biblical Adam and Eve are told to complete the good work that the Lord God had already started). The result is so beautiful that, consistent with Flieger's "splintered light" thesis of irretrievable loss noted earlier, not even the Ainur themselves are said to have since "made any music like to this music." Yet in the same breath the narration anticipates a day when "a greater still shall be made before Ilúvatar by the choirs of the Ainur and the Children of Ilúvatar after the end of days.

Even the discord introduced into the Music by Melkor ultimately serves not to lessen its beauty, but provides Ilúvatar with the occasion to enter again into the Music and make it more beautiful still. Where the Ainur's Music alone is concerned, therefore, the pattern is clearly not the metaphysically entropic one of an inescapable loss of beauty or being, but rather a progressive, eschatological movement from glory to greater glory.

This same progressive pattern within the Ainur's Music is also what characterizes the transition from the Ainur's Music to the Ainur's Vision which follows after it. The Ainur's Vision has been surprisingly neglected by commentators of the *Ainulindalë* and yet, as we shall see, its significance in many ways eclipses that of the Music. At one level it would seem that the Vision does not in fact add anything to the Music, but represents – again, as the metaphysically tragic interpretation would require – merely a visual counterpart to the Music, a point almost implied in Ilúvatar's statement that in the Vision he has merely given the Ainur "sight where before was only hearing", and a little later, when he further explains that "each of you shall find contained herein, amid the design that I set before you, all those things which it may seem that he himself devised or added" (ibid. 17). As the Ainur quickly realize, however, the Vision is no mere superfluous or decadent repetition of the Music, but drastically goes beyond it in its depiction of a reality not at all anticipated by the Music:

> And so it was that as this vision of the World was played before them, the Ainur saw that it contained things which they had not thought. And they saw with amazement the coming of the Children of Ilúvatar, and the habitation that was prepared for them; and they perceived that they themselves in the labour of their music had been busy with the preparation of this dwelling, and yet knew not that it had any purpose beyond its own beauty. (ibid. 18)

The Vision not only contains "all those things" which the Ainur had "devised or added" in the Music, but also contains "things which they had not thought" in the Music.

There are a number of distinguishable levels at which the Vision goes beyond the Music, one of which is clearly theological or revelatory: although the Music itself had been a means by which the Ainur could grow in their knowledge of Ilúvatar, in the Vision's depiction of the Children of Ilúvatar in particular the Ainur are able to see "the mind of Ilúvatar reflected anew, and learned yet a little more of his wisdom, which otherwise had been hidden even from the Ainur" (ibid.). Through the Vision, in short, the Ainur receive a greater revelation of the Creator than what the Music alone had provided, a progression that, again, makes little sense when interpreted according to the Neoplatonic principle that every later stage or emanation of reality results not in an increased but a diminished capacity to reflect the divine. Related to this is the greater theodical power the Vision wields in comparison to the Music, providing the Ainur with a fuller disclosure of Ilúvatar's ability to bring about good from Melkor's evil. As Ilúvatar explains to Melkor after the closing of the Music, in the Vision he will

> see that no theme may be played that hath not its uttermost source in me, nor can any alter the music in my despite. For he that attempteth this shall prove but mine instrument in the devising of things more wonderful, which he himself hath not imagined[...] And thou, Melkor, will discover all the secret thoughts of thy mind, and wilt perceive that they are but a part of the whole and tributary to its glory. (ibid. 17)

In addition to containing the things which the Ainur had *not* thought, the Vision also reveals to them the ultimate truth of those things which they previously *had* thought. It is not the prior Music, therefore, that embodies the essential truth of the later Vision, but vice-versa. Adding to the Vision's theological and theodical supremacy over the Music is its apparent aesthetic excellence, a point brought home in the Vision when Ilúvatar explains to Ulmo (the Ainur to whom is given dominion over the sea) that the "bitter cold immoderate" caused by Melkor, far from destroying "the beauty of [Ulmo's] fountains, nor of [his] clear pools", has instead managed only to contribute to "the height and glory of the clouds", "the everchanging mists", and "the fall of rain upon the Earth." To this disclosure Ulmo responds with appropriate awe: "Truly, Water is become now fairer than my heart imagined, neither had my secret thought conceived the snowflake, nor in all my music was contained the falling of the rain" (ibid. 19).

Behind each of the aforementioned respects in which the Vision surpasses the Music, however, is the ultimately metaphysical consideration that the Vision simply implicates a greater degree of reality or being than the Music. In contrast to the Vision, as we shall see in the following section, for example, the Ainur were able to enjoy the Music for its own sake, not knowing "that it had any purpose beyond its own beauty." In this the Ainur's Music illustrates the kind of "perfect self-contained significance" and "inner consistency of reality" which Tolkien argues in his famous essay "On Fairy-Stories" to be one of the hallmark features of the true fairy-story. However, unlike the fairy-stories of

Tolkien's essay – one of whose functions, as we shall also discuss below, is at the same time to direct the individual's attention back towards reality – the Ainur's Music is conspicuous in that it does not suggest to the Ainur before the fact any existential claims or possibilities beyond itself (much less creatively or productively render those possibilities actual).

In one letter Tolkien instead describes the Ainur's Music as an "abstract form" (*L* 284), an account which, combined with the Music's existential indifference or disinterest noted above, invites comparison to the similarly abstract account of music St. Thomas gives, for example, in his commentary on Boethius's *De trinitate*. According to Thomas, music is closely associated with mathematics, as it derives its first principles from arithmetic and then applies these principles to natural things (Aquinas, *Division and Methods* 5.1 ad 5). Music thus represents a kind of "intermediate", he says, between mathematics and natural science, though it bears "a closer affinity to mathematics" since music is more "formal" and thus more separated from matter and motion than is the case in natural science: "music considers sounds, not inasmuch as they are sounds, but inasmuch as they are proportionable according to numbers" (ibid. 5.3). Behind Thomas's argument here is his teaching that, although both mathematics and natural science involve an act of mental abstraction which separates their intelligible principles from the physical, sensible substances in which these principles actually exist, mathematics and natural science nevertheless differ in their respective *degrees* of abstraction. In the case of a mathematical object such as a circle, for example, there is no reference in the concept of a circle to the kind of matter that real (i.e., non-mental) circles are actually made of, since circles can be made out of virtually anything (ibid.). The case is otherwise with concepts of natural substances such as *man*, for which the kind of matter the thing is made out of comprises an integral part of the substance's essence or form (ibid. 5.2). Thus, while the concept of man, like the concept of a circle, is produced by the mind's abstracting it from the determinate matter out of which individual men or circles are actually made, the concept of man nevertheless retains a notional reference to the kind of matter out of which real men are made, namely "flesh and bones." For Thomas, then, while music as we experience it is of course an inherently physical, sensible, and sensuous phenomenon, music itself abstracts from and is thus completely indifferent to the particular, material conditions under which music is actually experienced, and focuses instead on simply the purely formal qualities which constitute its sounds as musical, which is to say, as mathematically or numerically proportionate sounds. In a similar fashion, I suggest, the Music enjoyed and played by the Ainur, while exceedingly beautiful and containing the formal pattern for the subsequent history of the world, is at the same time an exceedingly "abstract form", so removed from the material conditions under which physical world and its history later exist that it leaves the Ainur, as we have noted, blissfully unaware of the Music's ultimately having "any purpose beyond its own beauty".

Metaphysics of the Vision

This abstract formalism and metaphysical indifference of the Music, however, finds itself radically transcended in the subsequent stage of the Vision. While the Music, as we have seen, leads the Ainur from a state of initial isolation into greater contact and communion with each other, it is only in the Vision that they are for the first time forced outside of their own minds and the comparative pure conceptuality of the Music and challenged with the possibility of the existence of something "other than themselves, strange and free", (*S* 18) challenged, that is, with the prospect of a reality whose intractable physicality cannot be reduced to an abstract form. To continue the analogy suggested above, if the abstract Music resembles in this regard St. Thomas's account of mathematics, the Vision might be compared – as Tolkien himself indirectly does, as we shall see in a moment – to Thomas's account of natural science, whose intelligible forms abstract from individual matter while retaining an intentional or notional reference to the kind or species of matter out of which natural substances are actually made. The link between the "otherness" of the Vision and the Aristotelian and Thomistic conception of natural science, defined as the theoretical knowledge of natural things for their own sake, is found in Tolkien's descriptions of the enigmatic figure of Tom Bombadil, whom Tolkien identifies in one place as "an 'allegory', or an exemplar, a particular embodying of pure (real) natural science: the spirit that desires knowledge of other things, their history and nature, *because they are 'other'* [emphasis Tolkien's] and wholly independent of the enquiring mind, a spirit coeval with the rational mind, and entirely unconcerned with 'doing' anything with the knowledge" (*L* 192). In contrast to the mathematically abstract Music, the Vision, like the natural science allegorized in the figure of Bombadil, embodies a knowledge "of other things [...] *because they are 'other'* and wholly independent of the enquiring mind [...]" The resulting contrast between the Music and the Vision is one that Robert Collins captures well in a fitting application of the Aristotelian terminology of Aquinas: "Whereas the music had established an abstract pattern, the vision had indicated the nature of Ilúvatar's translation of form to matter [...]" (Collins 261). This "translation of form to matter", moreover, anticipated in the Vision (and performed directly by Ilúvatar himself, as Collins rightly notes), far from involving a tragic "fall" of ideal or pure form into matter, implies rather the realization, perfection, or actualization of form in and through the material substances which it is the form *of*, a point we shall return to in the following section.

This question of otherness raised in the Vision and embodied in the character of Bombadil is an important Tolkienian theme in its own right and represents one of the more direct or obvious lines of influence extending from St. Thomas to Tolkien. As Alison Milbank has noted, behind Tolkien's stress on the "otherness" of things in his writings is the metaphysical realism of St. Thomas: "Only through the reality of the world can the mind, according to Thomas, reach out to otherness and become the object" (Milbank 2007: 17). Thus, more than merely presenting for the Ainur's consideration the abstract or hypothetical *possibility* of the extra-mental, physical world it portrays, as we have seen, the Vision goes further in eliciting in the Ainur the intense *desire* that this world should be made real by being given its own independent act of existence: "Then there was unrest among the Ainur; but Ilúvatar called to them, and said: 'I know the desire of your minds that what ye have seen should verily be, not only in your thought, but even as ye yourselves are, and yet other[...]'" (*S* 20). Ilúvatar "knows the desire" of the Ainur's minds because it is, of course, Ilúvatar's own desire. As St. Thomas explains, although there is a sense in which things have more reality in God than they do in themselves, even God is a "realist", desiring that created beings should exist for their intractable otherness. In *Summa Theologiae* 1.19.2, for example, Thomas argues that it is because God is supremely perfect and has no unfulfilled needs that it belongs to him especially to act for the benefit of, by communicating something of his own inherent goodness to, things other than himself, and thus to will the existence of "things apart from himself" ("alia a se"). And while there is, as has been said, a sense in which creation must invariably represent a finite, superfluous, and inferior reduplication of the divine being, it is precisely the voluntary, unnecessary, and gratuitous character of creation that makes its existence far more comic than tragic – not so much a metaphysical decadence as a case of divine excess.

This desire for the otherness of things which occurs in response to the Vision but is absent from the Music is of further significance as it suggests a parallel with the related literary distinction Tolkien draws in his essay between fairy-stories and what he simply calls the "Dream". As Tolkien explains in his essay, while the Dream and the fairy-story are alike in that in both "strange powers of the mind may be unlocked", he says he would nevertheless "condemn" the Dream as "gravely defective: like a good picture in a disfiguring frame":

> if a waking writer tells you that his tale is only a thing imagined in his sleep, he cheats deliberately the primal desire at the heart of Faërie: the realization, independent of the conceiving mind, of imagined wonder[...] It is at any rate essential to a genuine fairy-story, as distinct from the employment of this form for lesser or debased purposes, that it should be presented as "true" [...] But since the fairy-story deals with "marvels", it cannot tolerate any frame or machinery suggesting that the whole story in which they occur is a figment or illusion. (*OFS* 41-2)

Tolkien's opposition between the dream-device and the fairy-story links him with other literary Thomists of his day for whom the dream symbolized the antithesis of true art. Jacques Maritain, for example, in his *Art and Scholasticism* – a treatise developing a Thomistic theory of art which influenced many lay Catholic artists and writers of the early to mid-twentieth century, including possibly Tolkien[2] – contrasts genuine artistic inspiration, defined along the Thomistic lines of "reason exalted by an instinct of divine origin where human work controlled by a higher law is concerned", with the mere "aping [of] artistic inspiration[...] in dreams or the whole organic night below the level of reason" (Maritain 142). For American novelist Flannery O'Connor, a disciple of both Maritain and St. Thomas, the dream-image symbolized (as it did for Tolkien) the artist's temptation to impose his own, alien purposes, whether rational or otherwise, onto the work of art, rather than letting the work's own form come

---

2 See, for example, Milbank 2008.

to the fore (O'Connor 218). It is in another reader of Maritain, however, one whom we know to have greatly influenced Tolkien, that the most suggestive reference to the dream-image appears. In his acclaimed biography of St. Thomas, G.K. Chesterton writes how

> That *strangeness* of things, which is the light in all poetry, and indeed in all art, is really connected with their otherness; or what is called their objectivity. What is subjective must be stale; it is exactly what is objective that is in this imaginative manner strange. In this the great contemplative is the complete contrast of the false contemplative, the mystic who looks only into his own soul, the selfish artist who shrinks from the world and lives only in his own mind. According to St. Thomas, the mind acts freely of itself, but its freedom exactly consists in finding a way out to liberty and the light of day; to reality and the land of the living. In the subjectivist, the pressure of the world forces the imagination inwards. In the Thomist, the energy of the mind forces the imagination outwards, but because the images it seeks are real things. All their romance and glamour, so to speak, lies in the fact that they are real things; things *not* to be found by staring inwards at the mind. The flower is a vision because it is not only a vision. Or, if you will, it is a vision because it is not a dream. (Chesterton 182-3)

Whether Tolkien ever read Chesterton's biography of St. Thomas is unknown, yet the antithesis he draws between the vision and the dream – metaphors for the free artist whose "mind forces the imagination outwards" and the "selfish artist who shrinks from the world and lives only in his own mind" – is certainly striking, and provides circumstantial support for my suggestion that behind the relationship between the Ainur's Music and Vision may, in part, be the Dream/fairy-story polarity of Tolkien's essay. And while it would be an overstatement to say that the Music, like the Dream, "cheats" the "primal desire" for the otherness of things, what we do see in the Music is this essential desire going completely unrecognized, to say nothing of being unrealized. The Music is certainly beautiful for its time, "unlocking strange powers" in the minds of the Ainur, yet the trajectory of Tolkien's logic is hard to mistake: had Ilúvatar followed the Vision, not with the creation of the actual, physical world, but instead with a repetition of the Music which had preceded it, the Ainur would have perceived its self-contained, disinterested beauty as a "figment or illusion", i.e., as a dream.

Tolkien's further characterization of the Dream as a piece of "machinery" is also of some interest given that in Tolkien's bestiary the machine is usually associated with the tyrannical domination of nature. As Tolkien hints at in his essay, however, there is a sense in which the modern, technological enslavement of nature is in fact precipitated by a much more subtle, artistic, and intellectual form of "possessiveness" by which he says we "appropriate" things "mentally" (*OFS* 77). It is in this sense that the Dream "cheats" the primal desire for otherness: by deliberately suspending the question of the story's being or being made real, the Dream becomes a kind of instrument of intellectual domination, suppressing the objectifying otherness of the things which the story would relate and whose queerness it is the task of the true fairy-story to "recover". One of the questions that would seem to be obliquely raised by the Music, therefore, is the extent to which the will to dominate which arises in Melkor during the Music is in some small, initially innocuous way, already latent within the kind of pure conceptual or mental mastery the Ainur enjoy and exercise in their Music. If so, one wonders whether there is not a very limited yet important respect in which the Vision not only fulfills and surpasses the idealism of the Ainur's Music, but possibly even "saves" them from it.

Metaphysics of Eä

While the Vision may elicit in the Ainur the *desire* for things other than themselves, the fact remains that in itself the Vision is ultimately akin to the Music in that it represents at most a mental or intellectual form of existence, in contrast to the real, extra-mental existence at last bestowed by the Creator on the physical world of Eä, "the World that Is". The *Ainulindalë* itself points to this fundamental dialectic of mental versus extra-mental reality on the opening page when it is already anticipated that it will only be "after the end of days" that "the themes of Ilúvatar shall be played aright, and take Being in the moment of their utterance, for all shall then understand fully his intent in their part, and each shall know the comprehension of each, and Ilúvatar shall give to their thoughts the secret fire, being well pleased" (*S* 15-16). This contrast between the merely mental existence of the Music and the Vision and the real existence of the created physical world is also a recurring theme in Tolkien's letters, as when he analyzes his creation narrative in terms of the "story" of the world as contained in the Music and the Vision on the one hand, and the story as it later becomes "realized" in the creation of the physical world (*L* 235-6); or when he speaks of the Music and Vision together as a "cosmogonical drama" which is "perceived[...] as in a fashion we perceive a story composed by someone else", in contrast to the world we see "later as a 'reality'"; (ibid. 146) or when he speaks of the Music as the Ainur's

> work of Art, as it was in the first instance, [in which the Valar] became so engrossed with it, that when the Creator made it real (that is, gave it the secondary reality, subordinate to his own, which we call primary reality, and so in that hierarchy on the same plane with themselves) they desired to enter into it, from the beginning of its 'realization'. (ibid. 259)

Another letter similarly stresses the ontological equivalence between the physical world and the Ainur themselves when it describes the Music and Vision as a mere "Design" communicated to and then "interpreted" by the Ainur, "propounded first in musical or abstract form, and then in an 'historical vision'", after which "the One (the Teller [of the story]) said *Let it Be,* then the Tale became History, on the same plane as the hearers[...]" (ibid. 284). In the same place Tolkien again contrasts the story as "it 'exists' *in* the mind of the teller, and derivatively in the minds of hearers, but not on the same plane as the hearers", with the realized world which the hearers "could, if they desired, *enter into*" (emphasis Tolkien's). The common thread in each of these accounts is the same dialectical progression from the existence a thing it has in the mind alone to the "realization" or "achievement" of its existence in its own right in the act of creation.

We have already seen something of how the Tolkienian theme of the otherness of things, forecasted in the Ainur's Vision, has its roots in St. Thomas's metaphysical realism. What I want to draw attention to here is how Tolkien's antithesis between the reality things enjoy in their own existence and the existence they have as thought-objects in the mind serves further to illustrate the related principle of Thomas's metaphysical "existentialism", the insight widely regarded as constituting the heart of Thomas's metaphysical thought, namely that the act of existence, signified by the Latin infinitive *esse*, is the "actuality of all acts and the perfection of all perfections" (Aquinas, *Power* 8.2 ad 9). As existential Thomists of the last century emphasized, the privileging of the real, concrete, objectifying act of existence of things over their intelligible, contemplative essence or form represented nothing less than a revolution in metaphysics and epistemology which reversed the "essentialism" which had characterized much of the intellectual tradition both before and after St. Thomas. According to Thomas, just as it is through its essence or form that a given substance has its existence, so it is through the substance's act of existence that a given essence has its being. One consequence of this doctrine which has a special significance for our present understanding of Tolkien concerns Thomas's teaching that, although things have more being in the divine mind of God than they do in themselves, as was noted above, there is nevertheless another sense in which creatures – especially *material* creatures, Thomas emphasizes – are more themselves *as creatures* than they are in the divine mind, and that "[e]ven so a house has nobler being in the architect's mind than in matter; yet a material house is called a house more truly than the one which exists in the mind, since the former is a house in act, the latter only in potency" (Aquinas, *Summa* 1.18.4 ad 3). Thomas's positive evaluation of matter as a created, intelligible, and objectifying force, combined with the role he reserves for the body in the sensual perception of beauty, mean that, as Michael Sweeney has put it in a passage in keeping with the theme of this paper, "[i]nstead of rendering philosophy tragic, the inescapable corporeality of human life makes philosophy comic because matter is no longer an irrational given contrary to intelligibility but the created principle to which all human thought must return" (Sweeney 255).

As we have seen, it is this same basic, "comic", or to adopt Tolkien's own expression, "eucatastrophic" metaphysical principle – according to which things have *more* reality in themselves, in the objectifying "otherness" of their own act of existence, than they do in the minds that conceive them – that Tolkien is especially concerned to depict in the *Ainulindalë*. As will be familiar to many of Tolkien's readers, *eucatastrophe* is the paradoxical term (literally meaning "good catastrophe) which Tolkien coined in his essay "On Fairy-Stories" to express that peculiar but highly desired quality in "true fairy-stories" of "the sudden joyous 'turn'", when a "sudden and miraculous grace" of deliverance occurs (*OFS* 86). Behind his concept of eucatastrophe, as Tolkien explains elsewhere, is his belief in a universal divine providence according to which the Creator is always immanently present to and in control of his creation, accomplishing his ultimate purposes, not *despite* the seemingly hopeless circumstances that arise in history, but precisely *through* them. The chief effect of this divine subterfuge, as Tolkien explains further in his essay, is an intense sense of rescued "Joy beyond the walls of the world, poignant as grief" (ibid.). There is further respect, however, and one especially pertinent to the question of interpreting the *Ainulindalë*, in which Tolkien's metaphysics relates to the issue of eucatastrophe, for as Tolkien continues in the epilogue to his essay,

> The peculiar quality of the "joy" in successful Fantasy can thus be explained as a sudden glimpse of the underlying reality or truth[...] [I]n the "eucatastrophe" we see in a brief vision that the answer may be greater – it may be a far-off gleam or echo of *evangelium* in the real world[...] God redeemed the corrupt making-creatures, men, in a way fitting to this aspect, as to others, of their strange nature. The Gospels contain a fairy-story, or a story of a larger kind which embraces all the essence of fairy-stories. They contain many marvels – peculiarly artistic, beautiful and moving: 'mythical' in their perfect, self-contained significance; and among the marvels is the greatest and most complete conceivable eucatastrophe. But this story has entered History and the primary world; the desire and aspiration of sub-creation has been raised to the fulfillment of Creation. The Birth of Christ is the eucatastrophe of Man's history. The Resurrection is the eucatastrophe of the story of the Incarnation. This story begins and ends in joy. (ibid. 88-9)

According to Tolkien, what has happened in the Christian Gospel, the story of the Incarnation, death, and Resurrection of Jesus Christ, is that the Creator has taken up the "essence of fairy-stories", these stories about hope and the unlooked-for "sudden joyous turn", and he has made them *real* by giving them the reality of "History and the primary world", raising them "to the fulfillment of Creation". The Gospel, in other words, is not merely a real-life story "containing" a eucatastrophe or happy ending, but precisely in being real it constitutes for Tolkien the eucatastrophe or happy ending of all other fairy-stories, for in it all other fairy-stories have, in a sense, become *true*, have been graced with the special dispensation of real, historical, physical, created being.

As the reader will by now have little difficulty in appreciating, this eucatastrophic, gospel movement from a story in the mind to its actual "fulfillment of Creation" is none other than the story of the *Ainulindalë*, so much so that the latter might fairly be said to represent as much a mythical retelling and foreshadowing of the Christian story of salvation or *re*-creation (as Tolkien understands it) as it does a rehearsal of the story of creation itself. In Tolkien's hands the creation event has become a kind of *protoevangelion*: if the Music, as we suggested, is a sort of abstract, metaphysically disinterested "Dream", and the Vision a desire-inducing "fairy-story", then the actual creation of the physical world in its own, mind-independent existence turns out to be nothing less than an image of the Gospel, the fulfillment of all myths and fairy-stories. The pattern of the *Ainulindalë*, in conclusion, is a movement from Music to Vision to Reality, from intelligible essence or abstract form, to a story, to an existing, mind-independent reality, a motion that is metaphysically speaking not a tragedy, but a *eucatastrophe*, not a Fall, but a Fulfillment. Through his creation-myth Tolkien thus portrays the Thomistic insight into the real existence or being of things as a surpassing and gratuitous gift, anticipated in but never necessitated by their forms or essences alone, hoped for in the promising and received with joy in the giving, a gift freely given by a good, all-powerful, personal God who himself must transcend all conceptuality because he is Being itself.

About the Author

Jonathan McIntosh is a recent graduate of the Braniff Graduate School of Liberal Arts at the University of Dallas, Texas, and a Fellow of Humanities at New Saint Andrews College in Moscow, Idaho. His doctoral dissertation in philosophy is on J.R.R. Tolkien's and St. Thomas Aquinas's metaphysics of creation.

Tolkien References

TOLKIEN, J.R.R., *The Letters of J.R.R. Tolkien*, (ed. by Humphrey Carpenter with the assistance of Christopher Tolkien), Boston: Houghton Mifflin, 2000.

"On Fairy-Stories", In: *The Tolkien Reader*, New York: Ballantine, 1966.

The Silmarillion, (ed. by Christopher Tolkien), Boston: Houghton Mifflin, 1977.

References

AQUINAS, Thomas, *The Division and Methods of the Sciences,* questions 5-6 of *Expositio super librum Boethii De trinitate,* (transl. by Armand Maurer), Toronto: Pontifical Institute of Mediaeval Studies, 1986.

On the Power of God, (transl. by Fathers of the English Dominican Province), Eugene, OR: Wipf and Stock, 2004.

Summa Theologica, (ed. by Robert Maynard Hutchins, transl. by Fathers of the English Dominican Province), Vol. 19-20, In: *Great Books of the Western World*, Chicago: Encyclopedia Britannica, 1987.

BIRZER, Brad, *Tolkien's Sanctifying Myth: Understanding Middle-earth*, Wilmington, DE: ISI Books, 2003.

CANDLER, Peter, "Tolkien or Nietzsche, Philology and Nihilism", University of Nottingham Centre of Theology and Philosophy, www.theologyphilosophycentre.co.uk/papers/Candler_TolkeinNietzsche.doc (accessed March 31, 2009).

CHESTERTON, G.K., *St. Thomas Aquinas: "The Dumb Ox"*, New York: Doubleday, 1956.

COLLINS, Robert, "'Ainulindalë': Tolkien's Commitment to an Aesthetic Ontology", In: *Journal of the Fantastic in the Arts* 11 (2000), 257-65.

COX, John, "Tolkien's Platonic Fantasy", *Seven* 5 (1984), 53-69.

DAVIS, Howard, "Ainulindalë: The Music of Creation", In: *Mythlore* 9 (1982), 6-10.

EDEN, Bradford Lee, "The 'Music of the Spheres': Relationships Between Tolkien's *Silmarillion* and Medieval Cosmological and Religious Theory", In: Jane Chance (ed.), *Tolkien the Medievalist*, London and New York: Routledge, 2003, 183-93.

FLIEGER, Verlyn, *Splintered Light: Logos and Language in Tolkien's World*, 2nd ed., Kent, OH: Kent State University Press, 2002.

GRUBBS, David, "The Maker's Image: Tolkien, Fantasy & Magic", Cornerstone (October 2001). http://www.cornerstonemag.com/imaginarium/features/tolkien_magic.html (accessed March 31, 2009).

KOCHER, Paul, *Master of Middle-earth: the Fiction of J.R.R. Tolkien*, Boston: Houghton Mifflin Company, 1972.

LEITHART, Peter, *Deep Comedy: Trinity, Tragedy, and Hope in Western Literature*, Moscow, ID: Canon Press, 2006.

MARITAIN, Jacques, *Art and Scholasticism*, (transl. by Joseph W. Evans), New York: Charles Scribner's Sons, 1962.

MILBANK, Alison, *Chesterton and Tolkien as Theologians: The Fantasy of the Real*, Edinburgh: T&T Clark, 2007.

"Tolkien, Chesterton, and Thomism", In: Stratford Caldecott and Thomas Honegger (eds.), *Tolkien's "The Lord of the Rings": Sources of Inspiration*, Zurich and Jena: Walking Tree Publishers, 2008, 187-98.

O'CONNOR, Flannery, *The Habit of Being*, (ed. by Sally Fitzgerald), New York: Farrar, Straus, Giroux, 1979.

SWEENEY, Michael, "Stat rosa pristine margine: Umberto Eco on the Role of the Margin in Medieval Hermeneutics and Thomas Aquinas as a Comic Philosopher", In: *Proceedings of the American Catholic Philosophical Association* 72 (1998), 255-69.

Part B

Music in Tolkien's World

Steven Linden

A Speculative History of the Music of Arda

Music is important in Tolkien's legendarium. Formulaic phrases such as "songs are yet sung" or "it is said in song" are frequently encountered, conveying the fame of some event. But whereas certain aspects of the cultural history of Arda were spelled out in great detail – particularly the languages – very little is said about the music itself. This is to be expected; Tolkien was a professional philologist, but had little knowledge of music (though in his letters he expressed a fondness for Chopin and a strong dislike for popular music) (*L* 89). This results in some very large gaps in our knowledge of the music of Middle-earth; and, as with so many other gaps in the Legendarium, it is irresistibly tempting to try to fill them in.

There have been many musical compositions written that relate in some way to Middle-earth. These may be roughly divided into three groups. There are, first of all, popular songs with lyrics that make reference to Tolkien's works (the best known of which are certainly those by *Led Zeppelin*). Then there are the Middle-earth "soundtracks" as it were, some of which are actual soundtracks (Rosenman's for the Bakshi movie and Shore's for the Jackson movies) and others abstract program music (like de Meij's symphony). Neither of these categories concerns the topic at hand. Finally, there are actual musical interpretations of the songs from the Legendarium – such as Donald Swann's work, or that of the Tolkien Ensemble. We may group with these a few essays that address the question: what did the music of Middle-earth sound like? Notable among these are Gene Hargrove's essay and David J. Finnamore's webpage. The tendency in these essays is to ascribe to the music of Middle-earth a style generally similar to that of Medieval European music. Finnamore says:

> "Middle-earth is mostly modeled on medieval and Renaissance western Europe with a fantastical, mythical twist. Therefore, it makes sense to use European music from before the 17th century in a similar kind of way as a model for the music of Middle-earth."[1]

---

1 http://www.elvenminstrel.com/tolkien/memusic.htm

Hargrove says:

> "Although in a footnote, Tolkien warns that the adoption of these early medieval languages to represent languages in LOR – for example, that of the Riders of Rohan – 'does not imply that the Rohirrim closely resembled the ancient English otherwise, in culture or art, in weapons or modes of warfare, except in a general way due to their circumstances,' music, or singing, because of its close relationship to the evolution of language in the Middle Ages, is probably an exception to his general warning."[2]

This is certainly a reasonable approach. But there is a problem. Middle-earth is our earth, but not our Medieval earth. Middle-earth is supposed to be ancient. It seems more than a little strange, then, that its music should be the sort of music that is peculiar to the Dark Ages and Middle Ages. Of particular note is the matter of polyphony, or contrapuntal music. In the real world, polyphony was not really developed until the latter half of the Middle Ages; yet there does seem to be polyphony in Middle-earth. In Bag End, the Dwarves begin singing "first one and then another," (*H* 26) which suggests that they are singing different parts. In Rivendell, Frodo hears music of "interwoven words" (*LotR* 249). The musical situation in Middle-earth appears to be something like that of roughly the thirteenth or fourteenth century. But a musical idiom does not exist in isolation; it is bound up not only with the culture in which it arises but also with the older idioms out of which it came and the later into which it develops. It is therefore hard to understand this particular musical situation in anything but the context of the thirteenth or fourteenth century – the context of the gradual rise of polyphony. And it is quite incredible to suggest that such a situation existed not once in our history, but twice – once in the early Renaissance and once far, far earlier, before the rise of Rome or the fall of Troy.

A solution to this problem may be discovered through a consideration of the differences between Arda and our modern world with respect to art and technology. There is a modern tendency to view such things through the lens of "progress" (although it could be argued that there is simultaneously an opposite tendency). And this is not misguided. Today's technology is more advanced than that from a hundred years ago, and we are justified in thinking that a hundred

---

2 http://www.phil.unt.edu/hargrove/music.html

years hence, technology will be still further advanced. And it is valid, at least to a degree, in the history of music as well. Polyphony really did develop out of monophony, through a process of increasing sophistication and complexity. But that is not how things work in Middle-earth. There it is not a matter of making newer and better things. There, great things, once achieved, often can never be achieved again. So it is for Yavanna and the Trees, Fëanor and the Silmarils, the Teleri and their white ships. In Arda, decay and decline are dominant, even if they can sometimes be reversed in the short term; the history of Arda is the history of the "long defeat". Why should the same not apply to its music? Perhaps we ought to imagine the music of Middle-earth as declining through the ages, so that the songs of Gondor are less sophisticated than the songs of Númenor; and those are but meager echoes of the songs of the Eldar in Aman. If we view the music of Arda in this way, the situation becomes the reverse of the one we were considering above. Perhaps it does not represent the time at which polyphony was overtaking monophony; perhaps it represents the time at which polyphony was giving way to monophony, declining into monophony. Perhaps the evolution of music in the Renaissance ought to be thought of as the rediscovery of techniques and practices that were lost with the decline of Men and the departure of the Elves.

Let us adopt this conjecture as a premise, and attempt to tell a story about the evolution of the musical styles of Arda.

The first music, and the greatest, that we encounter in the Legendarium is the music of the Ainur. There has been debate over whether this "music" is to be understood literally or figuratively. I have always understood it literally, and I will operate on that assumption here (though without defending it). Prior to the great music there are some early songs of the Ainur:

> And he spoke to them, propounding to them themes of music, and they sang before him, and he was glad. But for a long while they sang only each alone, or but few together, while the rest hearkened; for each comprehended only that part of the mind of Ilúvatar from which he came, and in the understanding of their brethren they grew but slowly. Yet ever as they listened they came to deeper understanding, and increased in unison and harmony. (S 3)

This tells us a good deal. When they sang alone, it was obviously monophony (though presumably of a marvelous and surpassingly fair kind). But there is here a specific reference to "harmony"; it seems then that there is homophony in this early music as well (when they sang "but few together").

After these earlier essays, the Ainur make their great music. Ilúvatar declares a great theme to them and commands that they show forth their powers in adorning this theme. This brings to mind a type of music known as heterophony wherein, as with monophony, all the voices sing the same general line, but there are slight differences among the various voice parts. But there is evidence that the great *Ainulindalë* is more than heterophony. They have already practiced harmony, and in fact Ilúvatar says "I will that ye make in harmony together a Great Music" (*S* 3). And we can reasonably expect their song to be polyphonic as well, for several reasons. First, there are hints of polyphony to be found in the Third Age, and it violates our premise (as well as common sense) to suggest that this Third Age music was more sophisticated than the *Ainulindalë*. Second, the music is described thus: "[…] a sound arose of endless interchanging melodies, woven in harmony […]" (*S* 4). "Interchanging" and "woven" surely suggest polyphony. Third, there is patently more than one melody progressing simultaneously after Melkor decides to "interweave" his own music into the song, and Ilúvatar responds by adding a new theme of his own, and then another: "And it seemed at last that there were two musics progressing at one time before the seat of Ilúvatar, and they were utterly at variance" (*S* 5).

If the *Ainulindalë* was polyphonic, we might well expect that it was the very epitome of polyphony. Perhaps it is foolhardy to try to comprehend the actual sound of the *Ainulindalë*, but it is difficult to resist. In known musical history, there have been two periods that have reasonable claims to the title "height of polyphony", and two composers who have epitomized polyphony, each in his own way. These are Palestrina during the sixteenth century and Bach during the early eighteenth. Their differences illustrate the great change that occurred in western music around the year 1600. Palestrina's music may be thought of as first contrapuntal and secondly harmonic, while Bach's is first harmonic and secondly contrapuntal. In other words, Palestrina's music comes out of a very long tradition of giving primacy to the individual musical lines, and conceiving of polyphony as a result of the superposition of these lines. In this sort of polyphony, there are strict rules about the progression of any of the individual melodies, but there is comparative freedom (though of course not total freedom) with regard to which notes are sounding together at any given time. The unit of harmony here is the interval; in other words, the rules that determine which combinations of notes are permissible and which are not are based on the distance (interval) in pitch between two notes.

Bach's polyphony, on the other hand, is firmly harmonic and firmly chordal. The tradition in which Bach is embedded thought first of the harmony and then of the progression of the individual lines. In this sort of polyphony, there is great freedom with regard to the progression of the individual melodies but strict rules concerning which notes may sound together. And whereas for Palestrina (and his precursors) harmony was thought of in terms of intervals, by Bach's time it was thought of in terms of chords (three or more notes sounding together).

So, which style approximates the music of the Ainur best? Obviously, there is something to be said for Palestrina's style, for it is older and closer to the styles that we expect to find in Middle-earth itself. But there is a great deal of evidence for Bach's style as well. The Ainur, unlike the composers of the Renaissance, seem to have learned harmony before counterpoint (for there is reference to harmony even in the earliest songs of the Ainur). It would be natural, then, for them to continue to think harmonically when they sang the great *Ainulindalë*. And when the music ends, it ends in "one chord", terminology that suggests Bach's style. But either way of thinking about the music of the Ainur is probably too limiting. Bach and Palestrina may have been the greatest human composers of polyphony, but we are dealing here with angels (or gods). Perhaps it is best to imagine a synthesis, a fusion, of Palestrina's style with Bach's, and perhaps even with Mozart's and Beethoven's – a sort of music where neither harmony nor counterpoint must come first, because they are so perfectly crafted together, where every note is exactly right in both its melody and its chord, where nature and artifice become one.

We move now to Arda. The first music after that of the Ainur is that of the early Elves. It appears that song was first inspired among them by the sound of water, wherein, it is oft repeated, there lives an echo of the music of the Ainur. So we may imagine that the *Ainulindalë* had some influence on these primitive Quendian songs. Of course, the question arises: to what extent is water really musical, and to what extent can it be mimicked? Are we to believe that the music of the first Elves consisted of gurgling and tinkling sounds? Probably not. David Finnamore speculates on a sort of mathematical imitation of the sound of water, leading him to consider chaos theory as a basis for early Elvish song. (Finnamore) This is certainly an interesting avenue of speculation, but it seems to me that we ought not to stray too far from the norms of western music; for surely Tolkien seems to have thought entirely in terms of western music. Perhaps, then, the first songs of the Elves mimicked water more figuratively, through lines that rise and fall naturally and perhaps even through a clear, undisturbed quality of voice. These early songs were almost certainly monophonic, if the Elves even sang together at all.

The first great sundering of the Elves occurred when the Eldar departed for Aman. The Amanyar (and Sindar) were subsequently sundered from the Avari and from those of the Nandor that did not enter Beleriand until the Second Age. And when contact was reestablished, it was the Noldorin and Sindarin cultures that dominated the Avarin and Nandorin. We know, therefore, almost nothing about Avarin music. Of course, it is probably safe to assume that it remained less sophisticated than the music of the Elves of the west; but beyond that, all that can be made are poorly educated guesses.

The next great split among the Elves, and from our Beleriand-centric point of view perhaps the most important, is that between the Sindar and the Elves of Aman. It would be of great interest to know whether the use of musical instruments by the Elves began before or after this split. For if Sindarin and Amanyan instrumental practice developed from a common source, we might expect them to utilize the same, or similar, systems of tuning; if not, there would be no need for their respective tuning systems to have anything in common.

In Aman, Elvish music must have reached its peak. Here, in the period before the Darkening of Valinor, we can expect to find the most sophisticated, most complex music created by the Children of Ilúvatar. In Aman the Elves must have learned a great deal about music from the Valar. There would then have been a clash, and probably a synthesis, between the primitive, monophonic Elvish tradition (inspired though it was by the *Ainulindalë* via water) and the new style learned from the Ainur. This probably resulted in great diversity in Elvish music of this period. If the music of the Ainur was indeed a perfect synthesis of chord and melody, harmony and counterpoint, as I have speculated, it seems that the Elves would have had to assimilate this style in pieces rather than as a whole (for they could not achieve the perfection achieved by the Ainur). If primitive Elvish music included neither homophony nor polyphony (as seems likely) then the whole Elvish theory of harmony would be based on the music of the Valar; so, if our speculation concerning the *Ainulindalë* is correct, it would probably be based on chords. But unlike the music of the Baroque (and later periods) it may have been modal. That is, it may have employed more modes than the major and minor that have dominated since about 1600, and strayed less often beyond the boundaries of the particular mode it was in. And of course, the rules governing harmonic progressions may have been quite different. Alongside large polyphonic compositions modeled on the music of the Ainur, songs for single voice persisted from earlier days. These may have been enriched through exposure to the new style. Accompaniment, based on chords or intervals or both, would sometimes have been employed.

There are a few hints about Amanyan music in the texts. Of great interest is a passage in *The Book of Lost Tales*, when the Elves are gathering in Valmar for the festival. Of the Vanyar (here called the Teleri) it is said: "[…] the throbbing of their congregated harps beat the air most sweetly." Of the Noldor (here Noldoli): "[…] the music that their viols and instruments awoke was now more sweetly sad than ever before." And of the Teleri (here Solosimpi): "[…] their piping blent with voices brought the sense of tides and murmurous waves and the wailing cry of the coast-loving birds thus inland deep upon the plain" (*LT I* 158).

This tells us much about the music of the Elves in general and also about the music peculiar to each kindred. It confirms that all three kindreds had ensemble music of some kind at this point. The Vanyar have what appears to be an orchestra of harps. The Noldor too do not sing here, but play "viols and instruments" – which sounds suspiciously like a modern orchestra. These pieces were probably chordal and polyphonic, and may have resembled music of the early Baroque. The Teleri, on the other hand, play pipes – wind instruments – and mingle this sound with voices. There also seems to be a suggestion that the music of the Teleri retains the ancient water connection much more strongly than the others (as we would indeed expect). Perhaps, then, whereas the Noldor eagerly adopted the new "learned" practices of counterpoint and harmony, the Teleri integrated the new techniques more carefully and conservatively, so that they retained a greater freedom with respect to harmony and voice-leading and a more naturalistic sound.

Maglor is said to the be the greatest Noldorin minstrel, but we never hear of him playing a "viol". His preference appears, rather, to be for the harp. Perhaps this is because he is also a singer, and whereas for purely instrumental compositions the Noldor employed their orchestra, for vocal pieces they turned to the harp. It should be noted that the term "harp" is somewhat vague. Probably the term covers all manner of plucked string instruments, though perhaps excluding those of which the strings are artificially varied in length by means of a finger board (like a guitar or lute). As suggested above, songs for voice and harp may have adopted from the Valar a chordal approach to the accompaniment. But it seems unlikely that Maglor would have been content with a simple arrangement of melody against evenly strummed chords. He may have developed the chordal accompaniment on the model of the larger-scale Noldorin music, turning the harp into a little orchestra of its own and adding contrapuntal lines and subsidiary melodic figures. This may have resulted in a sound similar to that of the Renaissance or Baroque lute. But the vocal melodies would probably still have their roots in the old Elvish monophonic tradition. Indeed, perhaps at this time accompaniments were written for old songs that had been sung in Cuiviénen.

But we ought also to remember that monophony seems to have been preserved alongside the more sophisticated forms. In the Lost Tales, the Elves launch into a song "in unison" (ibid.) before the gates of Valmar; and we certainly have later examples of unaccompanied song. Nonetheless, the style of melody employed in these songs was undoubtedly influenced by the new techniques.

The music of the Sindar would probably be rather different, since their style never met the high style of the Valar. The development of homophony and polyphony would here be much more gradual and more natural, if it occurred at all. It seems likely that it did, for it is suggested that Daeron at times played his flute while Lúthien sang. The Sindar probably did not have chords (or rather, did not think of them as chords). If there was a formal theory of counterpoint at all, it probably dealt with intervals. But whereas it is easy to picture the Noldor writing treatises and studies on music theory, the Sindar would probably have adopted a more free and expressive idiom. But it is important not to think that Sindarin music was vastly less sophisticated than, or inferior to, the music of the Eldar in Aman. For, according to the Lay of Leithian, Daeron is the "mightiest of the three" great musicians (Maglor, Daeron, and Tinfang Warble) (*LB* 174). In what ways might Sindarin music surpass Noldorin? In partial contrast to Amanyan music, melody would be the most important element; and perhaps the rules concerning counterpoint would be unrestrictive enough that certain dissonances and rhythmic differences would be tolerated among the various parts. This would allow certain things to be done in Sindarin music that would sound wrong and out of place in Amanyan – for example, tension could be created through the use of dissonance. This lack of a strict formalism may also have resulted in freer and more frequent use of chromaticism. Daeron may simply have had a larger menu of notes to choose from than Maglor. This would be more likely if (as seems probable) Sindarin instrumental music retained a closer connection with vocal music than Noldorin did. For all sorts of chromaticism are open to the voice, which is not restricted to any particular mode or even tuning system, unless by conscious design. Daeron's solo flute pieces may have mimicked the voice quite closely, while bringing the ethereal, entirely un-voicelike tone quality of the flute to bear. They may have employed all sorts of chromaticisms and rhythmic complexities that we consider "romantic" or "modern", without ever straying from their naturalistic and supremely melodic roots. And when Lúthien's voice was added, a whole new vista of harmony and counterpoint would have opened up.

When the Noldor returned to Middle-earth, they must have left a part of their musical tradition behind. It is unlikely that their "viols and instruments" survived the passage of the Helcaraxë, or the burning of the ships at Losgar. They would have been forced to develop smaller-scale, more mobile forms of music. The solo song probably rose into a new prominence; polyphony may have survived in the form of music for small ensembles. "Harps" of various sorts may have been more mobile than other instruments, and thus come into wider use (these would of course resemble Celtic harps and lyres more than the large modern harp).

As the Noldor became more firmly established in Beleriand, their music probably evolved in two directions. The more mobile form discussed above probably persisted as a sort of "popular" style, while, particularly in such places as Gondolin and Nargothrond, there may have been a revival of Valinorean, "learned" styles. The popular style was probably minimally polyphonic, suited to a single voice with or without accompaniment. It was most likely influenced by the Sindarin style (and vice versa), though in what way it is difficult to guess. One wonders what Maglor made of Daeron and vice versa when they met at the Mereth Aderthad. Perhaps Maglor had to write a new treatise on melody and harmony to take into account the Sindarin practics he observed. And possibly allowance was made for new chromaticisms in his music. Daeron, for his part, would have found Maglor's approach a little too formalistic, but he may have come to a better understanding of the foundations of his own musical system as a result of the meeting.

It is difficult to guess whether the first humans developed music on their own or learned it from the Avari. The latter seems more probable, given that their earliest languages were apparently derived from the Avari. At any rate, they certainly had music of a sort by the time they entered Beleriand; Finrod finds a crude harp in their camp. There is very little evidence for what this early Edainic music sounded like, for the culture of the Edain became almost immediately dominated by that of the Noldor and Sindar. But it must be supposed that their music was non-chordal; they probably did not have much of a system of harmony at all. Harps may have been used as solo instruments, in which case the music may have been monophonic. If the harps were used to accompany singing, they could have been restricted to a few notes, interjected here and there, to reinforce the vocal line.

In Beleriand, the chief influence on the Edain was probably the popular style of the Noldor, with the Sindarin style a close second. The references we have to the music of the Edain suggest that solo song with harp accompaniment was a favorite style; this sort of harp-song was undoubtedly modelled on the Noldorin accompanied song. These songs probably employed chordal or semi-chordal harmony and may have sounded roughly like songs of the late Renaissance and early Baroque. The Edain probably had little contact with the more learned, "high" style of the Noldor, which would have been at its height in Gondolin and

Nargothrond. And even if they did hear this style, it is unlikely that the Edain could have imitated it, given their limited resources and their limited longevity. The Noldorin-inspired accompanied song was probably the most sophisticated of Edainic music. We hear only of the lords of the Edain practising this style: Tuor in Cirith Niniach, for instance, or Húrin when Lalaith dies (though in the event he is too grief-stricken to actually sing). Those of less high lineage may have retained more of the primitive Edainic musical style and insofar as they adopted the Eldarin idiom it may have been as a "corrupted" folk-style. This would have become increasingly true as the Edain fell on hard times. Perhaps the oppressed people of Hador developed a sort of slave music following the Nirnaeth (a style that did not require instruments and that was easily learned, and yet recalled the music of happier times).

What of Dwarven music? It seems probable, just as it did with humans, that the Dwarves learned music first from the Elves. Tolkien says that the Dwarves are "at once native and alien in their habitations, speaking the languages of the country, but with an accent due to their own private tongue [...]" (L 229). Perhaps they also sang the songs of their country, but with their own musical "accent". Or rather, they adopted the musical styles of those around them, but injected them with a uniquely Dwarvish quality. We have few references to their music in the First or Second Age. At the Nirnaeth, they bear up their fallen lord and leave the battle singing a slow dirge. This must have been quite chilling. It was probably a melody similar to those of the Elves, though undoubtedly lacking in certain Elvish subtleties; perhaps it was even in a mode peculiar to the Dwarves. It seems likely to have been monophonic: a great unison chanting by deep Dwarvish voices. It would have sounded roughly like Gregorian chant, but undoubtedly deeper and probably with more use of formal, repetitive figures. It would certainly need to be a well-known song, and an easy one both to remember and to sing.

Following the fall of Beleriand, the Elvish population in Middle-earth drastically declined and Elvish culture became increasingly backward-looking. It seems probable that very little stylistic development occurred in their music after the First Age. The one thing that seems most likely to have happened is further synthesis of the Noldorin and Sindarin styles. But instead of achieving a real unity between the two styles, the Eldar may have simply preserved both styles side by side, and used them interchangeably. Polyphonic techniques could have been imported from the Noldorin style into the Sindarin. The result may have been something sounding roughly like the music of Palestrina and his contemporaries. Perhaps this is the sort of thing Frodo heard in Rivendell. Solo songs (sounding like plainsong) were probably preserved in both traditions. The "A Elbereth Gilthoniel" chant heard in Rivendell seems likely to have been in something of a Sindarin vein (the language is Sindarin, at any rate); indeed, it seems to recall Lúthien's song "Ir Ithil ammen Eruchín [...]" (*LB* 354). It therefore probably sounded like a rather free variety of plainsong, tinged perhaps with Sindarin chromaticism. It may have resembled old Roman or Byzantine chant more than Gregorian. The same general remarks apply to the hymn to Elbereth sung by one from Gildor's company. Galadriel's songs, particularly "Namarië", would have been more Noldorin – more firmly based in some formal modal system and therefore more restricted, but also more structured and balanced. They probably resembled Gregorian chant fairly closely – we know, at least, that Tolkien thought of "Namarië" as sounding like Gregorian chant (Tolkien/Swann vi).

When the Edain removed to Númenor, they must have brought their Eldarin-dominated music with them, along with whatever "lower" styles they possessed. The largest population in Númenor was that of the folk of Marach, the third house of the Edain. These had suffered long enslavement by the Easterlings, probably forcing them to adopt a purely vocal style, easy to learn and easy to sing. This would naturally have become a large component of Númenorean music. But Elros, the first king, was the foster-son of Maglor. So, at least in the early days of Númenor, an imitation of Maglor's Amanyan style may have been the fashionable "court-style". This may have helped to maintain the harp-accompanied song as a favorite form. But it seems likely that chords would have come to be considered archaic, learned, and difficult. Perhaps when a Númenorean minstrel wanted to sound sophisticated, he strummed a full chord to each note of the song. As time went on, Númenorean knowledge (and understanding) of chords may have diminished. Harmony in terms of intervals may have begun to replace harmony in terms of chords. Perhaps droning (sustaining a single note or chord underneath the melody) became a common method of accompaniment. Of course, these techniques would differ from their counterparts in the real world in that they would be fragments and echoes of an older, fuller system of chordal harmony, whereas in the real world they were precursors of the chordal system. Nonetheless these may have sounded something like the songs of the late Middle Ages.

Given the resources available to the Númenoreans, and the length of time for which their civilization lasted, it would be surprising if they did not develop larger-scale musical forms. Choirs are likely to have been formed, and maybe even instrumental ensembles. Númenorean choral music was probably derived primarily from the Númenorean solo song, rather than directly from older Amanyan forms. If this is true, much of this music would be monophonic, or nearly so. But perhaps some of the more ambitious Númenorean composers adopted chordal practices and even counterpoint.

In the last days of Númenor, music with an Elvish bent was probably discouraged by the king and practiced only by the Faithful. It is hard to guess, though, what sorts of music might have been considered "Elvish" – for nearly all Númenorean music was ultimately derived from Elvish. Perhaps the stylistic strand descended from Hadorian slave music was preferred by the King's Men as more authentically "mannish", while the court-style of Elros's day, or such as was remembered of it, survived among the Elf-friends. In any event, it was the Faithful who survived, and thus the more Elvish idiom that was brought back to Middle-earth. In Gondor, the semi-chordal style that was popular in Númenor probably survived, largely intact, through the Third Age. In Arnor, however, as the kingdom deteriorated, the old music might have taken on a sort of "folk song" characteristic. The Elvish modes and the rules governing melody and harmony were probably forgotten, though many of the old songs written according to those rules were remembered.

There would also have been a great deal of influence from the music of the neighboring peoples – the Men that either had not entered Beleriand at all or had not gone to Númenor. Among these were the Éothéod, the ancestors of the Rohirrim. It is very difficult to make guesses about the music of the Rohirrim, since we know so little about their ancestors. Their music was undoubtedly a distant descendant of the same early Mannish music represented by the rude harp found in Bëor's camp. But in the intervening years it would have been influenced by Avarin music (about which we know nothing), Nandorin music (again nothing), possibly Dwarvish music, and maybe even Sindarin music, following the establishment of such realms as Thranduil's. One clue we have is that the songs of the Rohirrim are invariably written in alliterative verse. This suggests that their singing was not entirely unlike plainsong, with great rhythmic freedom. Their style was likely purely vocal and almost certainly monophonic. They had horns, but there is no indication that these were ever used as musical instruments (in fact, it is unlikely that their horns were capable of such use). Nonetheless, it is possible (though utterly fanciful) to imagine that their vocal style imitated the sound of horns in some way, perhaps relying on frequent leaps of a fifth or fourth.

The Hobbits would have inherited, first of all, the same sort of music as the Rohirrim; for the Hobbits and the Rohirrim originated in the same region and even have related languages. But the folk songs of Arnor probably also had a profound effect on them. The native music of the Hobbits is always represented as strongly English and somewhat rustic. If indeed the old Númenorean style turned into a folk style in Arnor, it would have become somewhat simpler and more formulaic (and thus catchy and memorable); and it is this sort of music that the Hobbits are likely to have picked up. As opposed to the music of the Rohirrim, their music would have been quite rhythmic (i.e. not rhythmically free) and would be rich in tunes with repeating motives and even numbers of measures. English folk songs of the Renaissance are perhaps not far off the mark.

The music of the Dwarves in Bag End probably sounded rather strange to Bilbo at the time. The Dwarves are a stubborn folk and their musical style, like their language, would not have evolved very much. Again, it seems probable that most of their music was derived from Elvish music – so it may be that the music they played and sang in Bag End is the Dwarvish equivalent of the contemporary music of Rivendell and Lindon. They clearly have a real instrumental ensemble, suggesting that such things also survived in Elvish music. For the instrumental music of the Dwarves, we might turn to the early Renaissance for counterparts. But there must be little or nothing in our music that can match the singing of the Dwarves.

That is just a rough outline of one possible way of imagining the evolution of music within Arda. Undoubtedly there are countless others. Particularly suspect, I must confess, is the game of searching for counterparts to the various styles of Middle-earth in the music of the real world in the last millennium and a half. But it seems that Tolkien, a non-musician, imagined the music of Middle-earth as something rather like the music of Europe in the past few centuries. Is there any point in this game? Possibly not, beyond the enjoyment of exploring the Legendarium and trying to fill in the gaps. But this whole discussion makes obvious an interesting fact. While there is a great deal of music about Middle-earth, there have been very few attempts at writing the music of Middle-earth – that is, the sort of music that was actually heard in Middle-earth. There is Donald Swann's music, which has the distinction of having been approved by Tolkien. But one must conclude that it is really quite inauthentic, in both the style (which is distinctly post-Baroque) and the instrumentation (surely there were no pianos in Middle-earth!). The music of the Tolkien Ensemble does a better job at capturing the feeling of Middle-earth, but again one can raise objections to its authenticity. Songs that were clearly sung a capella in *The Lord of the Rings* are given instrumental accompaniment, for instance. And moreover the music is in general quite firmly embedded in the post-1600 chordal tradition. Perhaps, then, it is time for someone to have a try at writing the "real" music of Middle-earth.

About the Author

Steven Linden graduated from Columbia College and is currently a graduate student at Yale doing research in neutrino physics. He has been an avid fan and student of Tolkien's writing ever since his mother read *The Hobbit* to him when he was about five. Other interests include (but are not limited to) music, history, languages and linguistics, science fiction, and analytic philosophy.

Glossary of Musical Terms

CHORD – the simultaneous sounding of three or more pitches. In western music, chords are almost exclusively built by superimposing intervals of a third. Such chords are called "triadic". Chords have formed the basis of harmony since about 1600, but before that formal theory was more concerned with intervals than with chords per se.

COUNTERPOINT – the technique of combining two or more independent voice-parts; the polyphonic aspect of a piece of music.

HARMONY – the technique of combining two or more different notes simultaneously; the homophonic aspect of music.

HOMOPHONY – Music in which the voices all execute the same or nearly the same rhythm but not the same notes, so that there is single melodic line in the lead voice-part supported by harmony in the other parts.

INTERVAL – the simultaneous sounding of two notes, so called because the name of the particular combination is based on the "distance" (or difference in pitch) between one note and the other.

MODE – The particular set of pitches within an octave used as the notes in a composition. The two modes most frequently employed in western music since about 1600 are the major and minor (though "minor" actually refers not to a single mode but to three closely related modes). Before this time, other modes (the old church modes) were commonly employed.

MONOPHONY – Music in which all the voices are in unison, resulting in a single melodic line without harmony.

POLYPHONY – Music in which the different voice parts have multiple, rhythmically independent, melodic lines.

VOICE-PART – a single line or strand of music.

References

FINNAMORE, David, http://www.elvenminstrel.com/tolkien/memusic.htm

HARGROVE, Eugene, http://www.phil.unt.edu/hargrove/music.html

TOLKIEN, J.R.R., *The Book of Lost Tales 1,* (ed. by Christopher Tolkien), New York: Ballantine Books, 1992.

The Hobbit or There and Back Again (rev. ed.), New York: Ballantine Books, 1975.

The Lays of Beleriand, (ed. by Christopher Tolkien), Boston: Houghton Mifflin, 1985.

The Letters of J.R.R Tolkien, (ed. by Humphrey Carpenter with the assistance of Christopher Tolkien), Boston: Houghton Mifflin, 1981.

The Lord of the Rings, Boston: Houghton Mifflin, 1991.

The Silmarillion, (ed. by Christopher Tolkien), New York: Ballantine Books, 1981.

(with Donald Swann), *The Road Goes Ever On,* London: HarperCollins, 2002.

Heidi Steimel

"Bring Out the Instruments!"
Instrumental Music in Middle-earth

Music is more than mere entertainment in Tolkien's Middle-earth. Readers of his books know that a song can tell a story or set the mood for a festive occasion; it can also weave a spell, win a battle and create a world.

What about instrumental music? Is the "magic" tied to words or voice, or can a melody be just as powerful? Numerous instruments are played throughout the Ages by various races and peoples of Middle-earth. I would like to look more closely at the kinds of instruments that appear in Tolkien's works, at those who construct and play them, at the effect they have, and at their significance within the narrative.

Ainur

The very first musician was Eru, the creator of Arda. He taught his first created beings, the Ainur, to sing. After a time of practicing to increase their skills and their understanding of one another, they were ready for the task he gave them – helping to create the world. He propounded a theme, the Ainur improvised on it, added to it, even changed it. The voices of the Ainur are described as sounding "like unto harps and lutes[1], and pipes and trumpets, and viols and organs, and like unto countless choirs singing with words[...]" (*S* 3). Originally, as written in Tolkien's early version of the story in *The Book of Lost Tales*, (*LT1* 53) the author intended them to actually play instruments. However, he dropped that idea later – wisely, in my opinion, as it certainly would have raised the question of the origin of physical instruments before matter was created in the Void.

---

[1] Except for the reference on the next page of this article, this is the only passage in Tolkien's works that mentions the lute, a Medieval string instrument that might normally have been expected to play a larger part in his canon of musical instruments.

What did the Great Music sound like? Tolkien speaks of "endless interchanging melodies woven in harmony that passed beyond hearing into the depths and into the heights" (S 3). This is polyphonic music in its highest form, multiple voices sounding simultaneously, perfect independence of melodic line combined with perfect harmony. Although only vocal music is specifically mentioned, the actual sound was that of a symphony orchestra and choir, a combination of music with and without words. Unfortunately, the story continued less harmoniously – Melkor introduced his own discordant melodies, disturbed the harmony and, as a result, marred creation.

Although there were apparently no instruments involved in the creation story, several instruments of the Valar, the Ainur who took dwelling in Arda, are mentioned in the *Silmarillion*: the trumpets of Manwë and two different horns, belonging to Ulmo and Oromë, respectively.

These are all wind instruments; the sound is produced by the player's breath. Except for singing, that is the most direct way to produce melodic music[2], and as breath is closely linked to life, it is very elemental. Both trumpets and horns are used primarily as signal instruments in Tolkien's works; the various notes of the traditional historic instruments are limited to the overtones that can be produced by changing the lip position and by increasing or decreasing the force of the player's breath.

It is quite fitting that a wind instrument should represent Manwë, the "Lord of the Breath of Arda" (S 16), although it is not said that he himself played. The trumpets may be considered symbols of his power, and it can be assumed that they were used for fanfares, as behoved a ruler. Eönwë, his banner-bearer and herald, may have been one of the players.

Ulmo's horns, the Ulumúri, are spoken of in the plural; they were made of white conch shells. This is appropriate to his status as "Lord of Waters" (S 17). Tolkien gave a detailed description of the instrument in his early account of "The Fall of Gondolin":

---

2 Percussive music is excepted here; like vocal music, it can also be produced directly by the musician's own body (in this case, primarily hands and feet) without instruments as additional means.

> Thither he bore too his great instrument of music; and this was of strange design, for it was made of many long twisted shells pierced with holes. Blowing therein and playing with his long fingers he made deep melodies of a magic greater than any other among musicians hath ever compassed on harp or lute, on lyre or pipe, or instruments of the bow. (*LT2* 155)

This description clearly shows that these horns can play melodies, producing music that is art, not merely a signal. Ulmo was the Vala said to be most deeply instructed in music; his element of water contained the echo of the Music of the Ainur more than any other substance, and his playing was said to awaken hearts to a desire for the sea. "Those to whom that music comes hear it ever after in their hearts, and longing for the sea never leaves them again. But mostly Ulmo speaks to those who dwell in Middle-earth with voices that are heard only as the music of water" (*S* 17).

Here it is that a builder of instruments is first mentioned. Ulmo did not construct his horns himself; they were made by the Maia Salmar (*S* 34). Whether he invented them for his lord, or whether Ulmo had the idea and requested him to carry it out we do not know.

Oromë, the hunter, also had a horn, the Valaróma; its sound chased away evil and is described as being like a scarlet sunrise or lightning (*S* 20). In *The Book of Lost Tales* (*LT1* 99) it is said that his horn blasts brought forth forests. The author does not tell of which material the horn was made; it is possible that it was the horn of a hunted animal, such as the earliest horns of our own music history. Later, hunting horns were made of metal; the Valar smith Aulë could have crafted a horn that imitated the original natural form.

These two very different horns have an effect that could be called "magical" – their music is filled with power, having a supernatural effect on objects or persons. They figure prominently in the battle between good and evil in Arda, although they were not always victorious; we read that "the sound of the Valaróma faltered and failed" when the riders of the Valar encountered the Darkness of Ungoliant (*S* 81).

Elves

Of the Children of Ilúvatar, the Elves were awakened first. The sound of water, Ulmo's element, inspired them to sing. There is no mention of instruments in the early age of their lives. When the Elven groups went separate ways, their musical development also took different directions. Various instruments played by the Elves in Valmar are mentioned: the Vanyar played congregated harps; the Noldor viols and instruments; and the Teleri played pipes blended with their voices (*LT1* 143-4). This confirms that musicians played together in orchestras. It is not said if they all played simultaneously, though there is a passage that tells us of singing "in unison".

Gender differences are also recorded: Elven females played instruments; Elven males invented and made instruments and composed music (*MR* 214). Musical notation is never specifically mentioned in Middle-earth. If it existed, it was most likely developed by the Elves. Rúmil "first achieved fitting signs for the recording of speech and song" (*S* 63). We are not told if this means the words of songs or the musical notes as well. Both oral and written traditions are possible for preserving and transmitting music.

Tolkien names three Elves as the greatest musicians of all. In *The Book of Lost Tales* he writes of Tinfang Warble, who played his flute so enchantingly that it affected all who heard him. Eriol said,

> "[...] the hearts of those that hear him go beating with a quickened longing. Meseemed 'twas my desire to open the window and leap forth, so sweet was the air that came to me from without [...]". (*LT1* 95)

Maglor, one of Fëanor's sons, was said to be the greatest minstrel of the Noldor. As both singer and player, he naturally preferred the harp as an instrument which was played with the hands, so that he could accompany himself.

The mightiest of the three, Tolkien says in the "Lay of Leithian", was Daeron, the piper of Doriath, a Sindarin Elf (*LB* 174). Now, when Tolkien uses the word "mightiest" it is not necessarily clear how he meant it. Was Daeron a virtuoso on his instrument, having the best playing technique? Or was he the best composer of new melodies? At any rate he often accompanied Lúthien when she sang, or played when she danced. She was his inspiration, and his unrequited love for her must have produced creative peaks which made him great.

There is no mention of any special powers that these players and their instrumental music had; is it because they did not have the powerful nature of the Valar, or is it a result of the diminishing creativity that we find throughout Tolkien's works? Are the words of vocal music necessary to produce supernatural effects?

Trumpets and horns were also used by Elves, predominantly in battle situations. They were used to issue a challenge to battle: Fingolfin let silver trumpets be blown (*S* 111); he himself blew his horn to challenge Morgoth to combat (*S* 178); both a great trumpet and horns are mentioned in connection with Fingolfin's son Turgon (*S* 225, 227).

In *The Hobbit* and *The Lord of the Rings*, the instrument most often mentioned in connection with Elves is the harp. It was used to accompany their singing, the most important kind of Elven music. Elrond had a silver harp, which he took with him on his journey to the West, and Galadriel also played the harp as she sang. Instruments appear to have played a secondary role in the music of the Elves.[3]

The Dwarves also had musical instruments, although they are rarely mentioned. The most important occurrence is at the "Unexpected Party" in *The Hobbit*; I will come back to this account later, as it has some unique information on instrumental performance.

Men

When Men, the second-born Children, awakened, they developed independently of other influences at first. They must have made music; Tolkien writes of a "rude harp" that they had when the Elf Finrod Felagund found them. (*S* 163) Afterwards, Men were influenced by the Elves' music and learned from them. Like Elves, the Edain are said to have preferred the harp for accompanying their songs. In Numenor, it was the men's part to play instruments, while the women sang (*UT* 250).

---

[3] For more information on the harp in Middle-earth please read the chapter by Norbert Maier in this book, page 107.

Horns and trumpets are frequently mentioned instruments among Men in *The Lord of the Rings*. They were used for signals rather than for musical enjoyment and entertainment.[4] Several horns are specifically mentioned: the horn call of Buckland was raised by Fredegar Bolger when the Black Riders attacked Crickhollow. Apparently its use was restricted to dire emergencies, as it had not been sounded for a hundred years. The notes carried a very clear meaning, probably with different intervals signifying its messages: "AWAKE! FEAR! FIRE! FOES! AWAKE!" (*LotR* 231). The signal was echoed and answered by other horns; the sound was strong enough to be heard over distances, providing an effective warning system.

Boromir carried his inherited family heirloom horn with him at all times and blew a signal when the Fellowship's journey began in Rivendell. Poignantly, his horn, calling for help when the Orcs attacked on Parth Galen, also signalled the Breaking of the Fellowship. It is called a "war-horn" (*LotR* 363) and is described as great in size, ornamented with silver (*LotR* 312). We later discover that it was a wild-ox horn (*LotR* 988). It was broken by the orcs who killed Boromir, and its arrival in Minas Tirith brought news of his death to his father Denethor.

It is not surprising that the Rohirrim, as a warrior people, had horns. One is especially mentioned at the fortress of Helm's Deep. The great horn of Helm sounded as King Théoden and his men rode out on their last stand. We read that Théoden bids "men" to sound it; it appears to have been a very large instrument, perhaps even stationary within the fortress, that required more than one person to sound. There is an acoustic singularity about this horn; its echoes did not die, but rather grew louder, giving the impression that there were many horns sounding throughout the valley. Its effect was unexpectedly strong: "All that heard that sound trembled. Many of the Orcs cast themselves on their faces and covered their ears with their claws" (*LotR* 705).

Rohan's horns played a vital part in the battle in Gondor. Their sound signalled the turning of the tide, bringing hope and preventing the Witch King from entering Minas Tirith. Who is not stirred when reading, "Horns, horns, horns [...] Great horns of the North wildly blowing. Rohan had come at last" (*LotR* 1085).

---

4 One reason for this is that the book primarily tells the story of the War of the Rings; the life of its characters was different than it would have been during a time of peace.

King Théoden himself was able to blow the horn and did so quite memorably on the battlefield.

> With that, he seized a great horn from Guthláf his banner-bearer, and he blew such a blast upon it that it burst asunder. And straightway all the horns in the host were lifted up in music, and the blowing of the horns of Rohan in that hour was like a storm upon the plain and a thunder in the mountains." (*LotR* 1096-7)

In the following chapters, horns and trumpets are mentioned repeatedly in the battle scenes, and it is not always clear which side used them.

Near the end of the story, Merry Brandybuck received the Horn of the Mark as a reward for his service. It was beautifully crafted:

> [...] an ancient horn, small but cunningly wrought all of fair silver with a baldric of green; and wrights had engraven upon it swift horsemen riding in a line that wound about it from the tip to the mouth; and there were set runes of great virtue [...]. It was made by the Dwarves and came from the hoard of Scatha the Worm. (*LotR* 1280)

This description has a marked similarity to that of "magical" ancient heirloom weapons. It is, as far as I have found, the only instrument mentioned which carried runes upon it, and the Dwarves had apparently imbued it with special qualities. It had the effect of striking enemies with fear, bringing joy to the hearts of friends, and summoning help – virtues which were needed in the Scouring of the Shire.

All of these horns had a strong emotional effect on those who heard them; do horns have a special role within Tolkien's world? Can this effect be called magical? It certainly seems that horns have an extraordinary role among instruments played by Men.

Gondor, a country at war, used signal trumpets from the pinnacles of the White City to announce the comings and goings of soldiers and important persons. A trumpet announced the closing of the Gate at sundown (*LotR* 1009)[5]. These were apparently specific signal calls, much like bugle calls in modern military camps. Events or the identity of persons could be known by the melody that

---

5 Bells, which can also be counted as musical instruments, announced the time of day and called to meals.

was played. The "sound of a trumpet ending on a long high note" (*LotR* 1058) was identified by Beregond as Faramir's call. Trumpets sounded signals for attack and retreat (*LotR* 1073).

Aragorn blew a silver horn, given to him by Elrohir, at the Stone of Erech (*LotR* 1033). With that sound he summoned the Dead to fulfil their oath. He also had trumpeters who blew fanfares in the lands through which his army passed on the way to the final stand at the Black Gate. This preceded the announcement of his rulership over the conquered country (*LotR* 1158-9). Trumpets were then blown at the Black Gate, demanding the capitulation of the foe.

At the end of the War of the Ring, when victory was celebrated on the Fields of Cormallen, horns and trumpets were played. Then at the coronation of Aragorn, skillful musicians came from Dol Amroth to play. The variety of instruments and the addition of those, i.e. harps, viols and flutes, which were not of military nature, emphasize the advent of times of peace to the kingdom.

Other branches of the race of Men also had instruments. The Drúedain used drums for communication, much as some African tribes or native American Indians did "[…] thus they talk together from afar" (*LotR* 1087).

Of Hobbit instruments not much is said; except for the previously mentioned Horncall of Buckland[6], they appeared only at Bilbo's long-expected birthday party, where musical crackers were given away: trumpets, horns, pipes, flutes and others – "instruments, small, but of perfect make and enchanting tones" (*LotR* 38). They came from Dale, which suggests that they were of Dwarven make. At least some of the Hobbits must have been skilled and experienced players, since they made up an impromptu orchestra and played dance tunes.

This is the only occasion at which a Baggins is said to have played an instrument: Bilbo took one of the horns and blew three loud hoots to get everyone's attention (*LotR* 38). The aesthetic value of this performance is certainly debatable!

Horns and trumpets are mentioned as belonging to the enemies during battle scenes. Since it is never said elsewhere of Orcs that they have and play such

---

6 This Horncall again plays a role at the end of the story in the Scouring of the Shire.

instruments, it is fairly certain that they must have been used by Sauron's human allies: Easterlings, Haradrim and others.

Ents

As for a further race, the Ents, it is told that they made sounds like instruments – horns and drums, for example – without actually having instruments. Treebeard "raised his curled hands to his mouth so that they made a hollow tube; then he blew or called through them. A great *hoom, hom* rang out like a deep-throated horn [...]" (*LotR* 624). When the Ents marched to Isengard "[...] a marching music began like solemn drums, and above the rolling beats and booms there welled voices singing high and strong" (*LotR* 631). One could say that they had wooden instruments – woodwinds and percussion – since they used their own bodies to produce instrumental sounds.

Orcs

There is one more race in Middle-earth which had a form of music – the orcs, or goblins. The songs that they sang have short, rhythmic lines and snappy consonants.

> Clap! Snap! the black crack!
> Grip, grab! Pinch, nab!...
> Clash, crash! Crush, smash!...
> Swish, smack! Whip crack!
> Batter and beat! Yammer and bleat! (*H* 72)

This would suggest a strongly percussive music. They kept time with their feet, a typical characteristic of a race dedicated to warfare. Marching songs and chants are common to both soldiers and captives. Perhaps whips were also used percussively; in the Rankin-Bass animated *Return of the King* movie, the Orc song "Where there's a whip, there's a way" is a notorious example of that possibility.

In Moria, the "drums in the deep" gave signals, apparently providing a method of communication over distances. Other than that, the orcs used their weapons as percussive instruments, clashing their shields (*H* 76) and clashing spear shafts against shields (*H* 122).

Dwarves – The Unexpected Concert

I would like to highlight the one orchestral performance of which Tolkien writes in detail.[7] In *The Hobbit*, Bilbo's unexpected guests, the thirteen Dwarves, were musicians who had six different instruments with them. All together, they formed a string and wind ensemble with percussion. The unexpected party became an unexpected concert.

Let us look more closely at the instruments mentioned in this passage. The assumptions I make concerning them are similar to those of numerous other readers and musicians; based on the relationship between the languages and customs of societies in Middle-earth and aspects of our Middle Ages, I consider both the music and the instruments to be much like Medieval ones were.

> Although in a foot note, Tolkien warns that the adoption of these early medieval languages to represent languages in *The Lord of the Rings* – for example, that of the Riders of Rohan – "does not imply that the Rohirrim closely resembled the ancient English otherwise, in culture or art, in weapons or modes of warfare, except in a general way due to their circumstances," music, or singing, because of its close relationship to the evolution of language in the Middle Ages, is probably an exception to his general warning. (Hargrove 125)

Fiddles, the precursors to the modern violin, are wooden instruments; since Dwarves, as miners, would more likely have chosen metal for their instruments, this material suggests that the fiddles could originally have been Elvish instruments. Though fiddles are never specifically mentioned in connection with Elves, they are related to viols, which are spoken of both at the creation of Arda, thus being established as instruments played by the Ainur, and in the above-mentioned passage about the Noldor. They are melody instruments with several strings (normally four nowadays) that are usually played with a bow but can also be plucked. Since they are small, they would be relatively high-pitched.

Though the word "fiddle" is customarily used for either historical instruments or those used to play folk music nowadays, Tolkien preferred the English word to the Italian "violin" even when speaking of modern instruments.[8]

---

[7] For more on this musical event, I refer to my article "The Dwarven Philharmonic Orchestra" in *Hither Shore 5*, the 2008 yearbook of the German Tolkien Society, Scriptorium Oxoniae, Düsseldorf. The lecture on which that chapter is based was held at the Tolkien Seminar in Jena in April 2008.

[8] "I love music, but have no aptitude for it; and the efforts spent on trying to teach me the fiddle in my youth, have left me only with a feeling of awe in the presence of fiddlers." (*L* 173)

Three of the Dwarves carried flutes inside their coats; this indicates that the instruments were both sturdy and fairly short. They would have produced high notes and could have been made of reeds, of hollowed wood, or of metal.[9] They would almost certainly have had several holes, thus being able to produce melodies. If they were like played like "recorders" in our Middle-Ages, they would have been held vertically, though a transverse flute would also have been possible.

The next instruments mentioned are clarinets, brought from among the walking sticks. Clarinets are reed woodwinds that have a slightly lower playing range than that of the flutes and fiddles, possibly providing an alto melody to complement them. The inclusion of this instrument in Tolkien's story is problematic in the light of music history – the clarinet is a modern instrument, with a complicated mechanism, and therefore anachronistic in Middle-earth. Several alternative possibilities have been suggested: "crumhorns" or "chalumeaus", the medieval ancestors of the clarinet (Finnamore), or perhaps even the double-reeded oboe, which has a longer history. Tolkien apparently did not notice the discrepancy and merely chose an instrument which could go unnoticed among the walking sticks.[10] In the *History of the Hobbit*, Rateliff says that the author's original intention was to have the instruments produced magically; walking sticks would be turned into clarinets (*HH* 36, 54). He later changed that idea.

The drum is the only non-melodic instrument in this ensemble, and there is only one Dwarf who plays it here. It must have served the function of keeping the players together by sounding the beat. There is an interesting connection between the instrument and its player in this passage: "'bombur' means *drum* in Old Norse" (*HH* 784), a fact that the linguist Tolkien certainly knew. No further information is given on the size of the instrument, whether it was held horizontally (as in Medieval times) or vertically, and how it was played – with the hands or with one or more sticks.

---

9 Though their origin goes back to the natural materials, it is very possible that the Dwarven versions were made of metal.
10 Actually, Tolkien did not invent the walking stick instrument – the Romantic age brought forth such curiosities, supposedly to give those who walked in Nature's beauty an opportunity to express their emotions on location. "Even on a solitary walk one had to be prepared to react to sunsets or ruins, for which occasions there were canes that in a twinkling could be transformed into flutes, clarinets, violins" (Sachs 390).

Viols are the next instruments mentioned, as big as the Dwarves themselves. They could be compared to the string basses we know today, since the Dwarves would have had to stand rather than sit to play them. Historically, a viol is the "viola da gamba", a large wooden string instrument played like a cello. The low tones of the instruments would provide the bass line for the ensemble. These were probably the largest of the Dwarves' instruments – the most unwieldy to transport, as well as the most susceptible to damage because of the material of which they were made.

Finally there is a harp – only one, and it is played by the leader of the group, the Dwarves' king by hereditary right. This instrument has a very old history and was often associated with kings and their courts. Here it is said to be made of gold, an expensive and therefore valuable material. It is beautiful, so it must have been made by expert craftsmen who shaped it to be aesthetically pleasing both visually and audibly.

How many strings Thorin's harp had, and whether those were plucked melodically or strummed harmonically is not known. With so many melody instruments already included in the group, I would like to imagine that the harp was played in chords to accompany them. It could have been played differently for various occasions and styles. At any rate it allowed its player to sing simultaneously, since only the hands were used for playing.

Now the instruments are all assembled; their players are ready to commence. What follows is an unusual account in Tolkien's works – music that is at first, for a length of time, only instrumental before being joined by voices in song. We can compare the performance to the overture of an opera – hinting at the themes to come and preparing the way for the vocal drama, yet a work of art in its own right.

Were the instruments played in unison or in harmony? Medieval music was most often sung and played in unison[11], but I would like to imagine that the

---

[11] "The musical usage of the Middle Ages was limited to very few elements [...] Music essentially consisted of unison singing [...] Purely instrumental music was so rare that it cannot be considered the normal case. In a much greater measure than today, musical instruments had an accompanying function: They served (usually playing in unison) as a support, as guidance for the human voice" [my translation].
"Die musikalische Praxis des Mittelalters beschränkte sich auf wenige Elemente[...] Im wesentlichen war Musik einstimmiger Gesang [...] Reine Instrumentalmusik war so selten, daß sie nicht als Normalfall gelten kann. Musikinstrumente hatten in weit höherem Grade als heute eine begleitende Funktion: Sie dienten (meist im unisonen Spiel) als Stütze, als Orientierungshilfe für die menschliche Stimme" (Schulz 12–13).

various instruments could have been played polyphonically with interweaving melodies that generally harmonized with each other. That sounds complicated, but could have been as simple as canons, with one instrument beginning and the others setting in a bit later.

The effect of the playing on its audience – in this case, Bilbo – is described as "sudden and sweet" (*H* 17), sweeping him away to strange lands. The Dwarves must have played for quite awhile, since we are told that it became dark before they began to sing. Twice the narrative says that the Dwarves "still played on" (*H* 17), though daylight faded into darkness. Then we read that they began to sing while the playing continued, first one, then another.

The effect of the music became stronger with the inclusion of words: Bilbo felt within himself the spirit of the Dwarves and awakened to an understanding of their nature. This identification with his guests made it easier for him to join in their adventure subsequently. The music had an important part in preparing him for what was to come. Without the music, there might never have been a "There and Back Again"!

Once again, music has a creative function – not a world, this time, but a literary adventure begins with music.

There are a few further references to musical instruments of the Dwarves in *The Hobbit*. We read that they found harps and other instruments in Smaug's hoard near the end of the story and were thus able to play again.[12] Those were golden harps, strung with silver, which stayed in tune magically.

> Fili and Kili were almost in a merry mood, and finding still hanging there many golden harps strung with silver they took them and struck them; and being magical (and also untouched by the dragon, who had small interest in music) they were still in tune. The dark hall was filled with a melody that had long been silent. (*H* 277)

Additionally, in "Far over the Misty Mountains" the Dwarves sing of hammers which fell like ringing bells. This could be a hint of a secret kind of instrument known only to them, perhaps made of metal bars or tubes like

---

12 Their own instruments were lost when they were captured by orcs earlier in the story.

chimes or xylophones. Both the material and the method of playing such an instrument would seem very logical for a mining race.[13]

The song also says that the Dwarves carved harps of gold for themselves, so it is obvious that they made their own instruments. The fact that most of the instruments named are the same as those of the Elves suggests to me that the Dwarves did not invent them, but adopted the instruments of the Elves for their own use just as they used the language and letters of the Elves.

Conclusion

Music is significant in Tolkien's writings, especially song, which has great power. Instrumental music seems less powerful. It does influence emotions and set moods, yet it seldom has an immediate, supernatural effect on persons and objects.

For many of Tolkien's readers music has become an important expression of their love for his works. Many have composed music for his poems. Some of those, like Swann's officially sanctioned classical songs, or a number of heavy metal recordings, are interpretations that would have been out-of-place in Middle-earth, using instruments that would have been entirely foreign to Arda. Others do their best to capture the medieval flavour evoked by the spirit of the stories, with the appropriate instrumentation.

All that we can do today is to compare a secondary world to our own, explaining in our languages and concepts music that could have been completely different. Only the creator of Middle-earth knew what it was like, and even he was limited by his own knowledge and experience in the primary world. Yet our efforts to fill in the gaps can inspire us to creativity. In this way, the song of the Ainur that created a new world and echoed through the Ages of Middle-earth continues with ever new melodies today.

---

13 I am reminded of the Anvil Chorus in Verdi's opera "Il Trovatore" when reading this passage.

About the Author

Heidi Steimel was born and educated in the U.S.A. and holds a Bachelor of Music from Grace University, Omaha, Nebraska. She now lives in Germany, where she has served as a church musician, piano teacher, translator and interpreter.

Tolkien References

TOLKIEN, J.R.R., *The Book of Lost Tales, Part I*, (ed. by Christopher Tolkien), London: HarperCollins, 2002.

The Book of Lost Tales, Part II, (ed. by Christopher Tolkien), London: HarperCollins, 2002.

The Hobbit, London: HarperCollins, 2006.

The Lays of Beleriand, (ed. by Christopher Tolkien), London: HarperCollins, 2002.

The Letters of J.R.R. Tolkien, (ed. by Humphrey Carpenter with the assistance of Christopher Tolkien), London: HarperCollins, 1995.

The Lord of the Rings, London: HarperCollins, 2007.

Morgoth's Ring, (ed. by Christopher Tolkien), London: HarperCollins, 2002.

The Silmarillion, (ed. by Christopher Tolkien), London: HarperCollins, 1999.

Unfinished Tales of Númenor and Middle-earth, (ed. by Christopher Tolkien), London: HarperCollins, 1998.

References

FINNAMORE, David J., *Essay on the Development of Music for Middle-earth*, http://www.elvenminstrel.com/tolkien/memusic.htm (14.09.2008)

HARGROVE, Eugene C., *The Music of Middle-Earth*, Denton, Texas: Old Forest Sounds, 2001.

RATELIFF, John D., *The History of the Hobbit*, London: HarperCollins, 2007.

SACHS, Curt, *The History of Musical Instruments*, Mineola, New York: Dover Publications, 2006.

SCHULZ, Georg Friedrich, *Alte Musikinstrumente*, München: Schuler Verlagsgesellschaft, 1973.

Norbert Maier

The Harp in Middle-earth

"Then the voices of the Ainur, like unto harps and lutes [...]"

Many artists have concerned themselves with Middle-earth in the decades since the publishing of *The Lord of the Rings*, especially in the field of painting. Geology has been a focus as well: there are maps, even complete atlases. Linguists also concern themselves with Quenya and Sindarin. Since this was J.R.R. Tolkien's particular specialty, Middle-earth has become an accessible object of research.

It is astonishing to find out how often musical instruments can be found in Tolkien's works, when one has begun to take note of them. Of course the focus in the mythology of the ancient ages is on the Silmarils, later on the Great Rings. Many other valuable treasures of Numenor exist – such as the Palantíri, the Stone of Erech, Galadriel's phial, and heirlooms of the Noldor and the Men of the West. These we all known, and they are of great importance. Yet throughout all ages musical instruments are mentioned. One of them is the harp.

What is it like to actually attempt to build an object from Middle-earth here in our world? The reproduction of an object that is only mentioned in a fictional story is a risky undertaking. Aside from the "Red Book of Westmarch", we have no records.

Allow me to insert something personal at this point. Everyone who is familiar with the story of *The Lord of the Rings* knows, or at least can remember, that Galadriel stands in a boat when saying farewell to the Fellowship – with a harp in her hand. I once made a discovery: in the illustrated book *Realms of Tolkien – Images of Middle-Earth* I found a painting that shows exactly this scene: "The Swan Ship of Lorien" (15). It is a colored sketch by the Italian Maura Boldi – and Galadriel is holding a lyre in her hand. This may seem to be merely a minor matter, for the composition of the painting is wonderful and unique. However, I belong to the guild of musical instrument builders and it does make a difference to me if it is a harp or a lyre. Those who know

Tolkien realise with what love of language and accuracy in the choice of words he described situations. What is the reason for the harp – and not a lyre? That is the subject of this essay.

On our search for clues we will first ask several questions, hoping that the answers will give us some suggestions for the replication. The art of building instruments is the basis for the conclusions I make from the following criteria:

Of which materials are they made? How large were the harps and which shape did they have for the various peoples of the Elves, Humans, Hobbits, and Dwarves? Above all I am interested in the question: How did the harps sound?

Let us begin with the word "harp".

Although the Elves gave all things in Arda names, we have no exact term for this musical instrument in either High-Elven or in Sindarin. Only in the etymology of the Elven languages can we find two enlightening hints in the list of linguistic roots (*LR* 391, 420). The first we find in connection with the hypothetical root "BOR". In Quenya the syllable "voro" is established as meaning: "always", "continuously". This is used as a prefix, for example, in *vorogandele* – "always playing the same thing with the harp" as a synonym for "continuous repetitions". The second reference leads us directly to the harp: the root ÑGAL- or ÑGÀNAD- means "to play" – specifically, a string instrument. From that the following developed: "ñande" (Quenya) a harp; "ñandelle" – little harp; "ñandele" – harping; "ñandaro" – harper; in Noldorin (related to Sindarin) the root developed into "gandel" or "gannel" – a harp; "gannado" or "ganno" – play a harp, and "talagant" – harper (derived from the hypothetical "tyalangando"). From this the male name "Salgant" developed, for example. In the story "The Fall of Gondolin" (*LT2* 192) an Elven warrior bears this name. He was the leader of a group in Gondolin that was called "the people of the harp". Their heraldic device showed a silver harp on a black ground, but Salgant's emblem showed a golden harp. However, let us not anticipate too much in advance!

Why is the harp mentioned most out of all instruments? Tolkien was *the* specialist for Old English. During his years as a student he had already read the

Beowulf epic in the original text. He was attracted to it not only because of his historical interest in the early version of his own language, but also because this work appeared to him to be one of the most unusual poems of all times. Later *Beowulf* was a source of inspiration and rich material for work and teaching as well. Humphrey Carpenter describes the following in his biography of Tolkien:

> The most celebrated example of this, remembered by everyone who was taught by him, was the opening of his series of lectures on *Beowulf*. He would come silently into the room, fix the audience with his gaze, and suddenly begin to declaim in a resounding voice the opening lines of the poem in the original Anglo-Saxon, commencing with a great cry of 'Hwaet!' (the first word of this and several other Old English poems), which some undergraduates took to be 'Quiet!' It was not so much a recitation as a dramatic performance, an impersonation of an Anglo-Saxon bard in a mead hall, and it impressed generations of students because it brought home to them that *Beowulf* was not just a set text to be read for the purposes of an examination but a powerful piece of dramatic poetry. As one former pupil, the writer J. I. M. Stewart, expressed it: 'He could turn a lecture room into a mead hall in which he was the bard and we were the feasting, listening guests.' Another who sat in the audience at these lectures was W. H. Auden, who wrote to Tolkien many years later: 'I don't think I have ever told you what an unforgettable experience it was for me as an undergraduate, hearing you recite *Beowulf*. The voice was the voice of Gandalf.' (Carpenter 179)

The instrument "harp" is mentioned repeatedly in pivotal passages of *Beowulf*. This could indicate that the name of the harp belongs to an instrument which was brought to the British island from the continent in the $4^{th}/5^{th}$ century. In Anglo-Saxon the harp was paraphrased with a kenning. ("Beowulf" is such a kenning for bear: Beowulf = bee-wolf = bear). It is the syllable *gleó-* in the Anglo-Saxon word *glig-béam*, later *glee-beam*: that is the harp. The line in Beowulf says: *Næs hearpan wyn, gomen gleobeames* – "The pleasure of the harp is no more, the joyous sound of the singing wood" (*Beowulf* verse 2263, transl.: Bradley 471) In another passage we read: *þær wæs gidd ond gleo* […] *hwilum hildedeor hearpan wynne, gomenwudu grette*[…] – "There was talk and song[…] now and then a happy warrior touched the wooden harp" (Beowulf verse 2263, transl.: Crossley-Holland 126-7).

The harp plays a significant role not only in Anglo-Saxon literature but also in the German poetry of the High Middle Ages. This instrument is of great importance in the adaptation of the Tristan material by Gottfried of Strassburg.

Tristan is here just as much a highly gifted musician, singer and composer as a well-bred courtier, brave knight and cunning warrior.

Even in the old Greenlandic Atli song (verse 65) of the Edda we find the harp:

> Gunnar took his harp, moved it with his foot-twigs;
> plucked as well as he knew how to, so that the ladies wept;
> the men sobbed, those who heard it most clearly;
> he related his fate to the powerful woman, so that the rafters split.
> (transl.: Larrington 227)

Now the question is, to which instrument did the name belong before the 10th/11th century? In the pictorial material that has been passed down, the harp with the front bar does not appear until the High Middle Ages. This cannot be due to the lack of social prestige of the instrument, since the name "harp" is attested since the 6th century in sociologically comparable literature. Not until the 10th century do the object "harp" and the name "harp" belong together. Since the name "harp" existed previously and was differentiated from other string instruments in continental literature, we can assume with some certainty that it indicated a certain instrument in that time. This does not, however, limit the use of the verb "to harp", which can be used in general to indicate the plucking of string instruments; it is merely proof of the great age of both name and object.

Tolkien was aware of this problem, as we know from his letters. On May 4, 1958 he wrote:

> [...] words can be invented, or borrowed and may closely resemble older words in either case. The formal equivalent (the only known one) of our *harp* is Latin *corbis*. (The Romance *arpa* etc. are borrowed from Germanic.) But the poor philologist will have to call on some archaeological expert before he can decided whether any relationship between 'harps' and 'baskets' is possible – supposing Gmc. *harpo* always meant 'harp' or *corbi-s* always meant 'wicker basket'! *corbita* means a fat-bellied ship. (L 270)

The second aspect is that of literary effect. When we read a text today in which the word "harp" appears, each reader naturally has his own personal concept of it. These associations are different in nature. We are (almost always) capable of imagining an instrument, or the way it could sound.

The way in which a harper handles her/his harp also depends on the instrument's construction. We have perhaps seen pictures of minstrels with their small travel harps or have noticed the large concert harp in the middle of the orchestra at a symphony concert. Just as these two images are different, so does the sound of the two instruments differ – and that within the cultural interval of "only" a millenium. In comparison with that we are concerned with harp development in Middle-earth through endless years of the Elves in Valinor and the following seven millenia of the Three Ages in Middle-earth.

First and foremost, and this will be shown to be helpful for our consideration here, we almost always have an inner experience of hearing from memory when we read the word "harp". For this reason we are able to allow those feelings that we had when we previously heard the harp to be relived – consciously or unconsciously. We experience these inner moods of perfection and harmony in music as almost inexplicable wellbeing, when the harp is brought to our soul's eye in reading the text.

However, these feelings would be of a different nature if the author had put a lyre in place of the harp. We have no acoustic memories of the instrument. The associations are historically abstract and only of a pictorial nature. Perhaps we are familiar with Apollo with the lyre from Greek literature. We may also have experienced Emperor Nero with his lyre in the burning city of Rome – as a great cinematic event.

Having made these observations we are now ready to venture the step into Middle-earth. What we know from the Red Book of Westmarch comes from the Elves, who passed their knowledge on to Bilbo of the Shire. In these stories the Elves from the Ancient Ages utilise exactly the same association. The listener – in this case Bilbo – naturally has an idea of the sound of a harp at the end of the Third Age, though the legends of ancestral times date back approximately six thousand years. Even the Elves themselves describe the beginning of the world as it was transmitted to them, including associations of the sound of a harp – again relegated back through the Great Ages until the creation of Arda.

Dwarves

Now we come to the first big milestone of our journey to explore the harp. We turn our attention to the Dwarves.

The language of the Dwarves, which they entrusted to no one, is as much a secret as is their art of instrument building. There is no suggestion anywhere that the Dwarves adopted the harp from the Elves. Instead we could assume that the Dwarves learned their craftsmanship from Aulë himself, the Valar smith. Naturally precious metals and valuable crystals were utilised thereby. We find enlightening references concerning the Dwarves' harps in Bilbo's records of his journey to the Lonely Mountain.

Bilbo first saw a Dwarvish harp when Thorin Oakenshield appeared with his company and, after a substantial meal, old songs were sung. After the instruments of the other Dwarves were produced, Thorin unpacked his harp from a green cloth. It was a beautiful golden harp, and when Thorin began to play on it, the music sounded so suddenly and so sweet that Bilbo forgot all else. He was swept away to dark lands, under strange moons, far away over the water, very far from his hobbit hole. The Dwarves sang of their old kingdom, their longing for the treasures, for their golden harps, which lay there for a long time and which they wanted to win back (*H* 13).

In the end the Dwarves did win back their treasure under the Lonely Mountain. Fili and Kili were in especially good spirits when they rediscovered the many golden harps, strung with silver strings. Smaug had never touched these harps, since he had no interest in music. When the harps were played, they were still in tune, for they were magic harps. After Smaug's death, when the kingdom of the Dwarves was besieged and the Elves sang their songs with harp accompaniment, the Dwarves also took out their harps – if only to soothe Thorin somewhat.

In this passage we find a brilliant text composition. In the third stanza the second line says: "[…] while hammers fell like ringing bells […]" At the end of the next stanza we read: […] from twisted wire the melody of harps they wrung […]" (*H* 249).

The notable significance of these song lines for the reproduction of instruments becomes clear when we envision an historical Irish harp with metal strings.

There was a cultural era in our European history – I am speaking of the Gaelic Celts in Ireland and Scotland – which produced harp instruments that come close to these Dwarven harps. Only very few of these Medieval instruments remain in museums. The two most famous are the "Brian Boru harp" from the late 14th century in Trinity College in Dublin and the "Queen Mary harp" in the National Museum of Edinburgh. It is highly probably that both of these instruments were made by the same craftsman. The harps were strung with pure bronze strings. When a harp is strung with metal strings, the instrument builder must adhere to a precisely calculated string length and the curved line that results from it (the so-called neck curve), on which the strings are fastened with tuning-pins (similar to the curved frame of a piano). Since the tractive force of the strings is very high, these instruments had to be made fairly small, compact and robust. However, this places the instrument builder in a dilemma, since a certain string length is necessary to produce a pleasing tone in the bass range, which is not present in a short version. Therefore those old Irish craftsmen found a different solution: when using a short string, the weight of the string was increased. If brass or bronze was normally used in the bass range, there were two possibilities for achieving an increase in weight: using heavy precious metals, like silver or golden strings or twisting two thinner bronze strings to a thicker string.

The true marvel of these historic harps can be experienced when they are played: if these strings are not played with the finger tips, but rather with finger nails, they sound "like bells".

"The Irish harp [...] is beyond measure sweet in tone," Michael Praetorius wrote in the "Syntagma Musicum" in 1619 (Yeats 34).

J. G. Kohl wrote in 1844:

> "The music is wildly powerful, and the same time melancholy [...] rapid modulation and wild beauty [...] [Carolan's 'Fairy Queen'] is a charming piece of music, so tender, so fairy-like, and the same time so wild and sweetly playful." (ibid. 35)

Fig. 1: Dwarven Harp

Bilbo is likely to have experienced the Dwarves' harp playing in this manner. Therefore we can conclude the following from his description of Dwarven harps: The harps are relatively small, robust and built according to harmonic proportions. They were surely built of various kinds of hardwood. Ornaments of gold or mithril silver were certainly used. Very likely there were also inlays of valuable crystals and colored precious stones. The strings were of bronze, silver and gold or a compound of these metals. Twisted strings were used to give a pleasing sound. One possible way to build a Dwarven harp is shown in Figure 1. What kind of magic was used to keep the harps tuned permanently was not revealed by the Dwarves and is forgotten today.

Humans

It is not known since when the Men in Middle-earth played the harp. Sometime during their wanderings from the East in the First Age they encountered Elves and Dwarves. We do not know from whom they learned the art of craftsmanship and instrument building. It is likely that there were influences from both sides. If the harps were adapted from the Dwarves, the humans must have changed their construction, since they could not make finely wrought metal strings. For that reason it is more likely that they tended towards the harp construction of the Dark Elves, who lived in the wild forests of the East. When Men first wandered over the Blue Mountains to Beleriand, where Finrod Felagund found them sleeping by the fire, they had a small rude harp with them. Through the music of the harp and the songs that Felagund sang to Beor and his men, the humans became the closest Western allies of the Noldor. The construction of the Men's harps is likely to have remained relatively unchanged through the Ages since that remarkable meeting.

During a sick leave from the army in 1917 J.R.R. Tolkien wrote his first story: "The Fall of Gondolin". In this narrative the harp is mentioned seven times. Here are several examples:

> [...] but Tuor dwelt not with them, and lived alone about that lake called Mithrim, now hunting in its woods, now making music beside its shores on his rugged harp of wood and the sinews of bears. Now many hearing of the power of his rough songs came from near and far to hearken to his harping [...] (*LT2* 149)

> [...] as the stars came out in the narrow strip of heaven above the gully he would raise echoes to answer the fierce twanging of his harp. (*LT2* 150)

> [...] and to all these things he gave names of his own, and wove the names into new songs on his old harp [...] (*LT2* 154)

> Then he lifted up his voice, and plucked the strings of his harp, and above the noise of the water the sound of his song and the sweet thrilling of the harp were echoed in the stone and multiplied [...] (*UT* 31)

It is also said that the Elves of Gondolin were astonished at the size of the harp.

We hear of the harps of Men only very much later. The harp is mentioned again in connection with the Rohirrim at the end of the Third Age. They played for dances and sang the old festive songs and stories beside the fire and when riding to war. Their voices, accompanied by the harp, must have sounded similar to that of Tuor's singing two Ages earlier for the audience. This instrument was also played in some valleys of Gondor. In *The Lord of the Rings* we are told that the harp players of Gondor played their songs at the coronation of Aragorn (*LotR* 1001).

Today we would call Tuor's harp a travel harp or wander harp. Presumably the harps of Men in the Three Ages of Middle-earth were almost always built in a similar fashion. The Riders of Rohan could not have had very large harps if they took them, well wrapped in leather, along on their horses. Since humans, similarly to Dwarves, almost always had their harps with them on their wanderings in Middle-earth, these instruments must have had little weight. A slender, elegant construction with a resonance body made of a whole block of wood and strung with gut strings – we are no longer able to use bear sinews as string material – would achieve a tone such as Tolkien described throughout all Ages. We are familiar with harps of this kind from the Middle Ages to the Renaissance. Of course humans decorated their harps, as did the Elves, with ornaments and carvings. A royal harp of Numenor could very possibly have looked as shown in Figure 2.

Fig. 2: Royal Harp of Numenor

Elves

Now our research leads us to the Elves. Here we must go back further, for at this point we are dealing with the phenomenon mentioned at the beginning: when a harp is mentioned in a story, special associations are awakened, independently of the fact whether the harp actually exists or whether it is a literary device.

Let us come back to Tolkien. He himself never played the harp. However, he loved music very much. On December 2, 1953 he wrote to Robert Murray:

> I was sorry to hear that you are now without a 'cello, after having got some way (I am told) with that lovely and difficult instrument. Anyone who can play a stringed instrument seems to me a wizard worthy of deep respect. I love music, but have no aptitude for it; and the efforts spent on trying to teach me the fiddle in youth, have left me only with a feeling of awe in the presence of fiddlers. Slavonic languages are for me almost in the same category. (*L* 172-3)

So it came that music was the golden thread which is woven through Tolkien's whole literary work, and the mediators of this golden thread are the Elves!

In the very first outlines of the Legendarium, the "Lost Tales", Eriol is the first human to learn of the earliest events from Rúmil, an Elf. Ilúvatar set forth a musical theme and the Ainur responded with their music: "Then the harpists, and the lutanists, the flautists and pipers, the organs and the countless choirs of the Ainur began to fashion the theme of Ilúvatar into great music [...]" (*LT1* 53).

Though Tolkien abandoned this outline later, it is interesting that harp players are the first to be mentioned in the list of the quasi-divine musicians. At this point we return to the original question: Is this the way Elves experienced the old legends musically, or are we dealing with actual harps here? If we refer to the *Lost Tales*, the second possibility could be considered. Then it would be possible that the harp was played in Valinor by the Ainur and the Maiar. For in the further tales of Rúmil we read the following:

> In Valmar too dwelt Noldorin known long ago as Salmar, playing now upon his harps and lyres, now sitting beneath Laurelin and raising sweet music with an instrument of the bow. There sang Amillo joyously to his playing, Amillo who is named Ómar, whose voice is the best of all voices, who knoweth all songs in all speeches; but whiles if he sang not to his brother's harp then would he be trilling in the gardens of Oromë when after a time Nielíqui, little maiden, danced about its woods. (*LT1* 75)

In the Ainulindalë of the later *Silmarillion* we read in modified form that the voices of the Ainur sound like harps etc. (*S* 15).

Since these are the tales of the Elves we can assume that they were imagining or remembering a certain sound of harp music in order to describe the creation of the world in this way. The records of that are lost. However, we can certainly assume that the Elves already played the harp in Valinor. We find two references to this effect in the "Lost Tales", one about Meril-i-Turinqi, the Elven Queen of the lonely island. She says: "Often were the Noldoli with them and made much music for the multitude of their harps and viols was very sweet, and Salmar loved them […]" (*LT1* 126).

We know of a similar description by Lindo of Kór: "Now came the Teleri led by the white-robed people of the Inwir, and the throbbing of their congregated harps beat the air most sweetly […]" (*LT1* 143).

Though there are no direct references we can assume that there were even two Elvish developments of the harp. One type of harp can be found with the Elves who never went to Valinor. In the wide forests those Elves who instructed the Men in the East of Middle-earth in music continued to cultivate the playing of the harp themselves. This is hinted at in the passage in which Haldir speaks to Aragorn when the Fellowship arrives in Lothlorien and says that "our hands are more often upon the bowstring than upon the harp" (*LotR* 367).

The other line of development of the harp concerns those instruments which the Noldor brought from Valinor or new instruments which they built in Middle-earth with the knowledge of high craftsmanship from Aulë. The two instruments for high Elven rulers are prime examples: the harp which Galadriel held when saying farewell to the Fellowship (*LotR* 392) and the silver harp which Elrond had with him when the Fellowship undertook its last journey to the Grey Havens (*LotR* 1066).

How could these harps have looked or sounded? We can only recall a distant echo of these once great objects with our human instruments today. Yet let us make the attempt.

In the course of historical instrument construction in our western culture we find a type of harp that could conceivably do justice to the wonderful harps of the Noldor in Valinor. This is a special harp construction of the 17th century with three parallel rows of strings. These instruments were sometimes even larger than two meters and had approximately 80 to 100 strings. The consonance of these strings produces a harmony to which nothing on earth can be compared. Small harps of this construction, even with only one row of strings, can allow us to experience a sound that gives us an idea how Elvish music could have sounded. An example of this filigree Elven art can be seen in Figure 3.

One consideration that could inspire us to further research is the following: Let us assume that Aulë transmitted to the Dwarves the ability to build harps, along with all other magical craftsmanship. Let us further assume that the Noldorin Elves were also instructed in the art of harp construction by Aulë. Then all later harp instruments would have their origin in the Valar.

Now we have come full circle; once again I would like to refer to Professor Tolkien and his languages. He wrote a poem in the "fairy language" dated November 1915, March 1916. Here is an excerpt:

> Ai lintulinda Lasselanta
> Pilingeve suyer nalla ganta
> Kuluvi ya karnevalinar
> V'ematte singi Eldamar.

> "No translation survives, although the words *Lasselanta* ('leaf-fall', hence 'Autumn' and *Eldamar* (the 'elvenhome' in the West) were to be used by Tolkien in many other contexts." (Carpenter 108)

Ruth S. Noel writes:

> Humphrey Carpenter records a segment of one early poem for which no translation is given [...]. The poem contains the elements Eldamar and Valinor essential to *The Silmarillion*. It apparently begins with a characteristic Elvish bittersweet poignancy: "O swiftly sing of the Fall of Leaves." (Noel 5)

For the Elves the falling autumn leaves sounded like a mysterious music of the spheres. What could better express this sentiment than the music of a harp? With the correct metre and the rhyme the second line ends with "ganta".

Fig. 3: Elvenkings-Harp

I venture to claim that with this one word, the singing of autumn leaves is related to the sound of the harp – "ganta". Tolkien's love of music, the great importance of the harp in his whole work from its very beginning and the etymological roots of the Elven language indicate that.

Summary

Here now, at the end of our considerations, we look back once more. Through all Ages of Arda the harp was played, and the following understandable panorama presents itself:

Humans and Dwarves usually took out their harps when there was reason to celebrate, when there were heroes to be praised, when kings were crowned, in brief: right in the middle of life.

What about Elves? Here we learn from J.R.R. Tolkien that the harp sounded at the creation of the world and when the Elves are seated with the gods of the West, but also when things draw to an end – as in the farewell of the Fellowship in Lorien, or at the last journey to the Grey Havens – in other words: at the beginnings and the farewells.

We humans still play the harp in the middle of life today. What has remained of those moments of beginning and departure? We can experience an inkling of that in witnessing the seasons. We feel the time of awakening in the spring and the time of withering in autumn – those hardly perceived borderlines of the equinoxes. We also find this rhythm in the change of dawn and dusk after sunset. These seasonal times and twilight times are those of which the old myths say that the doors to the Elven world can sometimes be open in hidden places.

Perhaps you, dear reader, will take a journey to a forest. It is best to go at full moon when the gentle breezes brush the treetops at dusk and the air, still warmed by the sun, smells of bark and raised moss. Then it may be, if you are in the right state of mind, that the Elves grant you a special grace and you can hear their music. It sounds different to each person; perhaps it may sound like it was expressed by Tolkien in one of his earliest poems. It is an Elven song that remembers their home in the West, Kortirion. It carries the (unfortunately unfinished) title: *Narquelion la* [...] *tu y aldalin Kortirionwen* – "Autumn under the trees of Kortirion". The music of the Elves was never described more beautifully. There we read in the second stanza:

> Thou art the inmost province of the fading isle
> Where linger yet the Lonely Companies.
> Still, undespairing, do they sometimes slowly file
> Along thy paths with plaintive harmonies:
> The holy fairies and immortal elves
> That dance among the trees and sing themselves
> A wistful song of things that were, and could be yet. (*LT1* 34)

And when you then turn homewards again, with music and longing in your heart and the wish to be able to play this infinitely beautiful music, there is only one hope and one possibility: to play the harp.

About the Author

Norbert Maier developed an interest in fairy tales, stories, and Germanic and Celtic mythology while growing up in Tirol, Austria, where he lives with his family today. After being trained as a mechanical engineer and working in that trade for many years, he found his true calling as a player and builder of harps. His interest in Tolkien, particularly in Elves, influences his harp designs. It is his desire to come close to achieving the sound of Elvish music. His workshop is called *Elvenkings-Harp*.

Tolkien References

TOLKIEN, J.R.R., *The Book of Lost Tales, Part I*, (ed. by Christopher Tolkien), London: HarperCollins, 2002.

The Book of Lost Tales, Part II, (ed. by Christopher Tolkien), London: HarperCollins, 2002.

The Hobbit, London: HarperCollins, 1997.

The Letters of J.R.R. Tolkien, (ed. by Humphrey Carpenter with the assistance of Christopher Tolkien), London: HarperCollins, 1995.

The Lord of the Rings, London: HarperCollins, 1991.

The Lost Road, (ed. by Christopher Tolkien), New York: Ballantine Books, 1987.

The Silmarillion, (ed. by Christopher Tolkien), London: HarperCollins, 1998.

Unfinished Tales of Númenor and Middle-earth, (ed. by Christopher Tolkien), London: HarperCollins, 1998

References

BRADLEY, S.A.J., *Anglo-Saxon Poetry*, London: Everyman, 2000.

CARPENTER, Humphrey, *J.R.R. Tolkien: A Biography*, London: HarperCollins, 2002.

CROSSLEY-HOLLAND, *The Anglo-Saxon World: An Anthology*, Oxford: Oxford University Press, 1999.

LARRINGTON, Carolyne, *The Poetic Edda*, Oxford: Oxford University Press, 1999.

NOEL, Ruth S., *The Languages of Tolkien's Middle-earth*, Boston: Houghton Mifflin, 1980.

Realms of TOLKIEN – Images of Middle-Earth. London: HarperCollins, 1996.

Part C

Influences of Our World on Tolkien's Music

Gregory Martin

Music, Myth, and Literary Depth in the "Land ohne Musik"

O felix peccatum Babel! When J.R.R. Tolkien appropriated St. Augustine to celebrate the fall of Babel,[1] it was in the context of forwarding his belief that a person's linguistic preferences are a mark of their individuality, an extension of their genetic code, "as good or better a test of ancestry as blood-groups" (*L* 214). But it's rather difficult to not hear in this parenthetical exclamation a philologist's prayer of thanksgiving for the "fortunate sin" that gave us our plurality of languages. And it's close to impossible to not find this utterance redoubled when examining the manner in which he splintered the languages of Middle-earth, scattering their speakers to Rohan and Mordor and the woods of Beleriand. This sense of evolving language, the experience it contains, and the history it implies are just one aspect of the depth in Tolkien's work which was of such major concern to the author: he notes the success of the Beowulf poet in "surveying a past, pagan but noble and fraught with a deep significance – a past that itself had depth" (*MC* 27), and he avers in his essay on *Sir Gawain and the Green Knight* that a greater fairy-story is "not *about* those old things, but it receives part of its life, its vividness, its tension from them" (*MC* 73).[2] The multitude of maps, the shifting geography, the rise and fall of elves, men, and hobbits, and the cities they built – great and small – all contribute to this quality in Tolkien's work. But it was the words they used and the way they spoke that were the root of it all, the impetus for their entire condition. "The invention of language is the foundation," he

---

1 The quote attributed to Augustine which Tolkien references in "English and Welsh" (*MC*, 194) – "felix peccatum Adae" – seems to have been a favourite among the Inklings: C.S. Lewis claimed that "the whole of the ninth chapter [of *Perelandra*] is based on one of the great theological issues. In the fourth century St. Augustine gave classical formulation to the Church's belief that Adam's Fall brought more good than evil. His expression, *Felix peccatum Adae*, is rendered 'O happy fault, O necessary sin of Adam' in the Easter liturgy of the Catholic Church." (Green and Hooper, *C.S. Lewis: A Biography*, 200.) And Owen Barfield wrote in *Saving the Appearances*, "The whole depth and poignancy of Augustine's *Felix peccatum Adae!* would be lost on anyone who was not prepared to suppose, even for an instant, that Adam might not have fallen." (171)

2 For a protracted discussion, see Tom Shippey's *The Road to Middle-earth*, and *The Book of Lost Tales Part I*, especially pg. 1-7.

wrote, "the 'stories' were made rather to provide a world for the languages than the reverse" (*L* 219). This was Tolkien's love, his obsession, and this is why we know how the peoples of Middle-earth spoke and wrote and poeticized. But how did they sing?[3] Music and language are intimately related, and though details of musical structure or affect are vague – when present at all – in Tolkien's legendarium, "music and its apparatus" abound in Middle-earth, contributing more than a little space to this quality of literary depth. It is the intent of this essay to lay the groundwork of such an investigation, scratching the surface of this unexplored dimension of Middle-earth's scope, peoples, and history.

It may prove beneficial in such an investigation to do a preliminary survey of Tolkien's musical aesthetics in order to aid our look at the musics of the world he designed. It should come as no surprise to find throughout his letters a parallel between music and language: he writes of the music within him being "transformed into linguistic terms" (*L* 350), and references his "sensibility to linguistic pattern which affects me emotionally like colour or music" (*L* 212). Indeed, his entire approach to phonoaesthetics was rather like a musician's approach: the beauty in the sounds of individual words was dominant in his relationship to language, and the oft-cited discussion of the word "cellar" in "English and Welsh" is just the most famous example of this characteristic.[4] Similarly, he compared the "wizardry" of playing a stringed instrument with the mastery of Slavonic languages, a feat he never fully achieved (*L* 173). And though in an unpublished essay to the Lincoln Musical Society he confessed that "a man so little endowed by nature or less instructed by study in such matter would be hard to find" (*LMS*), he elsewhere admitted "music gives me great pleasure and sometimes inspiration" and credited his wife Edith with helping to draw the music in him out of its submergences (*L* 350). He studied the violin in his youth (*L* 173) and his daughter Priscilla remembers his constant whistling around the house.[5]

---

[3] By far the majority of documentation on music in Middle-earth pertains to vocal music, as opposed to instrumental genres; it is on the former that this paper will concentrate.
[4] It is worth noting that another pre-eminent 20th-century myth-maker seemed to have shared this philosophy: one of the foremost aspects of James Joyce's *Finnegans Wake* is its play with the sounds of words and the resonances implicit in them.
[5] Private conversation with the Ms. Tolkien.

He also seems to have developed rather definite musical tastes. The piano was "an instrument properly intended to produce the sounds devised by, say, Chopin" (*L* 89), and, being his wife's instrument, was the most prevalent one in his life. Edith's love of Grieg's music may have found Nordic sympathies in her husband, and if his relationship with Wagner's work was ambivalent, his admiration for *Rigoletto* was assured (*L* 223). It was with Priscilla, who inherited her mother's musical gift, that he attended a performance of Verdi's "perfectly astounding" opera in Venice during August 1955, and Tolkien and his wife often attended concerts in which their daughter was involved. One such occasion illustrates Tolkien's "very simple sense of humour" (*L* 289). During a performance of Haydn's oratorio *The Creation* at the Sheldonian Theatre in Oxford, in which Priscilla was a chorister, the professor was looking through his program notes when the opening C octave caught him off guard. The shock of the sudden music caused him to knock his glasses off, and so – as he related to his daughter after the concert – while the chorus was singing "Let there be light", he had been rendered unable to see! (ibid.) Tolkien found the cello to be a "lovely and difficult instrument", and when a neighbourhood rock band "aiming to turn themselves into a Beatle Group" would rehearse, he wrote "the noise is indescribable" (*L* 345). In the aforementioned Lincoln Musical Society lecture, he acknowledges his love of the harp; part of his attraction should come as no surprise: "It is an instrument of this *name* that is constantly associated with old (English) poetry." Then, as we would expect, the discussion turns philological:

> the *name* at least is Germanic, beyond doubt. It is common and ancient in all the northern Germanic tongues: of Iceland, Norway, Sweden, Denmark, North Germany, England; and when the name appears elsewhere (or with Romance languages) it is borrowed from the *North southwards*, not the reverse. That fact alone is possibly significant.

From here he moves to more familiar ground:

> In any case, the ancient harps of England have disappeared centuries ago, and not any echo of their strings can now be heard. On the other hand, many thousands of lines of verse have survived in manuscripts, mainly of the tenth century; and some of these poems were demonstrably composed at least 200 years earlier. We can in fact trace English recited verse back almost as far as St. Bede.

Much of the remainder of this unprinted essay deals with the metre of Old English verse, and metre is an aspect of more than a little relevance in the development of song.

In the wake of 18th and 19th-century linguistic and philological investigations, composers had begun to pay a different kind of attention to the nature of language. While care had always been taken (in varying degrees) with regard to recitative passages and matters of text-setting, the more scientific investigations of composers like Modest Mussorgsky were novel: His settings of Russian are rhythmically impeccable and yet vary according to the speaking style of each character. He wrote that "the mission of the art of music [is] the reproduction in musical sounds of not only the nuances of the emotions but, even more important, the nuances of human speech" (Kearney 2). Edvard Grieg set five different languages, and his conclusion that "the lyricism of, respectively, German, Danish and Norwegian poets is for the attentive observer so totally different that the music, too, must be equally varied in order that the contrasts among the several nationalities can be perceived" (Grieg 230) would certainly have met with Tolkien's approval. In *Den Bergtekne* (The Mountain Thrall) Op. 32, which takes its text from an Old Norse *stev*, Grieg "sought [here] to emulate the compact terseness of style that is expressed with such awesome power in the Old Norse poetry" (Grieg 235), and his collaborations with advocates on both sides of the Norwegian language debate – Ibsen and Bjørnson on the bokmål side, and Garborg and Vinje for *Nynorsk* – shows an artist with acute sensibility to language. Richard Wagner's appropriation of the Eddas and *Nibelungenlied* may have met with criticism from Tolkien, but the author must have taken some interest in Wagner's unique and unusual approach to German grammar and syntax, one aimed at getting to the emotional centre of each word and tying it so intimately to the music that one became indivisible from the other. Straddling the 20th-century is Leoš Janáček's opera *Jenůfa* (1894-1903), in which the composer's meticulous study of the rhythms and melodic inflections of spoken Czech are on display; Maurice Ravel applied similar procedures to the French language in works like the *Histoires naturelles*. But no one had better first-hand knowledge of how the metre of the English language had affected its respective music than Ralph Vaughan Williams.

On 4 December 1903, the still unknown composer collected his first folksong, *Bushes and Briars*, at Ingrave, near Brentwood, Essex. Over 800 more were to follow in the next decade, and he later reflected that

> I must have made my first contact with English folk-songs when I was a boy in the 'eighties, through Stainer and Bramley's *Christmas Carols, New and Old*. I remember clearly my reaction to the tune of the *Cherry-tree Carol*, which was more than simple admiration for a fine tune, though I did not then naturally realize the implications involved in that sense of intimacy. This sense came upon me more strongly in 1893 when I first discovered *Dives and Lazarus*. (Foss 32)

He wrote to the *Morning Post* on 1 December 1903 – three days before that fateful encounter in Essex – that "Every day some old village singer dies, and with him there probably die half a dozen beautiful melodies which are lost to the world forever" (Kennedy 36). But this was more a philosophy of innocence than of experience, as the composer later acknowledged:

> I was at that time entirely without first-hand evidence on the subject. I knew and loved the few English folk-songs which were then available in printed collections, but I only believed in them vaguely, just as the layman believes in the facts of astronomy; my faith was not yet active. (Vaughan Williams, *EF* 4)

But when VW heard Charles Pottipher sing *Bushes and Briars*, that one song "set all my doubts about folk song at rest" (Kennedy 29). Fifty years later he remembered "that sense of recognition – 'here's something which I have known all my life – only I didn't know it'" (Foss 32).

This kind of immediacy is a notion Vaughan Williams shared with Tolkien, whose natural affinity with Welsh, for example, is well documented. When VW wrote of his friend and colleague George Butterworth, who was killed at the Somme, "he could no more help composing in his own national idiom than he could help speak his own mother tongue" (Vaughan Williams, *NM* 242), the implication is something akin to what Tolkien called "native language" – one's "inherent linguistic predilections" (*MC* 190). But the composer and the philologist shared more than just this belief in a natural and uncontaminated expression, whether linguistic or musical.

Though it is doubtful that they ever met, there were personal connections. Priscilla sang several times under Vaughan Williams's baton, and Nevill Coghill

– English tutor at Exeter College, Oxford, and a member of the Inklings – directed the premiere of VW's magnum opus, the morality *The Pilgrim's Progress* at Covent Garden (26 April 1951). Robin Milford – the friend and composer of whom VW wrote, "if I wanted to show the intelligent foreigner something worth doing which could only possibly come out of England I think I would show him some of the work of Milford" – attended several Inklings meetings, and became friends with Charles Williams.[6]

But much more important than these peripheral intersections was the affinity of their artistic missions: Tolkien's "to restore to the English an epic tradition and present them with a mythology of their own" (*L* 231), and Vaughan Williams's to rediscover the authentic musical voice of the English people, whose nation had become known as "The Land without Music".

Both men were rooted in the pastoral idyll of late Victorian and Edwardian England and saw their vision of arcadia slowly overcome by industrialization, and then abruptly punctuated by the Great War, in which each served. The mark this experience left on their creative output is obvious and well-documented; there is no time to recapitulate it here. But it must concern us briefly that the intellectual component of industrialization – that is, the immediate processing and dissemination of information – had no small role in the decay of oral transmission. Little wonder that Tolkien viewed the "news" as "on the whole trivial and fit to be ignored" (Carpenter 121). Both Tolkien and VW were fully convinced of the importance of oral modes of communication, whether as a record of a culture's psyche or as a catalogue of its values (or for the sake of beauty alone). We have seen this already in VW's impassioned writings on the folksinger and his commitment to collecting and preserving their inheritance. We witness it in Tolkien's work in the proliferation of song and epic recitation by the peoples of Middle-earth. As Walter Benjamin noted,

> "experience which is passed on from mouth to mouth is the source from which all storytellers have drawn. And among those who have written down the tales, it is the great ones whose written version differs least from the speech of the many nameless storytellers". (Benjamin 84)

---

6 http://www.musicweb-international.com/classrev/2002/Aug02/Milford_centenary.htm VW in a letter to Adrian Boult.

Trying to distil this manner was at the very heart of Tolkien and Vaughan Williams's work.

There is the mutualism between music and language to which both Tolkien and VW attested. Tolkien's consistent equation of the two in his letters has already been noted. Similarly, Vaughan Williams linked music with language, contending that it arose from emotionally-charged speech. At an outdoor sermon on the Isle of Skye, VW – ignorant of the Gaelic with which the preacher spoke – began to focus instead on the increasing musicality with which he demonstrated, ultimately discerning individual pitches and pitch patterns. "The increased emotional excitement had produced two results, definition [of pitch] and the desire for a decorative pattern" (VW, *NM* 17). In his essay "Some Tentative Ideas on the Origins of Music", he attempts to investigate how the pitch patterns of excited speech inform a people's sense of melody, and identifies several folksongs which begin with those same melodic fingerprints he heard at Skye. Elsewhere, VW quotes H.C. Colles – "A people's music grows in contact with the people's mother tongue, from the emergence of the vernacular in poetry and prose literature speech stamps its character with increasing decisiveness in the music of that people" (VW, *NM* 60) – and in the epilogue to "Making Your Own Music", he parallels the development of English folksong with that of the English language, citing G.M. Trevelyan's *History of England*:

> As a result of Hastings, the Anglo-Saxon tongue, the speech of Alfred and Bede, was exiled from hall and bower, from court and cloister, and was despised as a peasants' jargon, the talk of ignorant serfs. It ceased almost, though not quite, to be a written language. The learned and the pedantic lost all interest in its forms, for the clergy talked Latin and the gentry talked French. Now when a language is seldom written and is not an object of interest to scholars, it quickly adapts itself in the mouths of plain people to the needs and uses of life. This may be either good or evil, according to circumstances. If the grammar is clumsy and ungraceful, it can be altered much more easily when there are no grammarians to protest. And so it fell out in England. During the three centuries when our native language was a peasants' dialect, it lost its clumsy inflections and elaborate genders, and acquired the grace, suppleness and adaptability which are among its chief merits. At the same time it was enriched by many French words and ideas. [...] Thus improved, our native tongue re-entered polite and learned society as the English of Chaucer's Tales and Wycliffe's Bible, to be still further enriched into the English of Shakespeare and of Milton. There is no more romantic episode in the history of man than this underground growth and unconscious self-preparation of the despised island *patois*, destined ere long to 'burst forth into sudden blaze,' to be spoken

in every quarter of the globe, and to produce a literature with which only that of ancient Hellas is comparable. (VW, *NM* 241)

Owen Barfield might add:

> the English language had at last become 'self-conscious'. In former times the struggle between different ways of saying the same thing [...] had generally worked itself out under the surface, amid the half-conscious preferences of the mass of the people. (Barfield, *HEW* 65)

VW wondered, "Could not this fable be told also of our music?" The parallel seemed obvious to him not just because of the intimate relationship of music and language, but especially because of their union within oral tradition. He notes that "the German words *sagen* and *singen* were in early times interchangeable", adding that

> to this day a country singer will speak of 'telling' you a song, not of singing it. Indeed the folk-singer (of course I am speaking of England only, the only place of which I have personal knowledge), the English folk-singer, seems unable to dissociate words and tune: if he has forgotten the words of a song he is very seldom able to hum you the tune and if you in your turn were to sing the words he knew to a different tune he would be satisfied that you knew the song, and I believe the same is true of dance tunes. A country musician, so Cecil Sharp relates, took it for granted that when his hearers had got the tune of a dance they would be able to perform the dance as well. (VW, *NM* 17)

His own field work afforded further proof, as he explained in the preface to *Eight Traditional English Carols*, wherein he acknowledges that in some instances "the text as sung was very corrupt owing to the singer being a gipsy [sic] and pronouncing the words phonetically without fully understanding their meaning."

That is, the sound of the words contributes at least as much to the music as does the meaning of the text; the music is in part an extension of the sound of the words. "Words when sung are sometimes only the framework for sound" (VW, *NM* 230). This first-hand recording of the place which the mere sound of a word holds in the unaffected and ever-evolving folk tradition would certainly have been endorsed by Tolkien, who contended "the very word-form itself, of course, even unassociated with notions, is capable of giving pleasure – a perception of beauty" (*MC* 207). And as the metre of English verse and the natural stresses of the language changed, so too did the music to which they were sung.

Music, Myth, and Literary Depth in the 'Land ohne Musik'   135

Related to this is the nature of their research. Tolkien's philological inquiries find a kinship with VW's investigations into the development of song, and while the composer did not actually try to reconstruct the original, ancestral guise of some folk tune or other in a way parallel to the manner of a philologist, he did do some comparable research. "Traditional music is a common stem on which individual leaves and flowers are constantly blossoming," he wrote in his comparison of different variants of the folksong *Shepherd's Hey* (VW, *On Music* 206). He likewise compares settings of *Greensleeves* in Ballet's Lute Book and Playford's *Dancing Master* with different Morris jigs built on the same tune: one in Dorian from Somerset, and another in Mixolydian from Gloucestershire (see Ex. 1).

Ex. 1a. "Greensleeves" from *Ballet's Lute Book* (c. 1600)

1b. "Greensleeves" from Playford's *Dancing Master* (7th ed., 1686)

1c. "Greensleeves", Morris jig from Somerset (Dorian)

1d. "Greensleeves", Morris jig from Gloucestershire (Mixolydian)

"How did the Morris men get hold of this tune?" he writes;

> "They certainly had not access to the libraries where Ballet's Lute Book and Playford's *Dancing Master* lay slumbering – it must have come down by an entirely separate tradition and be one offshoot of the same parent stem, of which the version used by Ballet so many years ago was another." (VW, *On Music* 207-8)

In an extraordinary work from 1939 called *Five Variants of Dives and Lazarus*, VW juxtaposed five different versions of the tune – from "[his] own collection and those of others" (note on the score) – side by side, showing simultaneously the common root-structure of the variants, as well as the flowerings that resulted from their development in separate locales. In doing so, he highlights the way a song may evolve in a number of different directions depending on the places to which it spreads. It is important to note that so many folksongs (and carols) bear as a name the location where they grew up; when VW wrote the music for "Come Down, O Love Divine", he upheld the tradition by naming the tune after the Cotswold village where he was born, Down Ampney. The importance of place names in Tolkien hardly needs mention; of the place names in The Shire, for instance, he wrote that they were "in fact devised according to the style, origins, and mode of formation of English (especially Midland) place-names" (*L* 360).

This mutual sensitivity to the power of names is significant.[7] Tolkien's beliefs are expressed succinctly by Oswin Errol in *The Lost Road*, when he says to his son, "I am afraid I called you Alboin, and that is why you are called it" (*LR* 37), and philosophically by Treebeard: "My name is growing all the time [...] Real names tell you the story of the things they belong to in my language" (*LotR* II 80). The value he placed on the study of names is further observed in the readings he assigned to his philology students, which included texts such as *The Survey of English Place Names*, Ekwall's *Place Names of Lancashire*, and *English River Names*. Likewise, VW expounded on the musical power native to a name. He points out that in *Tristan und Isolde*, Wagner reaches his musical heights by relying in part on the emotional potential latent in his protaganists' names. He continues:

> The names of places and people can give emotional intensity to a poem, even a mere recital of them. Here are the lines of 'Thyrsis', in which Matthew Arnold gives a list of the places he loved near Oxford:
>
>> Runs it not here, the track by Childsworth Farm,
>> Past the high wood, to where the elm-tree crowns
>> The hill behind whose ridge the sunset flames?
>> The signal-elm, that looks on Ilsley Downs,
>> The Vale, the three lone weirs, the youthful Thames? (VW, *NM* 231)

Again, overtones of phonoaesthetics arise: "The emotional value is enhanced, as if by music, by the singing quality of such words [as 'the three lone weirs']." (ibid.)

Ultimately, and regardless of the degree of symbiotic exchange between words and music, it is simply curious that during the English folksong movement and in the midst of the early 20th-century English Musical Renaissance, a man

---

7 In the Biblical tradition, the naming of animals was the first subjective act of Man. At the risk of opening the Pandora's Box that comes with the mention of Freudian thought, I quote from *Totem and Taboo*: "A human being's name is a principal component in his person, perhaps a piece of his soul" (15).

who by his own admission had "no aptitude" for music (*L* 173) should choose *music* as the foundation for the creation myth of a land that had so long relied on foreigners for its most public music-making that it had become known as *Das Land ohne Musik*. And this is especially relevant in that, even if the parallel stories of Atlantis and Númenor weren't ultimately destined to bridge Tolkien's sub-created world with our own in the way he had hoped,[8] the "Music of the Ainur", his creation myth from the *Silmarillion*, did offer, and continues to allow, a more venerable – if more ontological – link. As a student of medievalism, Tolkien would have been familiar with the mathematically-stressed presentation of music within the liberal arts, and, more specifically, as an acquaintance of Boëthius he would likely have had at least some familiarity with *De institutione musica* (On the Principles of Music), the standard text on music for the duration of the Middle Ages. Therein, Boëthius continued the Greek concerns with the music of the spheres (*musica mundana*), and elaborated on the work of, among others, Pythagoras, whose mathematics unveiled ratios in the musical overtone series that would later be found by men like Kepler and Galileo to reflect the layout of the solar system. This cosmological treatment of music, then, quite obviously placed Tolkien's myth in a tradition with real-world significance all-the-while mapping into the equation, through the introduction of the compositional and interpretative aspects of music, a mythopoeic explanation for the Christian reconciliation of Divine plan and free will. This reconciling is, not coincidentally, also a primary concern of Boëthius in *De Consolatione Philosophiae* (On the Consolation of Philosophy).

Perhaps it was that Tolkien had sensed the same inherent musicality in the English which VW and his peers had, and which they felt should be developed according to a quality "redolent of our 'air'." VW wrote parable-like:

> I am told that when grape vines were first cultivated in California the vineyard masters used to try the experiment of importing plants from France or Italy and setting them in their own soil. The result was that the grapes acquired a peculiar individual flavour, so strong was the influence of the soil in which they were planted. I think I need hardly draw the moral of this, namely, that if the roots of your art are firmly planted in your own soil and that soil has anything individual to give you, you may still gain the whole world and not lose your own souls. (VW, *NM* 11)

---

8 See, for example, Verlyn Flieger, *Interrupted Music*, especially 98-103, 125-30, and 137-39.

Elsewhere, he contends more immediately: "One day perhaps our 'native woodnotes wild' may cross the frontier hand in hand with Shakespeare, but they will not do so unless they are true to the land of their birth" (VW, *NM* 64). This position was one he had inherited from his teacher Hubert Parry, who addressed the inaugural meeting of the Folk Song Society in 1898 – a year before the world first heard Elgar's *Enigma Variations* – with the following words:

> True style comes not from the individual but from the products of crowds of fellow-workers who sift and try and try again till they have found the thing that suits their native taste [...] Style is ultimately national. (Kennedy 8)

In *Sir John in Love*, his opera based on *The Merry Wives of Windsor*, VW interpolated folk-songs and dances – most famously "Greensleeves" – to give the setting a more English color; he must have been elated by responses such as that of Bill Kenny, who wrote, "And of course it's not Verdi or Nicolai: instead it's our own – our *very* own [...]"[9] Another reviewer poignantly summarized the whole of VW's output in a manner that might as easily be applied to Tolkien: "His music is an atmosphere [...] the greatness of it comes from a certain order of our national way of living, independent and natural as a growth out of the earth, refreshed by all the weathers and humours and dispositions of the reserved but romantic English" (Kennedy 321). Such insistence on developing English music rather than modelling works on the successes forged overseas would not have been contested by Tolkien, who had no qualms about asserting that *The Lord of the Rings* "is English, and by an Englishman" (*L* 250), or warning translators that "its Englishry should not be eradicated" (*L* 299). The famous letter to Milton Waldman (no. 131) baldly lays out the Englishness at the heart of Tolkien's artistic mission, and in volume 2 of *The Book of Lost Tales*, he writes that England (here called Lúthien) is "even yet a holy land, and a magic that is not otherwise lingers still in many places of that isle" (*LT* 313).[10]

And what is Englishness? This is, of course, a thorny issue, but to Tolkien it was contained in the English language. An Englishman, he esteemed, is

---

9 http://74.125.95.132/search?q=cache:vEZVWNdwTYMJ:www.musicweb-international.com/SandH/2006/Jan-Jun06/sir_john0403.htm
10 This was, of course, the same "holy isle" to which Pope Gregory had sent Augustine in 595 with the mission of delivering its souls: *non Angli sed angeli* (Not Angles but angels).

any man who speaks English natively, and has lost any effective tradition of a different and more independent past. For though cultural and other traditions may accompany a difference of language, they are chiefly maintained and preserved by language. (*MC* 166)

And English being an amalgam of the languages used by the island's natives and invaders, the "English quality" in Tolkien's work has as much to do with a linguistic and topical assimilation from the sources that conspired to become England as it does with a self-conscious attempt to evoke a specific flavour.[11] This is part of why, I believe, his work feels English: by absorbing the languages of the contributing peoples, it reflects the actual socio-political history of the island. The literary depth which is so marked a feature of his stories owes as much to the cultural overtones of the Welsh, Scandinavians, and Anglo-Saxons within its structure as it does to the years of work (and consequent tremendous storehouse) from which Tolkien could draw. Included among these overtones must be each culture's music, especially given how often the personages of Middle-earth express themselves poetically and taking into account the music that goes hand in hand with the epics that catalogue the history of their peoples.

Immediately before Legolas notes the similarity between the language of the Rohirrim and the landscape from which it arose,[12] Tolkien writes that Aragorn "began to chant softly in a slow tongue, unknown to the Elf and Dwarf; yet they listened, for there was a strong music in it" (*LotR*, III, 112). This idea is echoed by Maurice Merleau-Ponty; as David Abram has summarized it: "It is this expressive potency – the soundful influence of spoken words upon the sensing body – that supports all the more abstract and conventional meanings that we assign to those words" (Abram, 79-80). He continues to demonstrate:

> If, for instance, one comes upon two human friends unexpectedly meeting for the first time in many months, and one chances to hear their initial words of surprise, greeting, and pleasure, one may readily notice, if one pays close enough attention, a tonal, melodic layer of communication beneath the explicit denotative meaning of the words – a rippling rise and fall of the voices in a sort of musical duet, rather like two birds singing to each other. Each voice, each side

---

11 A flavour reflecting "the clime and soil [...] Celtic" (*Letters*, 144). And while he observed that "the northwest of Europe [...] is as it were a single philological province, a region so interconnected in race, culture, history, and linguistic fusions that its departmental philologies cannot flourish in isolation" (*MC*, 188), he does note within this unit "underlying differences of linguistic heritage" (ibid.).

12 "That, I guess, is the language of the Rohirrim [...] for it is like to this land itself; rich and rolling in part, and else hard and stern as the mountains" (*LotR*, III, 112).

of the duet, mimes a bit of the other's melody while adding its own inflection and style, and then is echoed by the other in turn – the two singing bodies thus tuning and attuning to one another, rediscovering a common register, *remembering* each other. It requires only a slight shift in focus to realize that this melodic singing is carrying the bulk of the communication in this encounter, and that the explicit meanings of the actual words ride on the surface of this depth like waves on the surface of the sea. (Abram 80-81)

This forces a bit of an adjustment to VW's notion of song arising from excited speech, for pitch distinction certainly existed before functional language as we conceive of it. Additionally, VW's mention of the equation of *sagen* and *singen* finds balance in the fact that, for example, "the German word for magic formula is *galdr*, derived from the verb *galan*, 'to sing', a term applied especially to bird calls" (Abrams 89). The significance of this – and its analogous occurrences in so many aboriginal cultures – lies in the proliferation of words critical to shamanistic rituals, believed to have arisen from the song of animals, particularly birds; that is, many of the words central to primitive language seem to have been later products of consciousness than song. VW's observation must then be amended to respect the greater reciprocity that certainly exists between speech and song, and when he contends that "the musical style of a nation grows out of its language" (VW, *NM* 60), we must necessarily qualify this statement to pertain to relatively late linguistic and musical developments. The exchange to which VW refers is, rather, of a sort brought to the fore in the epic poetry of oral tradition, and in Tolkien's mind there was no more stellar example than *Beowulf*. With the Anglo-Saxon language imported to the Rohirrim would come the Anglo-Saxon manner of expressing its myths and stories, which Tolkien alludes to in the above mentioned lecture to the Lincoln Musical Society in which he notes the role of the harp in the performance of such verse. We can use what little information we have on how this was achieved to determine how (roughly) *Beowulf* would have been performed, and therefore how the epic poems of the Riders of the Mark would likely sound. But this is the practice of men, and this has been done elsewhere. We now turn our focus to the music of elves and hobbits, at least what we can divine of them.

To begin with, let us look at what we might be able to determine of the music of the Grey Elves, a study aided especially by their language, Sindarin. It is well known that this tongue is based on Welsh: "The 'Sindarin', a grey-elven language, is in fact constructed deliberately to resemble Welsh phonologically" (*L* 219, footnote). Beyond using the Welsh language as the model for Sindarin, there is, I believe, evidence to suggest that Tolkien in some regard equated the Elves in general with the Welsh. This is especially prominent with regard to place: "as far as geography goes," Tolkien writes, "Faery is situated (or its entrances are) westward" (*SWM* 85).[13] In any case, it remains that Sindarin was patterned after the Welsh language, a fact of no small weight in a world built on languages and one with special relevance in determining how that tongue would be set to music.

Given the air of antiquity with which Tolkien was trying to fill Middle-earth and the degree to which he consulted medieval manuscripts to do so, we would be advised to consult those texts in our effort to determine what we can about the musical practices of the Welsh. More than any other source, Gerald's *Description of Wales* elaborates on the performance of music by the medieval Welsh:

> In their musical concerts they do not sing in unison like the inhabitants of other countries, but in many different parts; so that in a company of singers, which one very frequently meets with in Wales, you will hear as many different parts and voices as there are performers, who all at length unite, with organic melody, in one consonance and the soft sweetness of B-flat […] the practice is now so firmly rooted in them, that it is unusual to hear a simple and single melody well sung; and, what is more wonderful, the children, even from their infancy, sing in the same manner. (Gerald 498)

In other words, the Welsh were employing counterpoint and polyphonic structure while most of the rest of the continent – and certainly the English, as Gerald later points out – were still singing monophonically. Tolkien's familiarity with Gerald's scholarship is attested by his translation of part of the same work cited above into a contemporaneous Middle English dialect of the Southwest Midlands for a paper by William Rhys Roberts, a colleague at Leeds University from 1920-23. It would be surprising if Tolkien never read the above description on Welsh song, especially as Gerald's comments on Welsh language and verse are couched between his discussions of their musical instruments and their mode of singing. Throughout the legendarium we discover evidence of elven superiority in intellectual and artistic pursuits; it only follows that their music should similarly excel – again parallel between the Welsh and the Elves. Gerald's account reveals a people whose part-writing is "habitually" more

---

13 Tolkien's spelling of "Faërie" fluctuated throughout his life.

complex than other nations, and which employs polyphony well earlier than it became common currency among peoples elsewhere in Europe. Given the way a people's music and language interact – in rhythm and melodic shape – it is certainly not too much to believe that a music founded on Sindarin would have characteristic similarities with one built on Welsh, especially when the craft of the Elves is administered.[14]

Now, Sindarin is, of course, the more vernacular of the two dominant Elven tongues in the legendarium. The other major language, Quenya, is of a more classical nature, and by the time of *The Lord of the Rings* it "had been a 'dead' [language] (sc. one not inherited in childhood, but learnt) for many centuries (act. about 6000 years)" (*L* 425). Tolkien referred to this hallowed tongue as "Elven-Latin" (*L* 176); we might expect, then, to find it sung to a more elevated or solemn mode of music, one commensurate with the way we commonly hear Latin performed in the primary world – that is, as chant. Indeed, such speculation is confirmed by Tolkien's own recording of "Namárië" (Farewell) (*LotR* I 394) and by his account of "reciting this *chant*." (Swann 69 – italics mine). But there is a more musically interesting aspect to Tolkien's recording than simply the Gregorian nature of the performance. Quenya is, as is well known, founded to a large extent on the Finnish language, a spark ignited by the author's youthful discovery of the *Kalevala*, a 19th-century collection of Finnish myth and folk-legend published by Elias Lönnrot (who shared more than a little of the authorial credit, and was largely responsible for the narrative thread of the work). The *musical* affinities between Finnish and Tolkien's "archaic language of lore" (*L* 176) find support in details such as their mutual tendency to stress the first syllable of each word, thus affecting contour and meter, and evince a more poetic, if not so quantifiable, kinship in the phonoaesthetic qualities they share, an aspect that, as has been discussed, was of a musical nature to Tolkien. And if he spoke of Anglo-Saxon as a language to be sung with a harp – which it was and which he did – then there is every reason to believe that he would have recognized the Finnish of the *Kalevala* as a musical language, as well,

---

14 This obviously does not include instances in which only a single elf is present. An example when multiple elves are gathered in song is found when the hobbits encounter a group on their way out of the Shire; we are told that "One clear voice rose now above the others" (*LotR* I 88). While this could be interpreted as one voice being louder than the rest, I read this as rising "above the others" melodically, not in terms of volume. This is indicative, then, of part-singing.

when used in such epic capacity. As a source of musical inspiration, the *Kalevala* has had no greater ambassador than Jean Sibelius, who used this collection as the topical (and textual) source for so many of his masterful symphonic tone-poems and vocal works. Most notable is the elaborate *Kullervo Symphony*, one of his first truly distinct works, an important artistic monument on the road to Finnish independence, and a programmatic piece founded on a story from Finnish mythology that also captured Tolkien's imagination (one of Tolkien's first creative efforts was a retelling of the tale of Kullervo). This work was written during Sibelius's awakening as to his artistic mission, and its preparations included research not unlike VW's. Most noteworthy was an excursion to Borgå (Porvoo), Finland to hear Larin Paraske (c.1834-1904), an Ingrian reciter of the *Kalevala* described by the composer as "an old rune singer [...] from Russian Karelia" (Goss XII). It is reported that Sibelius took dictation from Paraske, but these annotations have been lost (ibid.). His notes from performances by other singers, however, have survived, such as those of Pedri Schemeikka taken in the summer of 1892 (Ex. 2).

Ex. 2: Jean Sibelius's dictation of two *Kalevala* rune singers

Storytellers such as Paraske and Schemeikka used a series of melodic figures or recitation formulae to sing their tales, stringing musical patterns and vocal gestures together to construct larger, epic structures. When we examine Sibelius's field work in the context of Tolkien's recording of "Namárië", we notice a number of important similarities. The *Kalevala* singers and Tolkien both use a heightened delivery to draw attention to the difference between their elevated manner and the everyday uses of the language. Tolkien highlights this by adjusting the word-order when giving his translation: "The word-order and style of the chant is 'poetic,' and it makes concessions to metre. In a clearer and more normal style the words would be arranged [differently]" (Swann 66). And there is still further flexibility within the text: Paraske's recitals of the *Kalevala* were notably different from Lönnrot's published version – a tradition Sibelius upheld by his own textual alterations (Goss XIII) – and Tolkien notes of his performances of Galadriel's lament, "When myself reciting this chant, I usually begin it with an extra-metrical and extended version of *ai*! ("alas!"): āaaāĭ, and then repeat *ai* within the metre." Yet this is something he does *not* do on his recording, underscoring the fluidity of interpretation at the heart of oral performance. Tolkien's singing of "Namárië" also parallels Sibelius's records of *Kalevala* rune singers in its emphasis on and elongation of the end of words – syllables that in the spoken language are unaccented, and even clipped. This distinction is put in stark relief through a juxtaposed listening of Tolkien's sung version of the lament and his spoken recording of the same text. It can thus be seen that while Tolkien's singing of "Namárië" is often described as chant – a habit encouraged by our tendency to associate a certain way of singing with a particular repertoire, as well as by the author's own use of the word "chant" and referral of Quenya as a sort of Elven-Latin – his performance practice and mythological objectives bear a perhaps more significant resemblance to those of Karelian rune singers. This is appropriate for a language inspired by Finnish and modelled to no small degree on the storytelling potential exhibited in its most monumental text.

As Tolkien's recording of "Namárië" corroborates the musical implications of Quenya and its linguistic history, so does his recording of Sam's "Rhyme of the Troll" from chapter 12 of *The Fellowship of the Ring* confirm suspicions of hobbit song. In various contexts, Tolkien wrote of the parallels between hobbits and the "unadventurous" English: he likewise noted that The Shire "is in fact more or less a Warwickshire village of about the period of the Diamond Jubilee" (*L* 230), a place "based on rural England and not any other country in the world" (*L* 250). That is, hobbit-song should be roughly the same as the music Vaughan Williams encountered on his folksong-collecting expeditions in mid- and south England. And in fact, Tolkien's recording does share many features with this mode of music: a dance-like quality supported by marked and regular accents; a stress on the 5th scale-degree (in this case A), which acts as something of a reciting-tone; and a sort of musical budding, so common in folksong, in which musical ideas grow through repetition and extension (as opposed to more classical designs like antecedent-consequent; see Ex. 3). The first phrase is constructed of two parts, the second a slightly more elaborate restatement of the first. The dominant interval – an ascending 4th – is then isolated, initiating a short, interlocking sequence that finally spills over into a full triad, outlining the tonic, or home key (D major). After a brief liquidation and descending sequence, the second phrase is repeated with a full close. While this is a diatonic melody, many of the contours are heavily pentatonic (using 5-notes), a hallmark of so many folk-tunes. This adds further folk-color to the tune, as do words like "Tinbone/Thinbone", "Rover/Trover", "Hee now" and "Gum by". This use of nonsense syllables is common in English folksong and carols, and is seen crystallized in the refrains of many Christmas carols.

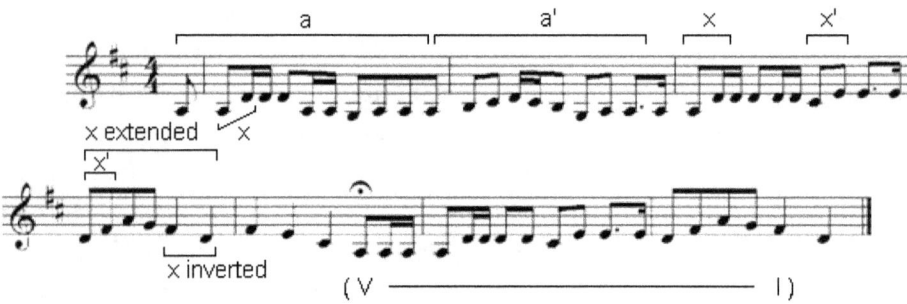

Ex. 3: Tolkien's melody for Sam's "Rhyme of the Troll"

The language again works in communion with the musical structure to act as an arbiter of cultural identity. As with the music of the Grey Elves and the few Noldor still remaining in Middle-earth by the time of *The Lord of the Rings*, hobbit-song serves to add variance and depth to the "vast backcloth" that the Ainur sang into existence millennia ago. In *Phantastes*, George MacDonald describes the music of fairyland as

> Words and tones coming together, and inseparably connected, as if word and tone formed one thing; or as if each word could be uttered only in that tone, and was incapable of distinction from it, except in idea, by an acute analysis. (MacDonald 69)

Likewise, in Rivendell Frodo stood "enchanted, while the sweet syllables of the elvish song fell like clear jewels of blended word and melody" (*LotR* I 250). This is what Wagner was after, and this is what Vaughan Williams recorded in his folksong collecting experiences. And, of course, this is akin to what Tolkien must have experienced when a linguistic pattern affected him "emotionally like music" or he was arrested by the sheer beauty of a phonetic sound. Middle-earth owes its existence, literally and mythically, to the impact of sound – in the languages Tolkien created, and in the music of Ilúvatar's imagination, a sound "of endless interchanging melodies woven in harmony that passed beyond hearing into the depths and into the heights" (*S* 15). In a very real way, we can echo both Augustine and Tolkien and exclaim "Felix peccatum Melkor!"

About the Author

Pianist Gregory Martin's playing has been noted for its "imagination, fire, and lyricism [...] a virtuoso performance." He holds a Bachelor of Music degree from the University of Cincinnati College-Conservatory of Music, and Master and Doctorate degrees from Indiana University (all in piano performance); additional post-graduate work was conducted at the University of Oxford. He has researched and written extensively on Edvard Grieg (of which a full-length study is forthcoming), the composers of 20th-century England, and the German Romantics, as well as Inkling studies, especially J.R.R. Tolkien. He is currently on staff at Western Illinois University, and is also active as a composer.

Tolkien References

TOLKIEN, J.R.R., *The Book of Lost Tales, Part I,* (ed. by Christopher Tolkien), Boston: Houghton Mifflin, 1984.

The Letters of J.R.R.Tolkien, (ed. by Humphrey Carpenter with the assistance of Christopher Tolkien), Boston: Houghton Mifflin, 1999.

Address to the Lincoln Musical Society, Bodleian Library, Oxford, A30/1.

The Lord of the Rings, 2nd ed., Boston: Houghton Mifflin, 1987.

The Lost Road and Other Writings, (ed. by Christopher Tolkien), Boston: Houghton Mifflin, 1987.

The Monsters and the Critics and Other Essays, (ed. by Christopher Tolkien), London: HarperCollins, 1997.

The Silmarillion, (ed. by Christopher Tolkien), London: George Allen & Unwin, 1977.

Smith of Wootton Major, (ed. by Verlyn Flieger), London: HarperCollins, 2005.

References

ABRAM, David, *The Spell of the Sensuous*, New York: Vintage Books, 1997.

BARFIELD, Owen, *History in English Words*, Gt. Barrington, MA: Lindisfarne Books, 1967.

Saving the Appearances: A Study in Idolatry, 2nd ed., Middletown, CT: Wesleyan University Press, 1988.

BENJAMIN, Walter, "The Storyteller: Reflections on the Works of Nikolai Leskov", In: Hannah Arendt (ed., transl. by Harry Zohn), *Illuminations*, New York: Schocken Books, 1968.

FLIEGER, Verlyn, *Interrupted Music*, Kent, OH: Kent University Press, 2005.

Foss, Hubert, *Ralph Vaughan Williams: A Study*, London: Harrap, 1950.

GIRALDUS Cambrensis (Gerald of Wales), *The Description of Wales*, In: *The Historical Works of Giraldus Cambrensis* (rev. and ed. by Thomas Wright), London: H.G. Bohn, 1863.

Goss, Glenda Dawn, Introduction to *Jean Sibelius: Kullervo, Op. 7*, Wiesbaden: Breitkopf and Härtel, 2005.

GREEN, Roger Lancelyn and Walter Hooper, *C.S. Lewis: A Biography*, (rev. and expanded edition), London: HarperCollins, 2002.

GRIEG, Edvard, *Letters to Colleagues and Friends*, (ed. by Finn Benestad, transl. by Williams H. Halverson), Columbus, OH: Peer Gynt Press, 2000.

KEARNEY, Leslie, *Linguistic and Musical Structure in Musorgsky's Vocal Music*, Diss., Yale University, 1992.

KENNEDY, Michael, *The Works of Ralph Vaughan Williams*, London: Oxford University Press, 1964.

MACDONALD, George, *Phantastes*, London: Azure, 2002.

MANNING, David (ed.), *Vaughan Williams on Music*, Oxford: Oxford University Press, 2008.

SHIPPEY, Tom, *The Road to Middle-earth*, New York: Houghton Mifflin, 2003.

SWANN, Donald, *The Road Goes Ever On*, 3rd ed., London: HarperCollins, 2002.

VAUGHAN WILLIAMS, Ralph, *National Music and Other Essays*, 2nd ed., Oxford: Clarendon Press, 1996.

English Folk-songs, London: EFDS, 1912.

Eight Traditional English Carols, Preface, Boca Raton, FL: Masters Music Publications, Inc.

Bradford Lee Eden

Strains of Elvish Song and Voices: Victorian Medievalism, Music, and Tolkien

> Rise, my true knight. As children learn, be thou
> Wiser for falling! walk with me, and move
> To music with thine Order and the King.[1]
>
> In hawthorn-time the heart grows light,
> The world is sweet in sound and sight [...]
> And all his life of blood and breath
> Sang out within him: time and death [...][2]
>
> I must follow in their train
> Down the crooked fairy lane
> Where the coney-rabbits long ago have gone,
> And where silvery they sing
> In a moving moonlit ring [...]
>
> O! the warmth! O! the hum! O! the colors in the dark!
> O! the gauzy wings of golden honey-flies!
> O! the music of their feet – of their dancing goblin feet!
> O! the magic O! the sorrow when it dies [...][3]

These poetic lines of Tennyson, Swinburne, and Tolkien, while encompassing about a 60-year time period (1842, 1896, and 1915, respectively), all refer to some type of musical allusions throughout not only these works, but many of these authors' other poetic and prose writings. Tennyson often uses the musical harmony/disharmony theme in his Arthurian works. Swinburne, often compared to and in competition with Tennyson and his writings during his lifetime, also incorporated musical themes and phrases throughout his works. Finally Tolkien picked up – consciously or unconsciously – the idea of music, song and dance as a structural element in his first published poetry.

This article will focus on the influence of English Victorian fiction on Tolkien's writing style, particularly in relation to musical-literary symbolism. There are

---

1 (Rosenberg 78) Lines 72-74 from Tennyson's *Idylls of the King*. "The interpolation serves to stress the motif of music versus discord that is especially prominent in "Balin and Balan" and that runs throughout the *Idylls*." ftnt.
2 (Swinburne 171)
3 (Tolkien, *Oxford Poetry* 65)

obviously many tangents and influences to follow when speaking of musical influence on Tolkien's writing style, including the romantic compositions of Richard Wagner, the works of medieval philosophers such as Plotinus and Augustine. One can also see parallels to theosophical writings current in the nineteenth century, the singing/enchantment/ancient origin tales such as the Finnish *Kalevala* (which we know had a strong early influence on Tolkien) and Icelandic sagas, to name but a few. It would be beyond the scope of a single article to discuss all these influences; the author is currently researching and writing a book that will examine the conscious and subconscious musical influences on Tolkien's writings. For this article, the writings of three major English Victorian fictionists are examined, and parallels between their use of musical-literary language and Tolkien's are illustrated.

Although Tolkien has been quoted as saying that he had never imitated anyone's writing style nor ever used current literature or events as analogies or metaphors in his works, careful study of Tolkien's writings shows an extensive predilection and use of musical language similar to the Victorian writers. The resurgence of Arthurian literature during the Victorian period, the rise of philology and the study of ancient and medieval languages as a discipline as well as the incorporation of rhyme and prosody into Victorian fiction all had an influence on Tolkien's writing style, whether he chose to admit it or not. Many of the great Victorian scholars and philologists also contributed to the wealth of Victorian fiction and fantasy that arose in the nineteenth century – in fact, Tolkien was the last in a long line of Victorian philologist/fiction writers. The interest in ancient languages, their sound and pronunciation, along with the discovery and translation of many medieval legends and myths, helped to feed the growth of fictional poetry and prose based on Arthurian legend and medieval myths. Although Tolkien grew up in Edwardian England, his writings indicate a strong predilection, use, and emulation of Victorian concepts and techniques, not the least of which is a strong emphasis on music and its power, music and its relationships, and music as a unifying concept and theme that consciously or unconsciously ebbs and flows throughout his writings, particularly his earlier endeavors to write fiction.

The concept of "medievalism" in the Victorian period comprised a wide range of artistic, cultural and political pursuits. In religion, the Oxford Movement sought to bring back the ancient liturgical and musical traditions once practiced in English cathedrals prior to the Dissolution. In painting, the works of Dante Gabriel Rossetti and the Pre-Raphaelite Brotherhood, while short-lived, served to inspire styles of painting well into the twentieth century. In historiography, the writings and constitutional work of scholars such as J. R. Green, William Stubbs, and Edward Freeman looked back into the English past. In social and aesthetic criticism, the essays of Victorians such as John Ruskin, William Morris, Thomas Carlyle, A. W. Pugin, and Benjamin Disraeli were constant and politically motivated. Even in their physical environment, the Victorians sought to emulate the Middle Ages. Neo-Gothic law courts and town halls, cathedrals and churches, railway stations and public buildings, were built to contrast dramatically with factory smokestacks and commercial industry. Finally, in literature, Alfred Tennyson, Algernon Charles Swinburne, and William Morris sought to emulate ancient and medieval prose and poetry, as well as use Arthurian romances and themes, to transport their readers into a "heroic age" where things such as honor, virtue, and chivalry were the norm rather than the exception. It was this heritage into which Tolkien was born and in which he grew up; even the university environment of Oxford itself was reflective of the medieval culture from which it had first emerged. Ultimately, Tolkien's profound distaste for all things related to technology and his love of trees and nature can trace its source back to the Victorians and their concept of medievalism [...].

> The association of such ideas as nature, harmony, creativity, and joy with medievalism points up the other major aspect of the medieval revival, its attempt to create a coherent world view. As we have seen, medievalism was a response to historic change and to the problems raised by the various revolutions and transformations of the eighteenth and nineteenth centuries. But medievalism was also simultaneously a part of that vast intellectual and emotional response to change which we somewhat fuzzily denominate Romanticism. As such it had links to the renaissance of interest in nature, primitivism, and the supernatural and to the increasing valuation placed upon the organic, the joyous, and the creative. Just as medievalism was very much a part of the desire to give man a sense of social and political belonging, so it was also an attempt, in the decline of any transcendental order, to naturalize man in the universe and make him feel related to it. It was opposed to the Newtonian and Lockean view of the universe as a vast machine in which man was a subordinate mechanism moved by pleasure and pain. As part of the Romantic contradiction of these concepts, medievalism substituted a picture of man as a dynamic and generous creature, capable of loyal feeling and heroic action. Far from being isolated from nature,

medieval man was seen as part of it, and his chivalry mirrored its benevolence. In its hostility to a mechanistic metaphysics, medievalism as a philosophical movement thus paralleled its opposition to machinery on economic and social grounds. Both aspects of medievalism – the political and the metaphysical – saw materialism and mechanization as inimical to the human. The return to the Middle Ages was conceived of as a homecoming. (Chandler 7-8)

The three Victorian writers whose works best illustrate the blending of medievalism with musico-literary symbolism were Alfred Tennyson, Algernon Charles Swinburne, and William Morris.[4] All three incorporated musical themes and motives throughout their fiction, especially in relation to their Victorian "resetting" of the medieval Arthurian and French epic tales.

Alfred Tennyson

Alfred Tennyson (1809-1892) started writing poetry at a young age, and is best known as the Poet Laureate of England from 1850 until his death, and for his epic tale of King Arthur and the knights of Camelot, *Idylls of the King* (1859-74). Throughout the *Idylls*, Tennyson weaves musical ideas such as harmony and discord into a number of the Arthurian stories, especially into the tragic tale *Balin and Balan*, composed in 1885 (the last story in the *Idylls* to be written). In this tale, which is recounted in the Old French *Suite du Merlin* and Malory's *Morte d'Arthur*, the twin brothers Balin and Balan are cursed by fate, and eventually end up killing each other. Balin, in particular, is instrumental in the downfall of Arthur's Camelot. He wounds King Pellam with the sacred spear that pierced the side of Christ – the blow known as the Dolorous Stroke from the Fisher King story in the Grail epic. Balin also wields and will not give up a sword of which it has been prophesied to him that it will slay the man he loves most in the world, and bring about his own destruction. In the end, Balin fights his own brother, Balan, whom he does not recognize, and both are fatally wounded. Tennyson makes Balin an important figure in developing some of the major themes in *The Idylls of the King*. His Balin is known as "the Savage"

---

4 Douglas A. Anderson, in his recent book *Tales before Tolkien* (New York: Ballantine, 2003), comments on the many writers whose influence on Tolkien is both recorded or implied, especially George MacDonald. MacDonald's influence on Tolkien's writings can be specifically attributed to Tolkien's concept of children's literature and especially the production of *The Hobbit*, but I can find no direct influence of MacDonald on Tolkien's early mythological writings.

(Malory called him "Balin Le Savage") and occupies a major role in the struggle of Arthur to destroy the bestial, both in the realm and in his subjects, and thus to raise them and himself to a higher level, the level of the angels.

To illustrate some of Tennyson's use of music and language in his Arthurian epic, it is essential to mention some lines of *Balin and Balan*. For instance, immediately upon introducing himself to Arthur, Balan says:

> They followed; whom when Arthur seeing asked
> "Tell me your names; why sat ye by the well?"
> Balin the stillness of a minute broke
> Saying "An unmelodious name to thee,
> Balin, 'the Savage'--that addition thine--
> My brother and my better, this man here,
> Balin [...]⁵

There are constant references to music in the court at Camelot, music that is harmonious and orderly, just like Arthur's lofty goals and dreams for his realm:

> Thereafter, when Sir Balin entered hall,
> The Lost one Found was greeted as in Heaven
> With joy that blazed itself in woodland wealth
> Of leaf, and gayest garlandage of flowers,
> Along the walls and down the board; they sat,
> And cup clashed cup; they drank and some one sang,
> Sweet-voiced, a song of welcome, whereupon
> Their common shout in chorus, mounting, made
> Those banners of twelve battles overhead
> Stir, as they stirred of old, when Arthur's host
> Proclaimed him Victor, and the day was won.

Even after Balin is granted the boon of bearing the Queen's crown-royal upon his shield, the power of music is weaved into Balin's personality at that moment, both in his achievement and in his ultimate fate:

> So Balin bare the crown, and all the knights
> Approved him, and the Queen, and all the world
> Made music, and he felt his being move
> In music with his Order, and the King.
>
> The nightingale, full-toned in middle May,
> Hath ever and anon a note so thin

---

5 Quotes from *Balin and Balan* are taken from the The Camelot Project, available at http://www.lib.rochester.edu/camelot/idyl-bal.htm

> It seems another voice in other groves;
> Thus, after some quick burst of sudden wrath,
> The music in him seemed to change, and grow
> Faint and far-off.

As Balin begins to lose his sanity, especially after discovering the Queen and Lancelot in a secret tryst, the musical language used to describe him becomes more discordant and twisted. Balin's personality begins to turn into that of a raging beast, aptly described by Tennyson, as Balin attacks and wounds King Pellam, and fights the anonymous knight whom he eventually discovers to be his own brother. The tenderness and emotion as the two brothers die in each other's arms have a considerable effect on the reader:

> "O brother" answered Balin "Woe is me!
> My madness all thy life has been thy doom,
> Thy curse, and darkened all thy day; and now
> The night has come. I scarce can see thee now.
> Goodnight! for we shall never bid again
> Goodmorrow--Dark my doom was here, and dark
> It will be there. I see thee now no more.
> I would not mine again should darken thine,
> Goodnight, true brother."
>
> Balan answered low
> "Goodnight, true brother here! goodmorrow there!
> We two were born together, and we die
> Together by one doom": and while he spoke
> Closed his death-drowsing eyes, and slept the sleep
> With Balin, either locked in either's arm.

Algernon Charles Swinburne

Algernon Charles Swinburne (1837-1909) was born into the British aristocracy, and early on was trained by his grandfather and mother in the French and Italian languages. As a student at Oxford, he acquired a detailed knowledge of religion and the Bible, and established friendships with Dante Gabriel Rossetti, William Morris and Edward Burne-Jones. Swinburne was in frail health most of his life and of slight build (he was under five feet tall). Throughout the 1860s and 1870s he was in an alcoholic stupor, until finally in 1879, he was able to give up alcoholism, but remained ill for the remainder of his life. He was quite the personality within Victorian society. He challenged all of the norms and conventions of his time. He openly flaunted his homosexuality and his masochistic tendencies, and these appeared often in his writings. He introduced Victorian society to medieval French troubadour poetry and contemporary French literature (especially Bautier, Baudelaire, and Hugo), and even promoted the works of American writers such as Edgar Allan Poe and Walt Whitman. His poems are on tragic love and heroism, dominated by strife and frustrated love, by fickle men and women who are victims of a malevolent fate. Furthermore, he was a scholar in the truest sense; he revived medieval forms such as the rondel, the alba, and the ballad.

In 1896, Swinburne published his own version of the Arthurian tale of Balin and Balan, called *The Tale of Balen*. This poem was written in direct opposition to Tennyson's recent version of this Arthurian tale. Far from portraying the Victorian's obsession with medievalism as an idyllic or "golden age", Swinburne actively wrote on the desperate passions and hatreds of the human psyche that were contained in the Arthurian legends. As such, his use of musical imagery is even more vivid and dramatic than Tennyson's.

Again, examination of the work itself is essential to understanding the extensive use of imagery that Swinburne incorporates throughout this work. The opening of *The Tale of Balen* is provided at the beginning of this article; it seeks to symbolize the musical harmony inherent in the Arthurian realm prior to the tragedy of Balen. His character contains the "Northern" spirit, that which is full of the sea and the wild:

> And all his life of blood and breath
> Sang out within him: time and death
> Were even as words a dreamer saith
> When sleep within him slackeneth,
> And light and life and spring were one.
> The steed between his knees that sprang,
> The moors and woods that shone and sang,
> The hours wherethrough the spring's breath rang,
> Seemed ageless as the sun. (Rosenberg 78)

When confronted by a knight who debased his Northern heritage at Arthur's court, Balen strikes him down and is cast from Arthur's court. The whole world of Balen is truly dolorous and strange, and no matter how virtuous his motives are, his actions inevitably generate suffering, if not tragedy. As a central symbol of fate, Balen obtains the sword that no one else in Camelot's court can conquer, but must accept the fate that he will slay whom he loves the most. By the end of the tale, Balen has killed the Lady of the Lake, Launceor, Garlon, and eventually his own brother Balan. The use of nature, sea, and musical imagery is very reminiscent of Tolkien's early mythological writings. Here is just a small sample of Swinburne's musical symbolism:[6]

> But bright and dark as night or noon
> And lowering as a storm-flushed moon
> When clouds and thwarting winds distune
> The music of the midnight, soon
> To die from darkening star to star
> And leave a silence in the skies
> That yearns till dawn find voice and rise,
> Shone strange as fate Morgause, with eyes
> That dwelt on days afar.
>
> As morning hears before it run
> The music of the mounting sun,
> And laughs to watch his trophies won
> From darkness, and her hosts undone,
> And all the night become a breath,
> Nor dreams that fear should hear and flee
> The summer menace of the sea,
> So hears our hope what life may be,
> And knows it not for death.
>
> From choral earth and quiring air
> Rang memories winged like songs that bear
> Sweet gifts for spirit and sense to share:
> For no man's life knows love more fair
> And fruitful of memorial things
> Than this the deep dear love that breaks
> With sense of life on life, and makes
> The sundawn sunnier as it wakes
> Where morning round it rings.
>
> And there they laid their dead to sleep
> Royally, lying where wild winds keep
> Keen watch and wail more soft and deep
> Than where men's choirs bid music weep
> And song like incense heave and swell.

---

6 Quotes from *The Tale of Balen* are taken from the The Camelot Project, available at http://www.lib.rochester.edu/camelot/swinbal.htm.

And forth again they rode, and found
Before them, dire in sight and sound,
A castle girt about and bound
With sorrow like a spell.

In winter, when the year burns low
As fire wherein no firebrands glow,
And winds dishevel as they blow
The lovely stormy wings of snow,
The hearts of northern men burn bright
With joy that mocks the joy of spring
To hear all heaven's keen clarions ring
Music that bids the spirit sing
And day give thanks for night.

As toward a royal hart's death rang
That note, whence all the loud wood sang
With winged and living sound that sprang
Like fire, and keen as fire's own fang
Pierced the sweet silence that it slew.
But nought like death or strife was here:
Fair semblance and most goodly cheer
They made him, they whose troop drew near
As death among them drew.

And Balen rose again from swoon
First, and went toward him: all too soon
He too then rose, and the evil boon
Of strength came back, and the evil tune
Of battle unnatural made again
Mad music as for death's wide ear
Listening and hungering toward the near
Last sigh that life or death might hear
At last from dying men.

William Morris

William Morris (1834-96), in stark contrast to Swinburne, was the ideal Victorian medievalist. He was raised in a fantasy world in his home, Woodford Hall, which was a moated grange where medieval festivities were still actually celebrated. His parents presented him with a tiny suit of armor to wear about the family estate as a child. As a youth he became a devotee of Pugin and a disciple of Ruskin, whose work on medieval craftsmanship inspired Morris to base his life on that ideal. Morris designed all types of medieval materials in the nineteenth century, from architecture to painting and from furniture to gardens, and also carpets, poetry, calligraphy and even the translation of Icelandic sagas. His *News from Nowhere* (1890) is a story of a dream by a time-traveler who sees an England of the future – a future similar to the fourteenth century – after a violent revolution. The only difference is that there are no churches, no Christianity. Morris's influence on Victorian medievalism was profound and unique; his craftsmanship still survives today in various museums and galleries around the world.

Similarly to Tennyson and Swinburn, Morris also used poetry as his preferred device to depict the Arthurian romances. Through a number of poems, such as *The Defence of Guenevere, In Arthur's House, King Arthur's Tomb*, and *Sir Galahad: A Christmas Mystery*, he uses musical and sea imagery to great effect. Here are just a few samples of his musical symbolism:[7]

> "Nay Dame," he said, "I am but young;
> A little have I lived and sung
> And seen thy face this happy noon." *(In Arthur's House)*

> It chanced upon a day that Launcelot came
> To dwell at Arthur's court: at Christmas-time
> This happened; when the heralds sung his name,
> Son of King Ban of Benwick, seemed to chime
> Along with all the bells that rang that day,
> O'er the white roofs, with little change of rhyme. *(The Defence of Guenevere)*

> For no man cares now to know why I sigh;
> And no man comes to sing me pleasant songs,
> Nor any brings me the sweet flowers that lie. *(The Defence of Guenevere)*

> That very evening in their scarlet sleeves
> The gay-dress'd minstrels sing; no maid will talk
> Of sitting on my tomb, until the leaves,
> Grown big upon the bushes of the walk. *(Sir Galahad: A Christmas Mystery)*

J.R.R. Tolkien

J.R.R. Tolkien's writings, especially his early mythological and poetic endeavors, were strongly influenced by the musico-literary symbolism of Victorian fiction-

---

7 All quotes are taken from "The Camelot Project", available at http://www.lib.rochester.edu/camelot/cphome.stm.

ists. The conscious/subconscious use of musical language and symbolism arises not only from the Victorian tradition, but also from Tolkien's own personal background. His grandfather was a piano maker, and in his *Letters*, Tolkien refers to the fact that his family had musical talent, but that this predilection had unfortunately not surfaced in him. Carpenter's biography of Tolkien often makes reference to musical influences in Tolkien's life, especially his wife Edith's talent in piano playing (a prerequisite for all women in Victorian society), and how much Tolkien himself enjoyed the sound of music throughout his home.

An examination of Tolkien's early poetic endeavors reveals this predilection for musical symbolism. The poetry quoted at the beginning of the article was Tolkien's first published work at the age of 23. Cursory research of Tolkien's early published poetry illustrates the strong Victorian tendencies towards music symbolism:

> And songs long silent once more awake ("Iumonna" 130)

> Or shrill in sudden singing sheer [...]
> There melodies of music spill ("Nameless Land" 24-25)

> In mighty music from his monstrous head [...]
> Do neighbors musical in western lands ("Iumbo" 123-27)

> a sudden music came to her [...]
> Flutes there were, and harps were wrung, and there
> was sound of singing [...]
> They sang their song, while minstrels played on
> harp and flute slowly ("Firiel" 30-32)

> I'll sit and sing till the moon comes, as they sing
> beyond the mountains [...]
> and he sang a dirge for Higgins [...]
> A sad song [...] a dragon's song or colour ("Dragon's Visit" 342)

These are only a few of the musical allusions that are prevalent in Tolkien's early published poetry. His early mythological works continue these musical associations. Obviously, "Ainulindalë" in the *Silmarillion* was written early in Tolkien's career, and the musical nature of the creation of Middle-earth has been commented upon before.[8] *The Book of Lost Tales*, begun between 1916-17, contains not only the earliest versions of "Ainulindalë", but also much of the

---

8 Eden, "The Music of the Spheres".

foundation upon which Middle-earth would later be built. In addition, these early stories illustrate the broad influence of the Victorian period upon Tolkien's writing style, despite his comments to the contrary. Tolkien was influenced early on by the concept of chivalry and the idea of "loving from afar" which was very much a part of the trouvere/troubadour tradition in medieval music. Almost all of Tolkien's early work is done in the context of tales or stories as related or even sung to a listener or listeners. What we are reading is the documentation of that listening experience, again another strong indication that Tolkien was trying to portray the way medieval audiences would have heard and listened to the great stories of their past. On all accounts the use of, presence of, and reference to music in Tolkien's earlier versions of his mythology are so strong, that reading the published versions does not do justice to his imaginative power and both conscious and subconscious references to music. Here are a few of these examples:

Tinfang Warble: Tinfang Warble is the greatest minstrel in Middle-earth. His early appearance is in relation to the telling of the tales in *The Book of Lost Tales*, where he recounts some of the stories of the Valar that would eventually find their way into the *Silmarillion*. Tinfang does not appear in any published stories, but his early influence within Tolkien's legendarium is profound. In the list of the greatest minstrels ever, Tinfang takes first place above Maglor and Dairon. Part of his history is told in *The Book of Lost Tales* (*cf.* 107), but he appears in various other stories, particularly those related to the lay of Beren and Lúthien.

Dairon: In the first versions of the Beren and Lúthien saga, Dairon is Lúthien's brother, one whose power and use of music is even more profound than the published version of the story indicates. What is interesting is Tolkien's gradual diminishing of Dairon's musical role and power in the story, such that he eventually becomes a lover of Lúthien from afar, and not her brother. While his power as a musician is great, and is attested to by Tolkien in his listing of the three greatest musicians ever in Middle-earth, it is a fascinating personal account to follow the development of Dairon as a character in Tolkien's writings. In fact, the metered version of the lay of Beren and Lúthien contains some very powerful references to Dairon's power as a musician and his use of music to affect change in environment and circumstances.

Names of songs: More than any other topic, Tolkien names songs in his earlier writings, songs that he then proceeds to compose either in verse or prose. A list of some of these songs includes: "Song of the Valar", "Song of Aryador", "Song of Light", "Song of the Sleeper", "Flight of the Gnomes", "Song of the Sun and Moon", "The Siege of Angband", "The Bowman's Friendship", "Song of the Great Bow", "The Song of Tuor for Eärendel" (which exists in three versions and five different texts), and "Light as Leaf on Lindentree" (which Aragorn quotes from and sings on Weathertop). These are just a few of the titles. In addition, the *Lays of Beleriand*, the verse versions of the Beren and Lúthien story, are filled with some of the most powerful language this author has ever encountered in mythological literature on the use and power of music. Three of these musical/dramatic events, which are much more powerful here than in the published *Silmarillion*, are the battle of music and song between Finrod Felagund and Thû, the description of Lúthien's song to rescue Beren from Thû and destroy the prison where Beren is being held, and finally the description of Beren's song of farewell to earth and light after leaving Lúthien and Huan as he starts to enter Morgoth's domain. These are powerful and evocative musical events in which drama and music are interwoven and recited, similar to a musical composer using all the resources at his or her disposal to present a symphonic masterpiece, including melody, harmony, instrumentation, texture and volume. Indeed, Carpenter's and even Tolkien's references to powerful links between linguistics and music in his life are very apparent in these early writings.

One major story that does not appear in *The Silmarillion*, but for which Tolkien spent a lot of time writing and rewriting, was the legend of the making of the Sun and Moon. There is a long, detailed account in his early writings of the construction, launching, personalities involved, and even the end of days regarding the Sun and Moon. This legend, although I have not had sufficient time to examine and research it, also appears to hold many links to the philosophy of Plotinus, especially in regard to the Neoplatonist model of Vision vs. Reality. The published version in *The Silmarillion* does little justice to Tolkien's early efforts in writing this story.

Finally, the character of Túrin deserves mention. Tolkien's earlier stories and accounts of Túrin are powerful and again do little justice to his character in *The Silmarillion*. Not only are musical links extensive and vast, but Túrin's power as a musician and his training in Gondolin as a minstrel are truly dramatic in both the verse and prose versions of the "Fall of Gondolin" story, much of which never made it into *The Silmarillion*. Indeed, the song of Tuor for Eärendel, as stated previously, exists in three versions and five texts. Túrin's abilities as a minstrel and musician made him probably the greatest musician among Men, and most of his training was from the Elves in Gondolin, from meeting Ulmo and hearing his many-faceted musical instrument, and from the Music of the Ainur such as it still existed in the sound of the sea, where it was heard and felt most strongly by the Elves.

Conclusion

In conclusion, the Victorian predilection towards medievalism, and for musical symbolism in particular, had a strong influence on Tolkien's writing style. Whether he chose to admit it or not, he was influenced by Victorian writers. As for his musical leanings, Tolkien often referred in his *Letters* and other correspondence to the close relationship between linguistics and music, between philology and musical composition, between the sound and construction of words and the timbres and pitches of music. As Tolkien well knew, music was studied and respected as part of the quadrivium along with geometry, astronomy and arithmetic in the Middle Ages. It was such a common understanding that music guided and directed everything, that the discipline itself was studied as a scholarly pursuit rather than a practical application. Just as the medieval world saw music both consciously and subconsciously apparent in both the practical and the divine, so in Tolkien's writings the idea of music underlies yet intertwines all of the early verse and prose versions of his mythological world, much more so than is apparent in *The Silmarillion*. One quote in particular illustrates Tolkien's views on his early compositional process:

> This leads to the matter of 'external history', the actual way in which I came to light on or choose certain sequences of sound to use as names, *before* they were given a place inside the story. I think, as I said, this is unimportant: the labour involved in my setting out what I know and remember of the process, or in the guess-work of others, would be far greater than the worth of the results. The spoken forms would simply be mere audible forms, and when transferred to the prepared linguistic situation in my story would receive meaning and significance according to that situation, and to the nature of the story told. It

would be entirely delusory to refer to the sources of the sound-combination to discover any meanings overt or hidden. (*L* 383-84)

What is wonderful about this quote is not just Tolkien's opinion on how he created words in his languages, but the implication in the quotation of himself as a "composer of words", which is an apt analogy. Whether or not Tolkien thought of himself as a true composer in the musical sense, he certainly can be described as a composer of words, and in his own way his mythology and his stories are true symphonic works in the linguistic sense. Music was certainly part of his heritage, part of his personal, professional, and religious life, and to be sure it was a strong influence on his writing style, as it appeared in its many and varied guises throughout his mythology. The Victorian medieval/musical-literary heritage helped to inspire Tolkien's compositional process, his musical roots helped to nurture his interest in philology and the sound of words, and his own love of both music and linguistics combined to produce one of the greatest mythologies ever written.

About the Author

Dr. Brad Eden is currently Associate University Librarian for Technical Services & Scholarly Communication at the University of California, Santa Barbara. He has a masters and Ph.D. in medieval musicology, as well as an MS in library science. He discusses Tolkien's uses of music in terms of Boethian medieval music theory in *Tolkien the Medievalist* (Routledge, 2003).

Tolkien References

TOLKIEN, J.R.R., *The Book of Lost Tales, Part I*, (ed. by Christopher Tolkien), London: George Allen & Unwin, 1983.

The Book of Lost Tales, Part II, (ed. by Christopher Tolkien), London: George Allen & Unwin, 1984.

"The Dragon's Visit", In: *The Oxford Magazine* 55, no.11 (1937), 342.

"Firiel", In: *The Chronicle*, Convent of the Sacred Heart, Roehampton, 1934, 30-32.

"Goblin feet", In: *Oxford Poetry*, Oxford: B.H. Blackwell, 1915, 64-65.

"Iumbo, or ye Kinde of ye Oliphaunt", signed Fisiologus, In: *The Stapeldon Magazine* 7, no. 40 (1927), 123-27.

"Iumonna Gold Galdre Bewunden", In: *The Gryphon*, New Series 4, no. 4 (1923), 130.

The Letters of J.R.R. Tolkien, (ed. by Humphrey Carpenter with the assistance of Christopher Tolkien), London: George Allen & Unwin, 1981.

"The Nameless Land", In: *Realities: an anthology of verse*, (ed. by G.S. Tancred), London: Gay & Hancock Ltd., 1927, p. 24-25.

The Silmarillion, (ed. by Christopher Tolkien), London: George Allen & Unwin, 1977.

References

ANDERSON, Douglas A. (ed.), *Tales Before Tolkien: the Roots of Modern Fantasy*, New York: Ballantine Books, 2003.

Boos, Florence S. (ed.), *History and Community: Essays in Victorian Medievalism*, New York: Garland Publishing, 1992.

The Camelot Project, Available at http://www.lib.rochester.edu/camelot/mainmenu.htm

CARRUTHERS, Gerard and Alan Rawes (eds.), *English Romanticism and the Celtic World*, Cambridge: Cambridge University Press, 2003.

CHANDLER, Alice, *A Dream of Order: the Medieval Ideal in Nineteenth-Century English Literature*, Lincoln, NE: University of Nebraska Press, 1970.

CHAPMAN, Raymond, *The Sense of the Past in Victorian Literature*, New York: St. Martin's Press, 1986.

EDEN, Bradford Lee, "The 'Music of the Spheres': Relationships Between Tolkien's *Silmarillion* and Medieval Cosmological and Religious Theory", In: Jane Chance (ed.), *Tolkien the Medievalist*, London and New York: Routledge, 2003, 183-93.

FAY, Elizabeth, *Romantic Medievalism: History and the Romantic Literary Ideal*, New York: Palgrave, 2002.

FILMER, Kath (ed.), *Twentieth-Century Fantasists: Essays on Culture, Society and Belief in Twentieth-Century Mythopoetic Literature*, New York: St. Martin's Press, 1992.

GERVAIS, David, *Literary Englands: Versions of "Englishness" in Modern Writing*, Cambridge: Cambridge University Press, 1993.

HARRISON, Anthony H., *Swinburne's Medievalism: A Study of Victorian Love Poetry*, Baton Rouge: Louisiana State University Press, 1988.

LARRINGTON, Carolyne, "The Fairy Mistress in Medieval Literary Fantasy", In: Ceri Sullivan and Barbara White (eds.), *Writing and Fantasy*, London: Longman, 1999.

MCSWEENEY, Kerry, *Tennyson and Swinburne as Romantic Naturalists*, Toronto: University of Toronto Press, 1981.

PICKER, John M., *Victorian Soundscapes*, Oxford: Oxford University Press, 2003.

PRICKETT, Stephen, *Victorian Fantasy*, Bloomington: University of Indiana Press, 1979.

ROSE, Jonathan, *The Edwardian Temperament, 1895-1919*, Athens, Ohio: Ohio University Press, 1986.

ROSENBERG, John D., *The Fall of Camelot: A Study of Tennyson's "Idylls of the King"*, Cambridge, MA: The Belknap Press of Harvard University Press, 1973.

SHIPPEY, T.A., "The Undeveloped Image: Anglo-Saxon in Popular Consciousness from Turner to Tolkien", In: Donald Scragg and Carole Weinberg (eds.), *Literary Appropriations of the Anglo-Saxons from the Thirteenth to the Twentieth Century*, Cambridge: Cambridge University Press, 2000.

SIMONS, John (ed.), *From Medieval to Medievalism*, New York: St. Martin's Press, 1992.

SUSSMAN, Herbert L., *Victorians and the Machine: The Literary Response to Technology*, Cambridge, MA: Harvard University Press, 1968.

SWINBURNE, Algernon Charles, *The Complete Works of Algernon Charles Swinburne. Vol. IV: Poetical Works*, (Ed. Sir Edmund Gosse and Thomas James Wise), New York: Russell & Russell, 1968.

WADE, Stephen, *In My Own Shire: Region and Belonging in British Writing, 1840-1970*, Westport, CT: Praeger, 2002.

WAWN, Andrew, *The Vikings and the Victorians: Inventing the Old North in Nineteenth-Century Britain*, Woodbridge, Suffolk: D.S. Brewer, 2000.

Julian Eilmann

Sleeps a Song in Things Abounding: J.R.R. Tolkien and the German Romantic Tradition

> "Sleeps a song in things abounding
> that keep dreaming to be heard:
> Earth'es tune will start resounding
> if you find the magic word."[1]

With these poetic verses, full of linguistic magic and musicality, the poet Joseph von Eichendorff gives the fundamental poetological idea of German Romanticism a programmatic form. A poetic magic sleeps deep in the being of the world that surrounds us. Those who are aware of the magic and recognize it are the happy Romantic characters who know the secret of existence. Those who can furthermore awaken the magic are those chosen individuals who can open the door to a person's true inner being, the poets. Eichendorff's poem is significantly called "Wünschelruthe" (Divining Rod). Just as it is possible for a thirsty person to find water, the elixir of life, by using a divining rod, a poetic mind can trace by way of its artistic talent the crucial elixir of life for Romanticism, poetry. The world is to be brought to sing, a metaphor that points out that the magical poetic word stands in the centre of the Romanticist view of art and the world. It contains the hope of the changing power of poetry and with that the longing of Romanticist artistic work, to be able to disclose the secret of prosaic reality by way of the principle of Romanticising and so to come to the aesthetic, i.e. the true core of things:

> In Nature, however, in the dreams of forest loneliness as in the labyrinth of the human breast, a wondrous, undying song has ever slumbered, a bound, enchanted beauty, whose redemption is the deed of the poet.[2]

---

1 Translated by Walter A. Aue. http://myweb.dal.ca/~waue/index.html
"Schläft ein Lied in allen Dingen,
Die da träumen fort und fort,
Und die Welt hebt an zu singen,
Triffst du nur das Zauberwort." (Joseph von Eichendorff, Bd. I/1, 121)
2 *"In der Natur aber, in den Träumen der Waldeseinsamkeit wie in dem Labyrinth der Menschenbrust, schlummert von jeher ein wunderbares unvergängliches Lied, eine gebundene verzauberte Schöne, deren Erlösung eben die That des Dichters ist."* (Eichendorff, Bd. I/2, 224). Eichendorff also uses the metaphor of the sleeping song elsewhere: "Poor, bound Nature dreams of redemption, and speaks in a dream in broken, wondrous sounds, moving, childish, distressing, it is the ancient wonderful song that sleeps in

The magical poetic word has a vital significance in J.R.R. Tolkien's understanding of art. With the concept of sub-creation, which finds its full expression in the "enchantment" (*OFS* 53) of Elvish art, Tolkien has presented a poetological concept that has much similarity to Romantic understanding of art as it is encountered in Eichendorff's paradigmatic "Wünschelruthe". As my previous research on the function of poetry in Tolkien has shown, it is possible for the inhabitants of Middle-earth to make boundary expanding, even transcendental experiences through devoted presentation and enjoyment of songs and music (cf. Eilmann, *Lied* 122-133). So far, research has paid almost no attention to the fact that Tolkien also stands in the tradition of German Romanticism with his literary work and his concept of poetic enchantment. An evaluation of the state of research makes clear that a certain "romantic" quality in Tolkien's work is occasionally attested, though the identification and analysis of Romantic topics and concepts are mostly made in a manner that is hardly appropriate. Research has thus not achieved more than useless stereotypes.

The lack of critical literary studies on Tolkien and Romanticism is additionally due to an obvious fact: the majority of contributions to Tolkien research come from the Anglo-American world. Naturally we can assume that both the language barrier and a lack of knowledge of German studies impede any extensive research on this group of themes. For this reason some themes (e. g. the poetology of German Romanticism) never come into focus or are covered superficially and incorrectly, despite the unquestionable productivity and quality of Anglo-American Tolkien research. Accordingly, the poetological intersection of Tolkien and Romanticism has found almost no mention in English-language research literature. The situation of German-language research is similarly disappointing. Even though we could assume that the linguistic approach to the poetological texts of German Romanticism should be much easier to establish, this aspect of Tolkien research has been largely neglected in Germany as well. One exception is the remarkable study by Oliver Bidlo, who, starting from the emphatic interest that various generations of readers of *The Lord of*

---

all things. But only a pure, chaste mind, devoted to God, knows the magical spell that wakes it."
"*[D]ie arme, gebundene Natur träumt von Erlösung, und spricht im Traume in abgebrochenen, wundersamen Lauten rührend, kindisch, erschütternd, es ist das uralte wunderbare Lied, das in allen Dingen schläft. Aber nur ein reiner, Gott ergebener, keuscher Sinn kennt die Zauberformel, die es weckt*". (ibid.)

the Rings have had, deals with the longing of readers for Tolkien's mythology and thereby makes connections to German Romanticism. As meaningful and accurate as Bidlo's observation and analysis of a widely spread receptive attitude in Tolkien readers is, his discussion concerning Romanticist poetic theory is not entirely satisfactory. His study is limited to peripheral characteristics of the era, focussing especially on supposed antimodernist and antirationalist tendencies of Romanticism and thereby drawing on obsolete stereotypes rather than contributing to illumination. The depiction of Romanticists as lovers of nature and utopians (Bidlo 56, 64) gives a simplistic and incorrect impression and does not do justice to the historical significance of the ideas and artistic expression of this literary era.

In contrast to unproductive approaches of this kind, this study will focus on the analogy between the usage of songs in Tolkien's works and the poetology of German Romanticism, preserving terminological clarity and thereby pointing out the tradition of various poetry-theoretic characteristics of Tolkien. In this way the foundation shall be laid for a more intensive discussion of the literary historical line of tradition between Tolkien and German Romanticism[3] and it shall be made clear that Eichendorff's "Wünschelruthe" is also valid in Middle-earth: in Tolkien's mythology, a song truly sleeps in things abounding.

The Road Goes Ever On and On: The Walking Novel and Walking Song in Tolkien's Works

A significant characteristic of Romanticist verse which is also relevant for Tolkien's Middle-earth mythology consists of the contextual literary fixation of the poems. This fact was not adequately recognized for a long time even by German studies in relation to the literature of the Romanticist era, resulting in numerous misconstructions (cf. Fetzer 135). Because of the integration of

---

3 The emphasis of the following analysis lies on the connection between Tolkien and German Romanticism. Despite similarities common to the era concerning the poetic theory of Friedrich Schlegel or Novalis with Romanticists of other European nations, we should not lose sight of the differences specific to each country. For example, the poetology of German and English Romanticism are only conditionally comparable. Since the poetic theory of German Romanticism developed central avantgardistic views, which decisively characterised the ideal image of the Romantic in literature and art, German Romanticism is the focus of my analysis. Future studies should widen the spectrum to include Romanticist theory of art and literature in other countries.

poems in a superordinate literary context, the Romanticist novel was called a "poem of poems, a web of poetry"[4] by early Romanticist forward thinkers like Friedrich Schlegel. Why is the inclusion of poems in a prose novel so significant for the Romanticist theory of art? Beginning with an understanding of art as having an encompassing pervasion of artistic and social life as its goal, in order to make the poetic content of existence tangible, the mixture of literary genres signifies a decisive step toward the realisation of the Romanticist demand for "progressive universal poetry"[5]. In the concept of universal poetry Friedrich Schlegel sums up the utopian artistic goal to connect all areas of life with each other and to allow life itself to become poetry through art (cf. Uerlings 27). This fundamental programme of Romanticist poetry finds its expression in the famous 116th "Athenäum-Fragment" by Friedrich Schlegel:

> Romanticist poetry is a progressive universal poetry. Its purpose is not merely to unify all separated kinds of poetry and to bring poetry into contact with philosophy and rhetoric. It will and shall both mix and blend poetry and prose, genius and criticism, art poetry and natural poetry, make poetry come to life and become sociable and make life and society poetic, poeticise wit and fill and satisfy the forms of art with dignified cultural material of all kinds and animate through the vibrations of humour. It encompasses everything if it is poetic, from the largest system of art, in itself containing multiple systems, to the sigh, the kiss, that the versifying child breathes in artless song.[6]

In Romanticist novels this dictum finds expression in a permanent change of forms: narrative sequences are alternated with dramatic and dialogue passages; poems, songs or letters interrupt the flow of the narrative. Furthermore, the course of the narrative is repeatedly interrupted by smaller subtexts (fairy tales, digressions, memories, etc.). For example, Achim von Arnim's novel *Armut, Reichtum, Schuld und Buße der Gräfin Dolores* (*Poverty, Wealth, Guilt and*

---

4 "[Ein] Gedicht von Gedichten, ein ganzes Gewebe von Gedichten" (Schlegel, 160).
5 "progressive Universalpoesie" (Friedrich Schlegel, quoted by Uerlings 79).
6 "Die romantische Poesie ist eine progressive Universalpoesie. Ihre Bestimmung ist nicht bloß, alle getrennten Gattungen der Poesie wieder zu vereinigen und die Poesie mit der Philosophie und Rhetorik in Berührung zu setzen. Sie will und soll auch Poesie und Prosa, Genialität und Kritik, Kunstpoesie und Naturpoesie bald mischen, bald verschmelzen, die Poesie lebendig und gesellig und das Leben und die Gesellschaft poetisch machen, den Witz poetisieren und die Formen der Kunst mit gediegnem Bildungsstoff jeder Art anfüllen und sättigen und durch die Schwingungen des Humors beseelen. Sie umfaßt alles, was nur poetisch ist, vom größten wieder mehrere Systeme in sich enthaltenden Systeme der Kunst bis zu dem Seufzer, dem Kuß, den das dichtende Kind aushaucht in kunstlosem Gesang" (Schlegel, quoted by Uerlings 79).

Repentance of Countess Dolores), written in 1810, consists of almost 100 separate narrative elements (cf. Bausch 76ff).[7]

Tolkien's two Hobbit novels are also interspersed with numerous poems which are recited by protagonists at various occasions. In his detailed index "Songs and Verses" (*LotR* 1113-1115), Tolkien counted 64 songs and poems in *The Lord of the Rings*, even without including various citations and variations of the same poem. In the significantly shorter *Hobbit* there are still 16 poems as well as eight riddles. This relationship of songs and poems to the surrounding narrative text clearly shows the great importance of poetry in the literary cosmology of Middle-earth. The enclosed poems and songs should not be considered accidental attachments to an epic narrative. They are an integral element of the narrative and the removal of even a few poems from the complete text would constitute a massive diminution of its literary contents and quality.

The structural analogy between Tolkien's Hobbit novels and the Romantic novel consists not only of a similar relationship of poetry and prose. Above and beyond that, because of their structural and contentual similarity both *The Hobbit* and *The Lord of the Rings* can be understood as walking and artist novels in the tradition of Romanticism. Characteristic for the Romantic novel is a sensitive and artistically talented individual as its protagonist, who, driven by a dormant longing for aesthetic development and existential fulfilment, sets out into the world (cf. Hoffmeister, *Der romantische Roman* 213). Outstanding representatives of this type of novel are Ludwig Tieck's *Franz Sternbalds Wanderungen (Franz Sternbald's Wanderings)*, Novalis' *Heinrich von Ofterdingen* and with some reservations also Clemens Brentano's *Godwi*. Eichendorff's novellas *Ahnung und Gegenwart (Presentiment and the Present)* and *Aus dem Leben eines Taugenichts (From the Life of a Good-For-Nothing)* also mirror the typical Romanticist narrative situation of the subject who sets out into the world. In all of these texts the process of individual appropriation

---

7 Numerous passages and aphorisms on the mixture of literary genres can be found in the theoretical writings of the early Romanticists: "I can hardly imagine a novel that is not a mixture of narrative, song and other forms", "[I]ch kann mir einen Roman kaum anders denken als gemischt aus Erzählung, Gesang und anderen Formen" (Friedrich Schlegel quoted by Bausch 76). "Should the novel not be understood as including all kinds of style genres, variously connected in a common spirit.", "Sollte nicht der Roman alle (Arten) Gattungen des Stils in einer durch den gemeinsamen Geist verschiedentlich gebundenen Folge (enthalten) begreifen." (Novalis quoted ibid.)

of the world, a characteristic element of the classical travel novel, takes on a completely new meaning. The development of the protagonist does not only constitute a humanistic maturation process in the tradition of Goethe's epochal education novel (Bildungsroman) *Wilhelm Meisters Lehrjahre (Wilhelm Meister's Apprenticeship)*, but also moves the Romantic hope for a poetisization of the world into the centre of the poetry. I will go into this significant poetological concept of Romanticist thought and its relationship to Tolkien more closely in the second section.

It becomes obvious that Tolkien's Hobbit novels can be understood as walking and travel novels in the Romanticist tradition through the prominent position of the walking motive in the narrative structure of the stories. The protagonist's journey becomes the propelling momentum for the development of the narrative in both *The Hobbit* and *The Lord of the Rings*. The departure from the beloved homeland out into a promising world, in which dangers are omnipresent on the one hand, and on the other, the enchantment of adventure and poetry is potent, shapes the path of the Romantic hero. In accordance with the novel theory of the Romanticist era, Tolkien's wandering coincides with the plot of the novel (cf. Hoffmeister, *Der romantische Roman* 226). The chapter division follows the progressing journey of the four Hobbits for some time and later that of the Fellowship of the Ring.[8] Similar to the Romanticist novel with its particular window technique (ibid. 213), i.e. the successive opening of new spaces and landscapes by the protagonist, in every "book [and chapter] a new scene and a new world"[9] is brought forth in Tolkien's novels. The heroes open up a world and its secrets for themselves and the reader, a factor that has certainly contributed to the success of the book for many readers.

Further structural correlations between Tolkien's works and Romanticism become obvious in the respective exposition of the novels and the situation of the protagonists. This we can realize by bringing to mind the initial situation in Ludwig Tieck's *Franz Sternbalds Wanderungen*, written in 1798, a novel that entered literary history as one of the very first Romanticist walking and artist novels. In

---

8 Cf. Tolkien's chapter divisions in *The Lord of the Rings*, in which the respective geographical disclosure of the world is expressed: Book One: VI. The Old Forest, VII. In the House of Tom Bombadil, VIII. Fog on the Barrow-downs, IX. At the Sign of the Prancing Pony. [...] Book Two: III. The Ring Goes South, IV. A Journey in the Dark, V. The Bridge of Khazad-dum, VI. Lothlórien (cf. *LotR* vii).

9 "[Jedes] Buch [und Kapitel] bringt] eine neue Szene und eine neue Welt" (Kimpel, Wiedemann 97).

the first chapter of Tieck's book, the title character, who is on the point of leaving his home in Nuremburg and his master Albrecht Dürer "in order to widen his knowledge in foreign lands"[10], takes his leave of his friend and fellow craftsman Sebastian. The story's hero, leaving to strange lands, takes advantage of the farewell situation to express his longing for distant places in dazzling colours:

> I had painted the glory of Rome, the splendour of Italy, so often in my mind that I could lose myself in it completely while at work, that I imagined myself wandering on unknown footpaths, through shady forests, and then foreign cities and neverseen people met my sight; oh, the colourful, ever-changing world with its still unknown events, the artists I would see, the highly praised land of the Romans, where once heroes truly and actually roamed, whose pictures had already moved me to tears; see, all of this together had so often taken my thoughts captive that I at times knew not, where I was, when I arose again. [...] And then it was as if heart and spirit were enlarged inwardly and attempted to grasp with their arms the future time, to catch and seize it.[11]

A person's striving toward such a place of yearning, in this case explicitly associated with the city of Rome, but beyond that also the goal of all indeterminate Romantic longings and artistic ambitions of Sternbald, forms the basic motivating element of the novel's plot and finds its first prominent mention here. In the further development of the story Sternbald's longing for distant places is filled again and again with new contents, though in the end art and poetry are shown to be the actual destiny of the hero (cf. Hoffmeister, *Der romantische Roman* 226).

Similarly to the protagonists of the Romanticist novel, Bilbo and Frodo also find themselves in a condition of latent longing for distant places and inner restlessness at the beginning of their respective adventures. They experience their homeland as an attractive and beloved idyll on the border of world events, but in contrast to the prosaic dwellers of the Shire, both are aware of the en-

---

10 "Franz verließ jetzt Nürnberg, seine vaterländische Stadt, um in der Fremde seine Kenntnisse zu erweitern" (Tieck 12f)
11 "Ich hatte meinen Gedanken so oft die Pracht Roms, den Glanz Italiens vorgemalt, ich konnte mich bei der Arbeit ganz darin verlieren, daß ich mir vorstellte, wie ich auf unbekannten Fußsteigen, durch schattige Wälder wanderte, und dann fremde Städte und niegesehene Menschen meinem Blicke begegneten; ach, die bunte, ewig wechselnde Welt mit ihren noch unbekannten Begebenheiten, die Künstler, die ich sehn würde, das hohe gelobte Land der Römer, wo einst die Helden wirklich und wahrhaftig gewandelt, deren Bilder mir schon Tränen entlockt hatten; sieh, alles dies zusammen hatte oft so meine Gedanken gefangengenommen, daß ich zuweilen nicht wußte, wo ich war, wenn ich wieder aufsah. [...] Und dann war es, als wenn sich Herz und Geist innerlich ausdehnten und wie mit Armen jene zukünftige Zeit erhaschen, an sich reißen wollten." (Tieck 14f)

ticement of the great wide world beyond known regions, an enticement that is finally too strong to be resisted. The awakening of Romantic longing, the yearning for the adventurous appropriation of the world finds its expression in a central passage of *The Hobbit*. The Dwarves strike up the song "Far over the misty mountains cold" (*H* 14f), which has a leitmotiv function for Tolkien's first book, reflecting its central travel motive (There and back again):

> As they sang the hobbit felt the love of beautiful things made by hands and by cunning and by magic moving through him, a fierce and a jealous love, the desire of the hearts of dwarves. Then something Tookish woke up inside him, and he wished to go and see the great mountains, and hear the pine-trees and the waterfalls, and explore the caves, and wear a sword instead of a walking-stick. He looked out of the window. The stars were out in a dark sky above the trees. He thought of the jewels of the dwarves shining in dark caverns. Suddenly in the wood beyond The Water a flame leapt up – probably somebody lighting a wood-fire – and he thought of plundering dragons settling on his quiet Hill and kindling it all to flames. He shuddered; and very quickly he was plain Mr. Baggins of Bag-End, Under-Hill, again. (ibid. 16)

This passage of the book marks the beginning of the personal maturation of the title figure (cf. Eilmann, *Hobbit* 155f). The awakening of Bilbo's longing for distant places in *The Hobbit* by means of a song demonstrates the power of poetry for aesthetic enchantment of a person, an aspect that is of central importance for Tolkien's entire work (cf. Eilmann, *Lied* 122f) and which will be relevant for the further discussion of the relationship between Tolkien and the poetology of Romanticism. Bilbo's romantic streak is connected with his Tookish origin in this passage. The "Tookishness" (*H* 16) that gives Bilbo's thirst for adventure is also a synonym for the romantic, adventurous longing of the hero, long slumbering secretly and coming to the fore when needed, in the case of his cousin Frodo as well. Independently of their innate *Wanderlust*, both Hobbits are simultaneously bound emotionally to their homeland, similarly to Franz Sternbald[12], and can only take the decisive step for their development

---

12 The struggle that it took Franz Sternbald to leave his home is clearly emphasised in the farewell scene at the beginning of the novel: "Franz wished in his heart that the parting were over, it was as if his heart would be crushed by these present moments, he longed for loneliness, for the woods, to be able to weep his eyes out away from his friends." "Franz wünschte den Abschied im Herzen vorüber, es war, als wenn sein Herz von diesen gegenwärtigen Minuten erdrückt würde, er sehnte sich nach Einsamkeit, nach dem Walde, um dann von seinem Freunde entfernt, seinen Schmerz ausweinen zu können" (Tieck 18). He speaks for Sebastian, expressing his abiding love of his home by way of a vow: "I love you and my country and the parlour, in which our master lives, and nature and God. I will always cling to them, always, always! See, here on this old oak tree I promise it to you, you have

through outer circumstances. Thus, before his second journey Bilbo comments to Gandalf on Frodo's feelings, torn between the wish to stay and to leave:

> He would come with me, of course, if I asked him. In fact he offered to once, just before the party. But he does not really want to, yet. I want to see the wild country again before I die, and the Mountains; but he is still in love with the Shire, with woods and fields and little rivers. (*LotR* 32)

Accordingly the longings for home and for distant places are two diverging poles between which the Romantic hero constantly moves. Gerhart Hoffmeister's accurate analysis of Franz Sternbald's emotions could be applied to Frodo and Bilbo:

> The hero feels the parting from home as a loss of the idyll, the harmony of man and nature. [...] Sternbald sways between homesickness and the desire to see distant places until the latter asserts itself.[13]

Even Sam, a character who is a typical representative of the rustic Shire dwellers at the beginning of *The Lord of the Rings*, feels a latent longing for distant places and a yearning to get to know Elves:

> I heard [...] about an enemy, and rings, and Mr. Bilbo, sir, and dragons, and a fiery mountain, and – and Elves, sir. Lord bless me sir, but I do love tales of that sort. And I believe them too, whatever Ted may say. Elves, sir! I would dearly love to see *them*. Couldn't you take me to see Elves, sir, when you go?' (*LotR* 62)

Because of the close connection between the motive complexes Elves, art, and poetry in Tolkien's works[14], Sam's longing for Elves can be interpreted as a longing to integrate aesthetics and poetry in prosaic daily life, a wish that is obviously in the tradition of Romanticist thought, as shown above.

Of particular significance for our understanding of the Romanticist tradition in Tolkien's works is the fact that numerous songs in *The Hobbit* and *The Lord of the Rings* are walking songs in the Romanticist sense. Tolkien himself

---

my hand on it." "[I]ch liebe dich ja und mein Vaterland und die Stube, worin unser Meister wohnt, und die Natur und Gott. Immer werde ich daran hangen, immer, immer! Sieh, hier, an diesem alten Eichenbaum verspreche ich es dir, hier hast du meine Hand darauf." (ibid. 19)
13 "Der Held empfindet den Abschied von Zuhause als Verlust der Idylle, der Harmonie von Mensch und Natur. [...] Sternbald schwankt zwischen Heimweh und Fernweh, bis sich letzteres durchsetzt." (Hoffmeister, *Der romantische Roman*, 226).
14 "If I were pressed to rationalize, I should say that they [the Elves] represent really Men with greatly enhanced aesthetic and creative faculties, greater beauty and longer life, and nobility" (*L* 176).

explicitly called two of the songs listed in the Appendices of *The Lord of the Rings* "Walking Song" and "Old Walking Song" (*LotR* 1113). A characteristic trait of Romanticist walking novels is that the characters cite poems or strike up songs at various occasions. Sometimes the songs, in which Romantic longing is expressed by use of typical lyrical motives (posthorn sounds, rustling woods), extend over several pages (cf. Tieck 137-141 and 348-352 and Eichendorff, Bd. 3 147-152). In the light of numerous songs and poems in Romanticist novels and novellas we could exaggerate by saying that the distinctive ability to sing is a necessary prerequisite for a Romantic hero.

The characters in Tolkien's stories also sing at various occasions. When the Hobbits strike up Shire folksongs in an exuberant mood while walking through their homeland[15], this scene could have originated directly from one of Eichendorff's novellas. Similar to Franz Sternbald or Eichendorff's Taugenichts, Tolkien's characters are integrated in a lively collective culture of song (cf. Eilmann, *Kommunikation* 246). On the background of Romantic poetry, the distinctive poetic disposition of Tolkien's figures, their ability to rhyme extemporaneously even in existentially threatening situations (cf. ibid.), seems less strange. Obviously the above mentioned hallmark of the Romanticist novel as a mixture of all poetic genres plays a decisive role here. Of the walking songs in *The Hobbit* and *The Lord of the Rings*, the already mentioned "Old Walking Song" (*LotR* 1113) is the most outstanding. The "Old Walking Song" is sung in both *The Hobbit* and *The Lord of the Rings*, establishing an intertextual connection between the two novels. The song appears for the first time in the last chapter of *The Hobbit*. Gandalf's subsequent remark after Bilbo's singing, that he is no longer the same Hobbit who left the Shire with him at the beginning of the story (*H* 277), is appropriate in one decisive point: Bilbo has matured into a poet by the end of the story. The Hobbit's journey, as revealed in the undertitle of the novel, constitutes a circular movement (There and back again); however, in his own personal educational history, Bilbo himself has taken a significant step forwards in his development. It is in fact a different person who comes back

---

15 "They began to hum softly, as hobbits have a way of doing as they walk along, especially when they are drawing near to home at night. With most hobbits it is a supper-song or a bed-song; but these hobbits hummed a walking-song (though not, of course, without any mention of supper and bed). Bilbo Baggins had made the words, to a tune that was as old as the hills, and taught it to Frodo as they walked in lanes of the Water-valley and talked about Adventure." (*LotR* 76)

home. The song Bilbo sings at the sight of his home Bag End is, as far as the text indicates, the first poetic work of his beginning authorial career. "He took to writing poetry and visiting the elves" (ibid. 278), we are told concerning his further development at the end of *The Hobbit*. The fact that he dedicates himself above all to poetry after his return to the Shire is an idea that is only touched upon in *The Hobbit* yet is clearly present as a biographical element of Bilbo's character in *The Lord of the Rings*. The call to become a poet, the insight into his own poetic nature becomes a central element of the plot of the Romanticist novel, as shown earlier and made clear in Tolkien's books as well.

Bilbo's song, later known as the "Old Walking Song", has a leitmotiv quality for Tolkien's complete works, for it mirrors the walking motive that is constitutive in lyrical form for *The Hobbit* and *The Lord of the Rings*. The two central protagonists Bilbo and Frodo sing the song at crucial points in Tolkien's books, adapting it to the current situation and thereby reflecting their own position in the developing story. Even if it is remarkable that the lyrical first person is first utilised in the songs of *The Lord of the Rings*, explicit contextual indications emphasize the fact that the respective performer is speaking of himself (cf. Shippey 240).[16] The identification of the lyrical first person with the speaker is made obvious among other things by the immediate context; the narrator of *The Lord of the Rings* emphasizes the fact that both Bilbo and Frodo speak "as if to himself" (*LotR* 35, 72). This gives the impression that both speak thoughts and inner experiences out loud, which is emphasized by the reflective gesture of lyrical speech.

Bilbo's first version of the song says that "Roads go ever ever on" (*H* 303). Even if roads are spoken of in the plural here, I agree with Joanna Kokot, who points out concerning the road metaphor that it is always a single road without beginning and ending (cf. Kokot 329). Only the wandering, not the road can have an ending. The interpretation of the road as an individual's journey of life is adopted by the characters themselves in the process of the story and becomes obvious in the progression of the plot. So Frodo refers to his coming removal from the circles of

---

16 When Bilbo sings verses like "Over snow by winter sown,/ And through the merry flowers of June," (*H* 276) it is obvious that this refers to himself and his journey home, since it was June at this point of time in the narrative. The following verses are also to be understood as a reference to his successful adventure: "Eyes that fire and sword have seen/ And horror in the halls of stone/ Look at last on meadows green/ And trees and hills they long have known." (ibid. 277)

the world and the accompanying end of the wandering of his life when he sings Bilbo's walking song for the last time on the way to the Grey Havens.

I would like to take up one further thought by Joanna Kokot and link it to the Romanticist theory of poetry. In her discussion on the "Old Walking Song" Kokot reaches the conclusion that Tolkien refers to two levels of space and time in it. The road of the song shows the way above and beyond the current situation of the singer toward a time-transcending dimension. In this way the song links the *hic et nunc* (here and now) of the tangible world with the *semper et ubique* (anytime and anywhere) of the cosmos: "It introduces a constant and permanent order of the universe" (ibid. 329). This shift between temporal and timeless, of tangible experience and the eternity hidden behind the things is the central concern of Romanticist poetology, as shown in the next section, and has found its consummate expression in Eichendorff's "Wünschelruthe" (see above). It is in accordance with the transcendental quality of music and poetry in Tolkien's works that the "Old Walking Song" allows insight into the intrinsic structure of the cosmos and so makes possible the highest degree of transcendental experience, showing us the analogy to the poetology of German Romanticism.

Poetic Enchantment: Tolkien and the Principle of Romanticising

If a time-transcending order of things can be anticipated by poetic souls, the question arises how it is possible for an individual to awaken the sleeping song in order to look behind the veil of the objective world. The Romanticists give an unambiguous answer to this question: The metaphorical song can only be awakened through song itself, in other words, through poetry. In order to comprehend the fact that poetry has a similar power in Tolkien's Middle-earth, it is necessary to illuminate the Romanticist understanding of art more closely.

Of central importance for Romanticism as poetry, art, and world view is a poetological principle that found its clearest characterisation in the works of the early Romanticist theoritician and poet Novalis, the principle of Romanticising. What does it signify? In his typical aphoristic style, Novalis formulates in the "Logologischen Fragmente" (Logological Fragments):

> The world must become romanticised. So one can find the original purpose again. Romanticising is nothing other than a qualitative potentisation. The baser Self identifies itself with a better Self in this operation. [...] In giving a high purpose to that which is base, a mysterious esteem to that which is common, a neverending glory to that which is finite, I romanticise it – Reversed is the operation for that which is higher, unknown, mystical, endless – [...] it gains a common expression. Romantic philosophy. [...] elevation and degradation in turns.[17]

The claim that Novalis makes here is both radical and utopian in its poetological aspiration and follows the ancient poets' dream of pushing forward to the essence of things with the help of the arts. Poetry is to be the means of transforming the world. However, this process of Romanticising does not mean an "indiscriminate romantic fogging of things"[18]. Instead, Novalis, Friedrich Schlegel, and the other theoreticians of the early Romanticist era believe that the unknown secret that is slumbering in the prosaic daily reality can actually be discovered (cf. Roder 414).

The concept of "qualitative potentisation"[19] is decisive for an understanding of Novalis' train of thought: Just as the world of absolutes is to be tied into daily life by way of the principle of Romanticising, so the known and everyday experiences recover the dignity of the unknown and are thereby spiritually enhanced. Romanticism combines the hope of finding the "original meaning"[20] hidden in the surrounding world, i.e. to find the poetic content of existence again (cf. Roder, 225f). Art is to receive a pivotal role in this process, for it alone is able to spiritualise the sensual and sensualise the spiritual (cf. ibid. 415 and Volkmann-Schluck 46f).[21] The sleeping song can only be awakened by the "magical word"[22] of the poet. Because of this "redemptive deed of poetry,

---

[17] "Die Welt muß romantisirt werden. So findet man den urspr[ünglichen] Sinn wieder. Romantisiren ist nichts als eine qualit[ative] Potenzirung. Das niedre Selbst wird mit einem bessern Selbst in dieser Operation identificirt. [...] Indem ich dem Gemeinen einen hohen Sinn, dem Gewöhnlichen ein geheimnißvolles Ansehn, dem Bekannten die Würde des Unbekannten, dem Endlichen einen unendlichen Schein gebe, so romantisire ich es – Umgekehrt ist die Operation für das Höhere, Unbekannte, Mystische, Unendliche – [...] Es bekommt einen geläufigen Ausdruck. romantische Philosophie. [...] Wechselerhöhung und Erniedrigung." (Novalis, Bd. 2 545)
[18] "willkürlich-romantisches Umnebeln der Dinge" (Roder 414).
[19] "Romantisiren ist nichts als eine qualit[ative] Potenzirung" (Novalis, Bd. 2 545).
[20] "[Den] ursprünglichen Sinn [wieder finden]" (Novalis, Bd. *2* 545).
[21] "The change of sphere is necessary in a perfect depiction – the sensual must be represented spiritually, the spiritual sensually." "Der Sfärenwechsel ist nothwendig in einer vollendeten Darstellung – Das Sinnliche muß geistig, das Geistige sinnlich dargestellt werden.[sic]" (Novalis, Bd. 2 283. Cf. also Roder 738).
[22] "Zauberwort" (Eichendorff, Bd. I/1, S. 121).

by which the silent world is brought to sound again"[23], poetry is superior even to philosophy:

> Where the philosopher organises, places everything, so the poet looses all bonds. His words are not universal signs – they are tones – magical words, that move around in lovely groups [...] His world is as simple as an instrument – yet just as inexhaustible in melodies.[24]

In the same way that the magic of the poet's word opens the supposedly profane external world for the light of the higher world, the process of Romanticising comes to fruition and merges the two seemingly separate spheres. To find the "original meaning"[25] again consequentially means transforming the world itself into poetry, or making human beings aware that the world is internally made of poetry and art.

This outstanding purpose of art[26] is the point at which Tolkien and Romanticism meet in their poetological views and hopes. Poetic enchantment is omnipresent in Middle-earth. Analogous to the principle of Romanticising, which is significant for Romantic poetry, Tolkien bases his authorial work on a concept that gives the magical word of poetry (Volkmann-Schluck 48) a similarly high value: "enchantment" (*OFS* 53), bewitchment through poetry. In his key poetological essay "On Fairy-Stories", Tolkien deals extensively with the possibilities and limitations of poetic linguistic magic. For the question we issue it is crucial that the magical word of the Elvish artist has a similar function to poetry in German Romanticism. Furthermore, through the genuine qualities of "elvish craft" (ibid. 53), "enchantment" (ibid.) can be seen as the fulfillment of the Romanticist poetic dream. Just what does Tolkien mean by enchantment? In differentiation to despotic magic, which is oriented only toward the acquisition of earthly power[27], Tolkien attributes aesthetic intentions to poetic enchantment:

---

23 "[Die] Erlösungstat der Dichtung, durch die die verstummte Welt wieder zum Erklingen gebracht wird" (Fröhlich 223).
24 "Wenn der Philosoph nun alles ordnet, alles stellt, so lößte der Dichter alle Bande auf. Seine Worte sind nicht allgemeine Zeichen – Töne sind es – Zauberworte, die schöne Gruppen um sich her bewegen [...] Seine Welt ist einfach wie ein Instrument – aber ebenso unerschöpflich an Melodien." (Novalis, Bd. 2 87)
25 "[Den] ursprünglichen Sinn [wieder finden]" (Novalis, Bd. 2 545).
26 "Art is the magic which frees the spirit, frozen in objectivity, to life, and uncovers nature in its true essence", "Die Kunst ist der Zauber, welcher den gegenständlichen erstarrten Geist zum Leben befreit und die Natur erst in ihrem wahren Wesen enthüllt." (Volkmann-Schluck 48)
27 "[Magic] is not an art but a technique; its desire is power in this world, domination of things and wills." (*OFS* 53)

> Enchantment produces a Secondary World into which both designer and spectator can enter, to the satisfaction of their senses while they are inside; but in its purity it is artistic in desire and purpose. (ibid.)

Elsewhere Tolkien calls the enchanting quality of poetry the "power of the Faerie" (ibid. 14), having found a modern expression appropriate for his own works for the ancient poetic aim not only to describe things, but also to actually create them by means of linguistic magic, so becoming sub-creative:

> In dreams strange powers of the mind may be unlocked. In some of them a man may for a space wield the power of Faerie, that power which, even as it conceives the story, causes it to take living form and colour before the eyes. (ibid.)

For Tolkien, the Elven artist is the one who is capable of giving shape and form to the things of the imaginative world through his "creative desire" (ibid.) and his creative potential. This artistic creativity, which distinguishes poetic enchantment, is called "*Olos*" (*UT* 396f) in one of Tolkien's notes:

> Olo – s: vision, 'phantasy': Common Elvish name for 'construction of the mind' not actually (pre)existing in Ea apart from the construction, but by the Eldar capable of being by Art (*Karme*) made visible and sensible. *Olos* is usually applied to *fair* constructions having soley an artistic object (i.e. not having the object of deception, or of acquiring power). (ibid.)

Tolkien's concept of poetic enchantment can best be illustrated in his own literary work. Thus Frodo, sensitive to poetry, experiences the enchanting effect of Elvish poetry numerous times in *The Lord of the Rings*. Both the singing of Tom Bombadil and Goldberry as well as the Elbereth song sung by Elven singers in Rivendell convey to the Hobbit the impression of being caught in a magic spell. In all of these scenes the term "enchantment" (cf. *LotR* 117, 121, 232) is used to express the impact of the poetry and music in words. Art transfers the subject into a boundary expanding and exhilarating condition which makes it possible for him to have a transcendental experience (cf. Eilmann, *Lied* 132f) and achieve a notion of the true structure of the cosmos. In this way the word of the poet constitutes in the truest sense of the word a "magical word"[28].

This poetic transformation process, which is the goal of Romanticist art, as above described, can be found in a neglected passage of *The Lord of the Rings*,

---

[28] "Zauberwort" (Eichendorff, *Vol I/1*, S. 121).

which is significant for an understanding of Tolkien's artistic concept: Frodo's musical dream in Rivendell. When Frodo is so deeply affected by a musical-poetical performance in this scene, that he sinks into it, metaphorically speaking, and has a transcendental experience, then the characteristic merging of art and reality which is typical for the principle of Romanticising takes place here:

> At first the beauty of the melodies and the interwoven words in elven tongues, even though he understood them little, held him in a spell, as soon as he began to attend to them. Almost it seemed that the words took shape, and visions of far lands and bright things that he had never yet imagined opened out before him; and the firelight hall became like a golden mist above seas of foam that sighed upon the margins of the world. Then the enchantment became more dreamlike, until he felt that an endless river of swelling gold and silver was flowing over him, too multitudinous for its pattern to be comprehended; it became part of the throbbing air about him, and it drenched and drowned him. Swiftly he sank under its shining weight into a deep realm of sleep. There he wandered long in a dream of music that turned into running water, and then suddenly into a voice. It seemed to be the voice of Bilbo chanting verses. (*LotR* 227)

In the Romanticist view of art, a song sleeps in all things abounding. Which significance this thought has for a poet like Tolkien becomes clear finally through the concept that the sleeping song constitutes the foundation of Tolkien's mythological world: In Arda and Middle-earth a song does actually sleep in all things, since the cosmos, created of music, is essentially itself music and poetry. Poetically gifted individuals like Frodo, who are enchanted by linguistic magic, can hence achieve for a brief moment an impression of the world in a romanticized condition. Those who hear the "magic word" (ibid.) can look behind the veil of things and so experience the fact that the song of creation has never faded since the beginning of days.

About the Author

Julian Tim Morton Eilmann studied History, German Philology, and History of Arts at Aachen and Nottingham and is working as a grammar school teacher for German and History in Aachen. Before his vocation to teach he worked as a journalist and author for a film production company and is winner of the German Youth Video Award. In addition, he is fulfilling the functions of a gallery owner, and conservator for an artists' foundation. His main research is Tolkien poetry.

Tolkien References

TOLKIEN, J.R.R., *The Hobbit or there and back again*, Boston, New York: Houghton Mifflin, 1996.

The Letters of J.R.R. Tolkien, (ed. by Humphrey Carpenter with the assistance of Christopher Tolkien), London: HarperCollins, [1981] 1995.

The Lord of the Rings, London: HarperCollins, 1995.

"On Fairy-stories", In: *Tree and Leaf*, London: Unwin, 1964, 1-81.

Unfinished Tales of Númenor and Middle-earth, (ed. by Christopher Tolkien), London: George Allen & Unwin, 1980.

References

AUE, Walter A. (Home Page), July 2008, 26 June 2009, http://myweb.dal.ca/~waue/index.html

BAUSCH, Walter, *Theorien des epischen Erzählens in der Deutschen Frühromantik*, Bonn: Bouvier, 1964.

BEHLER, Ernst, *Frühromantik*, Berlin: Gruyter, 1992.

BIDLO, Oliver D., *Sehnsucht nach Mittelerde*, Norderstedt: BoD, 2003.

CURRY, Patrick, "Enchantment in Tolkien and Middle-earth", In: Stratford Caldecott and Thomas Honegger (eds.), *Tolkien's The Lord of the Rings: Sources of Inspiration*, Zurich and Jena: Walking Tree Publishers, 2008, 99-112.

EICHENDORFF, Joseph v., *Sämtliche Werke des Freiherrn Joseph von Eichendorff. Historisch-kritische Ausgabe*, Begr. Wilhelm Kosch und August Sauer, Hrsg. Hermann Kunisch, Helmut Koopmann u.a., 18 Bde., Stuttgart: Max Niemeyer, 1993ff.

EILMANN, Julian, "Das Lied bin ich. Lieder, Poesie und Musik in J.R.R. Tolkiens Mittelerde-Mythologie", In: *Hither Shore* 2 (2005), 105-35.

"Lieder und Poesie als Teil der kulturellen Kommunikation Mittelerdes", In: *Hither Shore* 3 (2006), 246-59.

"Singen oder nicht singen. Lieder und Gedichte in J.R.R. Tolkiens *Der Hobbit*", In: *Hither Shore* 5 (2008), 142-59.

FETZER, John, "Die romantische Lyrik", In: Helmut Schanze (ed.), *Literarische Romantik*, Stuttgart: Kröner, 2008, 135-58.

FRÖHLICH, Harry, "Erläuterungen", In: *Sämtliche Werke des Freiherrn Joseph von Eichendorff. Hist.-krit. Ausgabe*, Begr. Wilhelm Kosch und August Sauer, Hrsg. Hermann Kunisch und Helmut Koopmann, Bd. I/2, Gedichte, Erster Teil, Kommentar, Stuttgart: Max Niemeyer, 1994, 223-24.

HOFFMEISTER, Gerhart, *Deutsche und europäische Romantik*, 2. durchges. u. erw. Aufl, Stuttgart: Metzler, 1990.

"Der romantische Roman", In: Helmut Schanze (ed.), *Romantik-Handbuch*, Stuttgart: Kröner, 1994, 207-40.

KIMPEL, Dieter and Conrad Wiedemann, *Theorie und Technik des Romans im 17. und 18. Jahrhundert*, Bd. 2: *Spätaufklärung, Klassik, Frühromantik*, 1. Aufl., Tübingen: Max Niemeyer Verlag, 1970.

KOKOT, Joanna, "Dynamics in correlation. Words and music in a song by J.R.R. Tolkien and D. Swann", In: *Inklings-Jahrbuch* 5 (1987), 311-33.

NOVALIS, *Schriften. Die Werke Friedrich von Hardenbergs*, Hrsg. Paul Kluckhohn und Richard Samuel, 5 Bde., Stuttgart: Kohlhammer, 1960ff.

RODER, Florian, *Novalis. Die Verwandlung des Menschen. Leben und Werk Friedrich von Hardenbergs*, 2. Aufl., Stuttgart: Urachhaus, 2000.

SCHLEGEL, Friedrich, *Kritische Friedrich-Schlegel-Ausgabe. Bd. 6. Wissenschaft der europäischen Literatur*, Hrsg. Ernst Behler, Jean Jacques Anstett und Hans Eichner, Paderborn: Schöningh, 1979.

SHIPPEY, Tom, *J.R.R. Tolkien. Autor des Jahrhunderts*, Übers. Wolfgang Krege, Stuttgart: Klett-Cotta, 2002.

TIECK, Ludwig, *Franz Sternbalds Wanderungen*, Studienausgabe 1798, Stuttgart: Reclam, 1994.

TURNER, Allen, "The Hobbit and Desire", In: *Hither Shore* 5 (2008) 83-92.

UERLINGS, Herbert (Hrsg.), *Theorie der Romantik*, Stuttgart: Reclam, 2000.

VOLKMANN-SCHLUCK, Karl Heinz, "Novalis' magischer Idealismus", In: Hans Steffen (Hrsg.), *Die Deutsche Romantik. Poetik, Formen und Motive*, Göttingen: Vandenhoeck & Rupprecht, 1967, 45–53.

Murray Smith

"They Began to Hum Softly": Some Soldiers' Songs of World Wars I and II and of Middle-earth Compared and Contrasted

Songs and poems by hobbits of the Shire in J.R.R. Tolkien's *The Lord of the Rings* and *The Adventures of Tom Bombadil* are entirely civilian, due to the nature of their society. Songs about war, in particular about fighting for their country, insulting or satirising an enemy or both, or complaining about military life are non-existent; because there was no need for them, the Shire barely existing as a state and having no military.

Despite this, we see some of these normally peaceful hobbits turning into soldiers, and using songs and poems in some of the ways the United Kingdom's mostly previously civilian soldiers in World Wars I and II used songs: to cope with terror and to raise their morale.

One might by contrast expect Gondor, due to its history, to have in its musical culture songs about people fighting for their country, and soldiers' songs grumbling about military life. One might also expect songs against Sauron, his followers and allies, that, if not obscene, would be insulting, satirical, or both. Gondorian songs and poems are, however, only quoted twice, a "national anthem" and a rhyme about a herb.

This paper is divided into three parts. The first is a look at some songs sung by servicemen in the UK's military in both World Wars, with an emphasis on the first, in which Tolkien served as a junior officer. The second is a look at some poems and songs in the *The Lord of the Rings* and *The Adventures of Tom Bombadil*, of hobbit and Gondorian background. The third will be an attempt to compare and contrast these various categories of songs.

Soldiers' songs

World War I

The United Kingdom that entered World War I was a musical society. At a time when recorded music, in the shape of gramophone records, was beginning to appear, a high value was set on the ability of people to play a musical instrument, sing (even if it was only the ability to carry a tune), or both. The most popular musical instrument was the piano. Every respectable household aspired to having one in the parlour; and there was an upright piano in every church hall, every boys' club, and nearly every saloon bar. As a result, there were thousands of accomplished pianists and many who could play by ear.

At this time, most were brought up to attend church regularly. Many organisations affiliated to the churches were open to all. Salvation Army and other bands provided tunes as free entertainment. As a result, many hymn tunes were popular, and later irreverently appropriated by soldiers (Palmer 2; Arthur xii-xvii).

As well as religious tunes, some soldiers who enlisted early in the war had still been brought up in an atmosphere of more traditional songs. Ivor Gurnet, a musician and poet who enlisted in 1915 as a private in the Gloucestershire Regiment, talked of a soldier called Fred Bennett:

> A great broad chested heavy chap who has been a morris dancer and whose fathers and grandfathers, uncles and other relations know all the folk songs imaginable. (Palmer 15)

Men from communities where such traditional songs had been eclipsed, the majority by World War II, brought with them the popular songs of the day, learnt from sheet music, the music hall, or later from records and radio. (ibid.)

After 1914, the music halls continued their long tradition of using patriotic rhetoric, part of a popular culture that was "even more uncritical, jingoistic, and patriotic in its attitudes" than elite culture. Soldiers, however, developed their own different, far more sceptical and fatalistic culture. They had their own satirical trench magazines and composed their own songs that often mocked or subverted this patriotic culture of the home front, dealing with the incompetence of civilians and politicians, their military superiors, and the miserable conditions of trench life, including bad food. Xenophobia towards the Germans was absent, with indeed a sympathy towards those in the other trenches (Robb 160-61, 166-67, 178-84).

In 1930, John Brophy and Eric Partridge, private soldiers during World War I, published *The Daily Telegraph Dictionary of Tommies' Songs and Slang, 1914-18*[1]. This *Dictionary* pointed out that young civilians, who joined up early in that war as their patriotic duty, were "compelled to undergo a preliminary process" that "involved an almost total surrender of personal liberty and an immediate, unconsidered obedience to orders" (Brophy and Partridge 13).

The Army, in order to keep morale high, encouraged the formation of new bands along with the regimental ones. Most army divisions sponsored concert parties and theatrical troupes, which staged performances like music-hall fare (Arthur xvii-xxix; Robb 179).

Brophy said, in the preface to his and Partridge's *Dictionary*, that if soldiers sang in the front line, it was "one at a time and under the breath, unless they had reached a tacit and reciprocal arrangement with the Germans opposite". When they sang on the march it was during a "route march for exercise or to shift quarters, and only after the successive commands had been given 'March at Ease' and 'March easy' […]. Singing, with intervals of silence or of whistling or humming, provided a distraction from the long, slow count of the heavy laden miles".

Another sort of song was sung during training, in camps and billets behind the line, and whenever soldiers had the opportunity and money to visit estaminets[2]. It was typically a piece rendered by one man, or by a trio, and sometimes told a story, often ribald (Brophy and Partridge 23-24). In many cases, such estaminets or canteen huts had an "acquired" piano for sing-songs (Arthur xx).

---

1 "Tommy Atkins" or "Tommy" was the term for an ordinary UK soldier, which although of earlier origin has been particularly associated with those in World War I (Brophy and Partridge 193).
2 An "estaminet" had the qualities of a pub, a café and a restaurant, was never large, and found only in villages and very minor towns. While some overcharged, "in general they provided for the soldier off duty behind the line many and many a happy hour" (ibid. 117).

Brophy also said that soldiers did little or no singing when "on their way to the line", but coming out after a tour of duty in the trenches was "another matter". As soon as the company had a mile or two of road behind them "a kind of *sotto voce* singing or some soft whistling would begin". The tune was what mattered, not the words. In battle "no one thought of singing" (Brophy and Partridge 25).

Such soldiers' songs were parodies or satires of popular songs and hymn tunes, as well as their own compositions. Brophy said that like mediaeval ballads, "these songs were anonymous", such parodies or satires being perhaps composed by someone of some literary experience in a unit, taken up by others if appreciated, and possibly added to (ibid. 15-16).

Brophy divided the songs into seven categories: Satire on War, and Mock Heroics; Satire on the Military System; Satire on Superior Officers; Panegyrics of Civilian Bliss, Past and Present; Celebration of Drink and other Comforts; Nonsense and Burlesque; and Sex Ribaldry (ibid. 17-23).

Regarding satires on war and mock heroics, Brophy said that "When the victims can mock Juggernaut even as they writhe under the wheels, then by so much do they subtract from his victory". Such songs

> satirized more than war: they poked fun at the soldier's own desire for peace and rest, and so prevented it from overwhelming his will to go on doing his duty. They were not symptoms of defeatism, but strong bulwarks against it. (ibid. 18; Palmer 2; Robb 181)

As examples of such songs, one attacking military incompetence was "If the Sergeant Steals Your Rum, Never Mind", adapted from a 1913 sentimental song by Harry Dent and Tom Goldburn, which went "Though your heart may ache awhile, never mind!" Soldiers transformed it into

> If the sergeant steals your rum, *never mind*.
> And your face may lose its smile, *never mind*.
> He's entitled to a tot but not the bleeding lot,
> If the sergeant steals your rum, *never mind*. (Palmer 103; Arthur 74-75)

One song sung on the march was "We're Here Because". It was sung to the tune of "Auld Land Syne":

> We're here
> Because
> We're here
> Because
> We're here
> Because we're here.

It was sung "with great gusto" because, almost always, the men who sang it had "no idea why they were 'here', or where 'here' was, or how long they would continue at it" (Brophy and Partridge 37). Songs praising drink included "Here's to the Good Old Beer", sung to an unknown tune:

> Here's to the good old beer,
> Mop it down, mop it down!
> Here's to the good old beer,
> Mop it down!
> Here's to the good old beer,
> That never leaves you queer,
> Here's to the good old beer,
> Mop it down! (ibid. 41)

A song criticising the rations received was "Plum and Apple", to the tune of "A Wee Deoch an' Doris", which was about the only kind of jam that reached the troops early in the war:

> Plum and Apple,
> Apple and Plum,
> Plum and Apple,
> Apple and Plum,
> There is always some.
> The A.S.C. get strawberry jam
> And lashings of rum.
> But we poor blokes
> We only get –
> Apple and Plum. (Palmer 106; Arthur 84; Brophy and Partridge 59)

A very popular song, both among the troops and at home was "Take Me Back to Dear Old Blighty"[3], written in 1916 by A. J. Mills, Fred Godfery and Bennett Scott, of which the chorus went as follows:

> Take me back to dear old Blighty,
> Put me on the train for London Town,
> Take me over there, drop me anywhere –

---

3 "Blighty" being a slang term for Britain.

> Liverpool, Leeds or Birmingham, well I don't care!
> I should love to see my best girl,
> Cuddling up again we soon shall be; whoa!
> Tiddley-iddley ight-y, hurry me home to Blighty;
> Blighty is the place for me. (Arthur 37; Brophy and Partridge 217)

A popular song that had an extra meaning for soldiers, written in 1917 by Glitz Rice, was "But For Gawd's Sake Don't Send Me", originally "The Conscientious Objector's Lament", made famous by its performance by Alfred Lester. It was done to ridicule conscientious objectors; but the chorus was sung with great sincerity by soldiers:

> Send out the Army and the Navy,
> Send out the rank and file,
> Send out the brave old Territorials,
> They'll face the danger with a smile.
> Send out the Boys of the Old Brigade,
> Who made Old England free,
> Send out me brother, me sister and me mother
> But for Gawd's sake don't send me. (Arthur 42-43; Brophy and Partridge 58)

Brophy and Partridge called this song "very popular and very typical", being sung on the march but more often in billets and estaminets (Brophy and Partridge 58).

Some songs were ribald in nature, including versions of romantic ballads (Palmer 1; Arthur 27-28). An example of such a ribald song sung on the march, in which a senior officer joined in, happened when General Sir Douglas Haig, later Commander-in-Chief of the British Expeditionary Force, was visiting a headquarters, and heard a song sung by a marching battalion. Unaware of his presence, the men were singing

> Do your balls hang low?
> Do they dangle to and fro?
> Can I tie them in a knot?
> Can you tie them in a bow?

Haig pursued the column on horseback, intending to talk to the colonel at the head of the battalion. As he drew level with platoon after platoon, the men fell silent, that senior officer singing on. When Haig caught up, the conversation included the remark that while he liked the tune, the words were "inexcusable" (Arthur 89; Palmer 9-10).

Tolkien later alluded to this background of song against which he seriously began his story of Middle-earth, in letters to his youngest son Christopher in World War II, the latter then serving in the Royal Air Force. In a letter of 30th April 1944, he said that he first began to write the "H.[istory] of the Gnomes[Noldor]" in "army huts, crowded, filled with the noise of gramophones" (*L* 77; Letter 64). In another, dated 6th May, he said that "lots of the early parts" and "the languages" of Morgoth and the History of the Gnomes were done "in grimy canteens, at lectures in cold fogs, in huts full of blasphemy and smut, or by candle light in bell-tents, even some down in dugouts under shell fire" (*L* 78; Letter 66).

World War II

Many of the soldiers' songs of World War I survived into peacetime. Some became known to civilians in the United Kingdom. By the time of World War II, there were differences in what soldiers sang. The influence of radio meant that the strength of their culture diminished, due to closer contact with official thinking and the musical culture of home (Palmer 16).

The subject matter of the songs sung in that war would have, however, been familiar to those who had served in the previous one. One, "Longmoor", was a Royal Engineers' song about Longmoor Camp in Hampshire. Sung to the tune of "The Mountains of Mourne", one verse had comments about the tea:

> There's plenty of Naffi tea, oh never mind,
> It's a brew I'm sure Brooke Bonds never designed.
> The flavour I'm sure no one could ever place,
> But really it's a mixture of polish and paste. (ibid. 47)

A song popular among soldiers and then among civilians was "Bless 'Em All". It was written in 1916 by Fred Godfery, when he was in the Royal Naval Air Service, and was possibly already in circulation. Jimmy Hughes and Frank Lake were responsible for an arrangement popular with civilians from 1940. Soldiers sang sanitised or scurrilous versions depending on the audience:

> Bless 'em all, bless 'em all,
> The long and the short and the tall.
> Bless all the sergeants and WO Ones,
> Bless all the corporals and their blinking sons,

For we're saying goodbye to them all,
As back to their billets they crawl.
You'll get no promotion this side of the ocean,
So cheer up my lads, bless 'em all. (ibid. 142-44)

The most popular song on both sides of World War II was "Lili Marlene". The words were written in 1915 by a serving soldier on the Russian front, Hans Leip, who called the poem *Song of a Young Sentry*, but not published until 1937. The poem was set to music by Norbert Schultze in 1938, and recorded by Lale Andersen in 1939, just before war broke out.

While it failed as an initial hit it had a new lease of life when broadcast to soldiers of the Afrika Corps fighting in North Africa. These soldiers loved the song, as did their Eighth Army adversaries. To deal with this, the lyrics were translated into English; and a de-Nazified version was broadcast from 1944 on, and recorded by many singers. The theme, which tells of a soldier's girlfriend waiting for him near the barracks gate, led to the song being universally accepted and often recorded (Liebovitz and Miller passim). Its tune was re-used for many soldiers' songs (Liebovitz and Miller, 155-57; Palmer 177-81).

Some Songs and Verses of Middle-earth

Hobbits of the Shire

Tolkien based the Shire on where he and his brother Hilary spent part of their early childhoods in 1896-1900, in a cottage in Sarehole hamlet, a mile outside Birmingham (Carpenter 20-24). The Shire was stated by him, in a 12th December 1955 letter, to be "more or less a Warwickshire village of about the period of the Diamond Jubilee [1897]" (*L* 230; Letter 178. See also ibid., 235; Letter 181; ibid., 288, Letter 213).

In the prologue to *The Lord of the Rings*, Tolkien pointed out that hobbits had hardly any government, owing only nominal allegiance to kings who had lost their lordship. The only real Shire official was the elected Mayor; and the only governmental services he had to bother about were the police and the post office, the latter being the "busier" of the two. No standing army existed; it was not needed as the hobbits were protected unaware by the Rangers (*LotR* 4-5; 9-10; Prologue).

Tolkien pointed out that "at no time" had hobbits been warlike, and they had never fought among themselves. The last battle before the War of the Ring was that of Greenfields, in 2747 Third Age. Despite this "ease and peace", the hobbits were left "still curiously tough" (ibid. 5; Prologue). They were

> if it came to it, difficult to daunt or to kill; and they were, perhaps, so unwearyingly fond of good things not least because they could, when put to it, do without them, and could survive rough handling by grief, foe, or weather in a way that astonished those who did not know them well and looked no further than their bellies and their well-fed faces. Though slow to quarrel, and for sport killing nothing that lived, they were doughty at bay, and at need could still handle arms. (ibid. 5-6; Prologue)

How sophisticated the hobbits of the Shire were can for example be seen in some of the presents Bilbo Baggins gave when he left the Shire for good: an umbrella; a waste-paper basket; a gold pen and ink-bottle; a round convex mirror; a book-case; and a case of silver spoons (ibid. 36-37; Book 1, Ch. I).

The question about the kind of songs sung by hobbits was later answered by Peregrin Took when Ruling Steward Denethor II of Gondor asked if he could sing. His reply was that while he could "well enough" (ibid. 788; Book 5, Ch. IV) for his own people,

> "[...] we have no songs fit for great halls and evil times, lord. We seldom sing of anything more terrible than wind or rain. And most of my songs are about things that make us laugh; or about food and drink, of course." (ibid. 789)

While Denethor asked why such songs should be "unfit" for his halls or such times, Pippin still "did not relish" the idea of singing "any song of the Shire" to the Lord of Minas Tirith, "certainly not the comic ones that he knew best; they were too, well, rustic for such an occasion". He was spared "the ordeal" and not commanded to sing. (ibid.)

By this time, readers will have seen the truth in Pippin's explanation. Very early on, there was evidence of a rich Shire musical culture at Bilbo's 111th birthday party, where "music" was one of the main activities. When he gave his speech, there were "noises of trumpets and horns, pipes and flutes, and other musical instruments". Some of his younger relatives, supposing he had finished "now got up an impromptu orchestra, and began a merry dance-tune". A young couple got on a table and "with bells in their hands" began to dance the "Springle-ring" (ibid. 29; Book 1, Ch. I).

After disappearing, but before he left Hobbiton and the Shire, Bilbo sang "softly" a version of his "Roads go ever ever on", a travelling song he composed on his return in *The Hobbit*. This time it began "The Road goes ever on and on". After singing that "far ahead" the Road has gone, he "must follow" it if he can, until it joins "some larger way". He ended with "And whither then? I cannot say". (ibid. 35)[4]

Years later, when Frodo prepared to leave the Shire with Pippin and Sam, he spoke "aloud but as if to himself" this song exactly (*LotR* 72; Book 1, Ch. III). Pippin asked if it was "a bit of old Bilbo's rhyming", or one of Frodo's "imitations". Frodo answered that "It came to me then, as if I was making it up; but I may have heard it long ago." (ibid.)

We later find these three hobbits beginning to "hum softly":

> as hobbits have a way of doing as they walk along, especially when they are drawing near to home at night. With most hobbits it is a supper-song or a bed-song; but these hobbits hummed a walking-song (though not, of course, without any mention of supper and bed). Bilbo Baggins had made the words, to a tune that was as old as the hills […]. (ibid. 76; Book 1, Ch. III)

The walking song, as advertised, started with "Upon the hearth the fire is red,/ Beneath the roof there is a bed". It had references to "meat and bread", then its last line ended with two references to bed. (ibid.)

The next hobbit-songs that followed were a drinking song, "Ho! Ho! Ho! to the bottle I go" (ibid. 88; Book 1, Ch. IV), and "one of Bilbo's favourite bath-songs", sung when they arrived at Crickhollow. It started with "Sing hey! For the bath at close of day/that washes the weary mud away!" It included the comment that "Beer, if drink we lack" was better to drink than cold water (ibid. 99, Book 1, Ch. V).

---

4 For the original song, see *H* 275-76; Ch. 19.

Before leaving, Merry and Pippin sang "Farewell we call to hearth and hall!" (ibid. 104), an adaptation of the dwarf song ("Far over the misty mountains cold", *H* 13-14; Ch. 1) that Bilbo heard on the eve of his adventure to the Lonely Mountain. When the hobbits were in the Old Forest, Frodo began a song "O! Wanderers in the shadowed land" against the "ill will of the wood pressing on them"; but his voice "sank to a murmur"; and at the line "For east or west all woods must fail[…]", when he said the last word "his voice faded into silence" (*LotR* 110; Book 1, Ch. VI).

Later, they were caught by Old Man Willow, from whom they were rescued by Tom Bombadil, who later taught the four hobbits a rhyme to sing "if they should by ill-luck fall into any danger or difficulty the next day" (ibid. 131; Ch. VII). This came to pass, when the four were captured by a barrow-wight; but Frodo sang Tom's song, "which had a full and lively sound", and "the dark chamber echoed as if to drum and trumpet" (ibid. 138, Ch. VIII).

Later in the Prancing Pony in Bree, Frodo sang "a ridiculous song" of which the words were composed by Bilbo. This song, "The Man in the Moon Stayed up Too Late" (ibid. 154-56; Ch. IX) is implied to be the origin of the nursery rhyme "Hey Diddle Diddle", and explains the behaviour of the characters of the latter by the Man in the Moon drinking too much.

On the way to Rivendell with Aragorn, the latter referred to the Elven-king Gil-galad. When Merry asked who he was, Sam "murmured" part of the lay *The Fall of Gil-galad*, which Bilbo had translated, ending "for into darkness fell his star/in Mordor where the shadows are" (ibid. 181; Ch. XI). Sam said that there was "a lot more, all about Mordor", which he didn't learn; because "it gave me the shivers" (ibid. 182).

After the party arrived at Weathertop and as night fell, Aragorn "began to tell them tales to keep their minds from fear". When Merry asked about the lay of Gil-galad Sam had sung, Frodo began by saying he and Elendil went to Mordor; but before that land was mentioned, Aragorn said that the tale should not be told now "with the servants of the Enemy [Sauron] at hand" (ibid. 186-87).

As an alternative, Sam asked him to tell them "some other tale of the old days, a tale about the Elves before the fading time" (ibid. 187). Aragorn obliged by telling some of the tale of Tinúviel, beginning to "chant softly". He then told some more of the love story of Beren and Lúthien: one a man, the other an elf who "died indeed" to be with the one she loved (ibid. 187-90).

At that moment in the narrative, this love song appeared to be of no more than historical interest; but readers later find out that Aragorn and Arwen, daughter of Elrond, were descended from Beren and Lúthien; and she, being an elf, had, like Lúthien, to choose mortality to marry him, a mortal man. We only know for certain of their relationship at the end of Book 6, Chapter V, after Aragorn's crowning, when he and Arwen were married on Midsummer's Day (ibid. 951; Book 6, Ch. V).

On that night, the party was attacked by the Ringwraiths, and Frodo was stabbed. Some days later, Merry asked if someone would "give us a bit of a song" while the sun was high. He pointed out that they "haven't had a song or a tale for days". Frodo said that it was "not since Weathertop". Sam then sang, "to an old tune", "The Stone Troll" (ibid. 201-03; Book 1, Ch. XII). The song was a comic one, of Tom finding a troll eating a shinbone of his dead uncle, and kicking that troll's behind; but because that part was "harder than stone", Tom's leg was "game" and his bootless foot was "lasting lame" as a result. This performance improved the party's morale.

Much later, when he was going through Ithilien with Frodo and Gollum, Sam recited a poem about oliphaunts, "a rhyme we have in the Shire" (ibid. 632; Book 4, Ch. III). When going through Shelob's lair, and after that spider had attacked Frodo, Sam touched the Phial of Galadriel, and cried out in Sindarian a song invoking Elbereth (ibid. 712, Ch. X).[5] With this help, Sam recovered. He angrily and uncharacteristically called Shelob "you filth!" Thinking Frodo dead, he took the Ring and began to go on, only to see orcs find and take Frodo's body. He stood gasping for a moment, then drew his sleeve across his face, wiping away the grime, sweat and tears, and said "Curse the filth!" referring to the orcs (*LotR* 713, 719; Book 4, Ch. X).

The most moving and significant song sung by a hobbit is Sam's, in the Tower of Cirith Ungol, when he despaired of finding Frodo, whom he discovered was

---

5 For a translation by Tolkien of the song, see *L* 278, Letter 211.

still alive: "[…] then softly, to his own surprise, there at the vain end of his long journey and his grief, moved by what thought in his heart he could not tell, Sam began to sing". His voice sounded "thin and quavering", and was "of a forlorn and weary hobbit". He "murmured old childish tunes out of the Shire" and "snatches of Mr. Bilbo's rhymes that came into his mind like fleeting glimpses of the country of his home" (ibid. 887-88; Book 6, Ch. I).

Then, "suddenly new strength rose in him, and his voice rang out, while words of his own came unbidden to fit the simple tune", which began:

> In western lands beneath the Sun,
> the flowers may rise in Spring,
> the trees may bud, the waters run,
> the merry finches sing.

Although "here at journey's end I lie/in darkness buried deep", Sam "will not say the Day is done,/nor bid the Stars farewell" (ibid. 888). His song was successful; when he began again, at line 11, "Beyond all towers strong and high", he stopped, thinking that he had "heard a faint voice answering him". He saw the orc Snaga going to the room Frodo was in, discovering it could be reached by a trap-door in the roof of the passage, accessible by a ladder. (ibid.)

When the four hobbits arrived back at Rivendell, a very old Bilbo "murmured" another version of his old walking song, which ended with letting others who can follow the Road. He will "turn towards the lighted inn,/My evening-rest and sleep to meet" (ibid. 965; Book 6, Ch. VI). A few years later, Sam with Frodo on the way to the Grey Havens, heard the latter "singing softly to himself" the "old walking-song", but a version mentioning a day when he "Shall take the hidden paths that run/West of the Moon, East of the Sun" (ibid. 1005, Ch. IX).

Tolkien claims *The Adventures of Tom Bombadil* to be a selection of verses from the *Red Book of Westmarch*, taken both from the main text and from writings in margins and blank spaces. He selected samples that had been written at the end of the Third Age, especially by "Bilbo and his friends, or their immediate descendants" (*FGH and ATB* 78). One critic rightly said they enable us to see into the mind of the Shire, "its rich though homely sense of humour and its typically hobbitean love of ancient tales, mythic beast-lore, and cracker-barrel wisdom" (Helms 115).

As well as many of the songs and poems already met in *Lord of the Rings*, we meet other works by familiar hobbits. Sam Gamgee is credited with the comic "Perry-the-Winkle" about a hobbit who makes friends with a troll, and "Cat", dealing with a fat cat at home on the mat dreaming of "his kin, lean and slim", who "feasted on beasts/and tender men". The editor said that at most Sam, in the latter work, "can only have touched up on older piece of the comic bestiary lore of which Hobbits appear to have been fond" (*FGH and ATB* 79, 119-23, 129). The piece "Fastitocalon" is also part of this comic bestiary lore, dealing with a sea-creature that is taken for an island, and which drowns people so foolish as to land on him (ibid. 127-28). An earlier piece, "Errantry", the most sophisticated in the collection, is "evidently" by Bilbo, dealing with the legends of Eärendil. The pieces "The Man in the Moon came down too Soon" and "The Last Ship", are based on Gondorian material; and "The Hoard" on the tale of Túrin and Mím (ibid. 79-80, 99-103, 111-15, 132-35). The earliest and least sophisticated pieces in the collection, "The Adventures of Tom Bombadil" and "Bombadil goes Boating", from Buckland, indicate that the inhabitants knew Bombadil, but thought of him as hobbits also thought of Gandalf, "mysterious maybe and unpredictable but nonetheless comic" (ibid. 80-81). The first has Tom in a number of situations which he deals with by rough humour. The second, said to be composed after the four hobbits visited him, dealt with him joking with his friends, who turn it back upon him, though with an element of fear (ibid. 81, 83-98).

To sum up, the songs and poems of hobbit origin that readers come across mostly deal with the themes of food, drink, bath and bed, overlapping with comedy and with bestiary lore. The more sophisticated ones, sung by hobbits who had travelled and had connections with elves and men, also include stories of those other peoples, as well as about travelling. This fits in with the peaceful nature of hobbits in general, including the hobbits we know most about.

Gondor

Because Gondor was the main opposition to Sauron for millennia, Gondorians developed a strong sense of nationality. Early on, Boromir pointed out that by their valour "alone are peace and freedom maintained in the lands behind us, bulwark of the West" (*LotR* 239; Book 2, Ch. II). When Galdor spoke of the "waning might of Gondor", he was rebuked by Boromir: "Gondor wanes, you say. But Gondor stands, and even the end of its strength is still very strong" (ibid. 260).

This pride in Gondor was also seen in Boromir's younger brother Faramir, who said that while war was necessary, he only loved what it defended, "the city of the Men of Númenor; and I would have her loved for her memory, her ancientry, her beauty, and her present wisdom" (ibid. 656; Book 4, Ch. V). Tolkien said that Faramir was the character most like him (*L* 232 fn, Letter 180).

This pride also existed among Gondorians in general, seen when Beregond, an ordinary soldier, told Pippin, "we have this honour: ever we bear the brunt of the chief hatred of the Dark Lord, for that hatred comes out of the depths of time and over the deeps of the Sea" (*LotR* 749; Book 5, Ch. I).

Gondor was sophisticated enough to distinguish between the kingdom and the king, still enduring as a state despite having a vacant throne, the kings' hereditary chief ministers ruling as hereditary regents, (ibid. 654-55; Book 4, Ch. V) experienced in person by Pippin in Book 5, Chapter I, when he arrived in Minas Tirith. When he agreed to swear allegiance, he first swore "fealty and service to Gondor" (ibid. 740; Book 5, Ch. I). His first question to Beregond, assigned to give him information, was about meal times, something that earned the latter's respect. Beregond calls him "an old campaigner", commenting how he had heard that "men who go warring afield look ever to the next hope of finding food and drink" (ibid. 744). Pippin later saw the evacuation of "the aged, the children and the women that must go with them" (ibid. 747).

The next day, Pippin found that food was now rationed; he was told his duties by Denethor II, and dressed in the "livery and gear of the Tower". After that day's duties, he and Beregond were out on the walls, Pippin having felt "imprisoned indoors". Now he was "one small soldier in a city preparing for a great assault, clad in the proud but sombre manner of the Tower of Guard". He complained to Beregond about "waiting hungry on others while they eat. It is a sore trial for a hobbit, that" (ibid. 788-90; Book 5, Ch. IV). Later, Denethor released Pippin from his service (ibid. 807), permitting him to go and warn Gandalf. Unlike Pippin, Beregond had to resolve the dilemma between saving the life of Faramir and deserting his post; because the Lord did not permit "those who wear the black and silver to leave their post for any cause, save at his own command" (ibid. 809).

It was mentioned above that Denethor asked Pippin if he could sing (ibid. 788). When Pippin was reluctant to sing, on the grounds that Shire songs would be inappropriate, Denethor asked why such songs should be "unfit": "We who have lived long under the Shadow may surely listen to echoes from a land untroubled by it? Then we may feel that our vigil was not fruitless, though it may have been thankless" (ibid. 789). This interest appears to run in the family; a later reference to Faramir said that he was a "lover" of music (ibid. 1031; Appendix A, iv).

This love of music was not just confined to the ruler and his family. Later, during the siege of Minas Tirith, when Denethor refused to do anything, Gandalf took command of the last defence. He and the Prince of Dol Amroth went to inspect the defences; and the latter and his knights reminded the soldiers that there was elvish blood in their veins, and that the people of Nimrodel lived there long ago. "And then one would sing amid the gloom some staves of the Lay of Nimrodel, or other songs of the Vale of Anduin out of vanished years" (ibid. 806; Book 5, Ch. IV).

After the victory, at the Field of Cormallen, a "minstrel of Gondor stood forth, and knelt, and begged leave to sing". His "lay" was called "Frodo of the Nine Fingers and the Ring of Doom". He was obviously a very good singer, his "clear voice" rising "like silver and gold", all men being "hushed" (ibid. 933; Book 6, Ch. IV).

When the eagle came out of the east with "tidings beyond hope" to the people in Minas Tirith, he told the people to "sing" four times; and "the people sang in all the ways of the City" (ibid. 942; Book 6, Ch. V). Among the people who came to the City from all parts of Gondor to the crowning of Aragorn were musicians:

> from Dol Amroth came the harpers that harped most skilfully in all the land; and there were players upon viols and upon flutes and upon horns of silver, and clear-voiced singers from the vales of Lebennin. (ibid. 944)

After the crowning, when King Elessar came to the barrier, these musicians and singers were referred to *directly*; "amid the music of harp and of viol and of flute and the singing of clear voices the King passed through the flower-laden streets[…]" (ibid. 947). After they returned to the Shire, there was a reference to Merry and Pippin "singing songs of far away" (ibid. 1002; Book 6, Ch. IX). Doubtless some were of Gondor, there being no language barriers between the Shire and Gondor, both speaking the Common Speech (ibid. 1107; Appendix F).

The Adventures of Tom Bombadil refers to two pieces, which although written by hobbits "must be derived ultimately from Gondor". They are "The Man in the Moon came down Too Soon", the "ancestor" of the "later" nursery rhyme of the same name, and "The Last Ship", dealing with a mortal woman, Fíriel, who refused the offer of elves to carry her to Elvenhome. There are geographical references in both poems to Gondor, and a use in the second of Fíriel, a Gondorian name of Elvish origin (*FGH and ATB* 79-81).

There are, however, only two Gondorian songs and poems quoted. The herbmaster of the Houses of Healing after the Battle of the Pellenor Fields recalled one of the "rhymes of old days" concerning athelas when Aragorn was looking for some. This poem started: "When the black breath blows" (*LotR* 847; Book 5, Ch. VIII). Earlier, Aragorn had sung a song in praise of Gondor, after looking at the White Mountains on its borders, and wishing he had looked on that country "in happier hour!" Not yet did his road "lie southward to your bright streams":

> Gondor! Gondor, between the Mountains and the Sea!
> West Wind blew there; the light upon the Silver Tree
> Fell like bright rain in gardens of the Kings of old.
> O proud walls! White towers! O wingéd crown and throne of gold!
> O Gondor, Gondor! Shall men behold the Silver Tree,
> Or West Wind blow again between the mountains and the Sea?
> (ibid. 412-43; Book 3, Ch. II)

Among the references to Gondor's geographical location and national symbols, there is also a reference to the Silver Tree. In 2852 T.A., when the White Tree died; and because no seedling could be found, the "Dead Tree" was "left standing" (ibid. 1063; Appendix B). Previously, Aragorn had served King Thengel of Rohan and Ecthelion II of Gondor in disguise (ibid. 1064). The song may be a composition of Aragorn's, or a partial and complete composition by another. If the latter, the song may have been written after the death of that White Tree, looking back to happier times before the event, when Gondor was stronger, and wondering if they would return again.

Despite their fierce opposition to Sauron, who "desired to be a God-King [...] if he had been victorious he would have demanded divine honour from all rational creatures and absolute temporal power over the whole world" (*L* 243-44, Letter 183), the Gondorians were quite mild in references to him and his followers and allies. At the Council of Elrond, Boromir called Sauron "him that we do not name" (*LotR* 237; Book 2, Ch. II). References to Sauron used the terms "Enemy" (for example, ibid. 652; Book 4, Ch. V), "Nameless" (for example, ibid. 653), "Unnamed" (for example, ibid. 656), or by a pronoun or adjective, such as "He", "Him", and "His" (for example ibid. 645, Ch. IV). He was also called the "Dark Lord" (for examples ibid. 864; Book 5, Ch. IX). In front of the Black Gate, the heralds call him the "Lord of the Black Land" (ibid. 869; Book 5, Ch. X).

In terms of references to the counry of Mordor, Gondorians again mostly use euphemisms. After he met Frodo and Sam, Faramir did not even refer to Mordor by name, but just pointed in its direction (ibid. 644; Book 3, Ch. IV). He later called it "the Nameless Land" (ibid. 676; Book 4, Ch. VI). On another occasion, Beregond told Pippin, after referring to Mordor by name, that "[w]e seldom name it", and later called it "yonder realm" (ibid. 748, 750; Book 5, Ch. I).

Actual cursing seems restricted to the Rangers Mablung and Damrod, who used phrases like "Curse them [the Men of Harad]!" and "Aye, curse the Southrons!" and "These cursed Southrons" (ibid. 645; Book 3, Ch. IV).

This Gondorian mildness of manner is shown when King Elessar treated his country's enemies leniently. He pardoned the Easterlings who had given themselves up "and sent them away free". He "made peace" with the peoples of Harad. He released the slaves of Mordor and gave them the lands around Lake Núrnen for their own (ibid. 947; Book 6, Ch. IV).

Although Gondor had fought against Sauron for so long, and despite being more like a nation-state of the early twentieth-century than any other Middle-earth country (in terms of its sense of patriotism, its legal and governmental structures and military); it is curiously not as "advanced" as the Shire, a peaceful, insular society. While there is a vibrant musical culture in Gondor, it is referred to indirectly in most cases, with only two songs or poems actually being quoted.

Comparisons

In comparing the types of UK soldiers' songs of the two World Wars with the hobbits' and Gondorian poems and songs, a few themes emerge.

Patriotism, But no Xenophobia

We have seen earlier that while there is a sense of patriotism among Gondorians, there is none in the Shire, due to their different histories. The song sung by Aragorn, "Gondor! Gondor", resembles a national anthem, which Gondor was sophisticated enough to have.

The song bears a resemblance to the Polish national anthem, *Mazurek Dąbrowskiego* (*Dąbrowski's Mazurka*), also called after its first line, *Poland Has Not Perished Yet*. It was written by Józef Wybicki to a popular folk-tune in 1797, two years after partition had removed Poland from the map. It was written for the Polish Legions commanded by General Jan Henryk Dąbrowski in the service of the French revolutionary army. It expressed the hope that the idea of a Polish nation would not die as long as Poles lived and fought for it:

> Poland has not perished yet
> So long as we still live.
> That which alien force has seized
> We at swordpoint shall retrieve.

This song has been the national anthem since 1926, after the re-emergence of Poland as an independent state in 1918 (Davies 12-13).

Tolkien was acquainted with Polish. In an 18th January 1944 letter to his son Christopher, he said that he found that language "rather sticky yet". He expected that "poor old Poptawski", a Polish officer who had consulted him a few weeks earlier, would "be wondering how I am getting on, soon. It will be a long time before I can be of assistance to him in devising a new technical vocabulary!!!" He referred to the situation of Poland in the next sentence, "The vocab[ulary] will just happen along anyway (if there are any Poles and Poland left) [...]" (*L* 67-68; Letter 55).

Here, Tolkien was referring to the occupation and partition of Poland between Nazi Germany and the USSR in 1939, and its later full occupation by the former from 1941. By 1944, it was clear that the USSR would remove the Germans from Poland; but Tolkien had no illusions about what Poles would endure under Josef Stalin, whom he had called a "bloodthirsty old murderer" (ibid. 65; Letter 53).

By contrast, the Shire had no sense of patriotism, none being necessary. In a note on W. H. Auden's review of *The Lord of the Rings*, which was printed on 22nd January 1956, Tolkien said that Frodo's duty was not a patriotic one:

> Frodo's duty was 'humane' not political. He naturally thought first of the Shire, since his roots were there, but the quest had as its object not the preserving of this or that polity, such as the half republic half aristocracy of the Shire, but the liberation from an evil tyranny of all the 'humane' – including those, such as 'easterlings' and Haradrim, that were still servants of the tyranny.
> (ibid. 240-41; Letter 183)

In a footnote, Tolkien explained that the word "humane" included "of course Elves, and indeed all 'speaking creatures'" (ibid. 241 fn.). When Sam sang in the Tower of Cirith Ungol, his quoted song did not refer to the Shire, but to "western lands" in general.

Neither hobbits nor Gondorians exhibited any xenophobia towards their enemies. Sam, for example, only really cursed at Shelob and particular Orcs. Gondorians not only refrained from any ribaldry or satire against their enemies, in particular Sauron; they only referred to him and those things and people associated with him mostly by euphemism. This was in keeping with a dislike felt by many soldiers of the flippancy of the music hall approach to World War I, with its overblown patriotic rhetoric (Robb 167).

Tolkien himself, while a patriot, was free of xenophobia, and imperialism whether political or cultural. While genuinely feeling a duty to king and country, he postponed enlisting until 1915, in order to finish his studies. His interest in matters "Germanic" might have been a factor, giving him a view on war different from that of many of his contemporaries (Garth 40-44).[6] His continuing pride in his German background, and how he found it compatible with his war service was shown in a letter of 1938, to be sent to a German publisher:

> I have been accustomed, nonetheless, to *regard my German name with pride*, and *continued to do so throughout the period of the late regrettable war*, in which I served in the English army. (ibid. 37; Letter 30) (my italics)

His patriotism and lack of xenophobia was still there in the middle of World War II, though now with two sons in the armed forces to worry about. In a 9th December 1943 letter to Christopher, he said:

> For I love England (not Great Britain and certainly not the British Commonwealth (grr!)), and if I was of military age, I should, I fancy, be grousing away in a fighting service, and willing to go on to the bitter end – always hoping that things may turn out better for England than they look like doing. (ibid. 65; Letter 53)

While detesting Adolf Hitler as a "ruddy little ignoramus" (ibid. 55; Letter 45), Tolkien, unlike many, had no illusions about the war. First, he knew the truth about USSR and Josef Stalin. Second, he opposed attacks on German civilians, and was disgusted at Allied propaganda (ibid. 93; Letter 81).

The problem for him was that, unlike in the book he was writing, there were orcs on both sides. He said in a letter of 6th May 1944 to Christopher that "we are attempting to conquer Sauron with the Ring. And we shall (it seems) succeed. But the penalty is, as you will know, to breed more Saurons, and slowly turn Men and Elves into Orcs. Not that in real life things are as clear cut as in a story, and we started out with a great many Orcs on our side" (ibid. 78; Letter 66).

---

6 See also *L* 53; Letter 43.

On 20th January 1945, with Germany's defeat drawing near, he wrote to Christopher, attacking the gloating over refugees moving West:

> We were supposed to have reached a state of civilization in which it might still be necessary to execute a criminal, but not to gloat, or to hang his wife and child by him while the orc-crowd hooted. (ibid. 111; Letter 96)

After the end of the war in Europe, when it appeared that Christopher might have to fight the Japanese, he said in a letter of 29th May 1945 that

> as I know nothing about British or American imperialism in the Far East that does not fill me with regret and disgust, I am afraid I am not even supported by a glimmer of patriotism in this remaining war. I would not subscribe a penny to it, let alone a son, were I a free man. (ibid. 115; Letter 100)

Satires on Civilian and Military Superiors and Military Discipline

Unlike in both World Wars, no such critical songs and poems exist among hobbits and Gondorians. With hobbits the explanation is, for the most part, easy. The Shire barely existed as a state, and was an insular society; so there was no question of encouraging or compelling its people to fight anyone. Frodo volunteered to take the Ring to Rivendell. Sam, Merry and Pippin volunteered to come with him. Later, at the Council of Elrond, Frodo again volunteered to take the Ring to Mordor in the Council of Elrond, with the other three demanding to accompay him once again.

Elrond said of Frodo that "[o]n him alone is any charge laid"; on the others accompanying him, "no oath or bond is laid on you to go further than you will" (*LotR* 273-74; Book 2, Ch. III). Thus the Fellowship of the Ring was not based on any form of oath, and cannot be compared to a "military" unit in any modern sense.

This changed when they encountered Rohan and Gondor. Merry was sworn to the service of Théoden; but it appears the oath was quite informal in nature. Merry's refusal of the monarch's order to stay in Rohan, was later readily forgiven. Things were quite different in Pippin's case. Readers are left in no doubt that he subjected himself to military discipline, and consequent penalties for any breaches of the same. Luckily, he was released from his service by Denethor, making him able to warn Beregond and later Gandalf of the steward's madness.

Beregond's case, however, shows the consequences of breaching such a military oath. Death would have been the penalty for leaving his post "without leave of Lord or of Captain" and spilling blood in the Hallows. Instead, King Elessar pardoned and promoted him (ibid. 947-48; Book 6, Ch. V).

As we have seen, Pippin did actually grumble about the new constraints that being part of the Gondorian military placed on him, although these complaints did not take the form of songs. They did however underline some of the deficiencies and he may be seen as a spokesman for his longer-serving comrades in arms. The lack of any such songs from Gondorians themselves, and the absence of criticism of civilian and military authority may reflect two things. First, if you are fighting someone who wants to be a God-King and is demanding not only complete temporal power bt also to be worshipped, you tend not to be as critical of those in authority as you would otherwise be. Two, those Gondorian leaders we see, from Denethor II downwards, appear to be competent, although there was some criticism of Denethor's treatment of Faramir.

Songs About the Comforts of Home and Comic Songs

As has been shown, the hobbit songs given deal overwhelmingly often with the comforts of home: food, drink (including alcoholic drink), the bath, and bed, and with comic themes, such as "The Man in the Moon Stayed up Too Late". These were the kind of songs soldiers of both World Wars would have agreed with and sung. Also, there is a hint that Gondorian soldiers might have sung similar songs, with the "The Man in the Moon came down Too Soon" talking about when the Man in the Moon came down looking for "song, and laughter long,/and viands hot, and wine" (*FGH and ATB* 113).

Songs Sung on the March

As mentioned previously, John Brophy said that when soldiers sung on the march, when coming from the trenches, a "*sotto voce* singing or some soft whistling" would happen after a mile or two. On a route march for exercise or to shift quarters, soldiers would sing "with intervals of silence or of whistling or humming". This reminds us of the hobbits singing. Bilbo, when leaving the Shire for good, sang his travelling song "softly"; the three hobbits "hummed" his walking song; Sam "murmured" his fragment of the lay of Gil-galad, and later "murmured" old childish tunes out of the Shire in the Tower of Cirith Ungol.

It is explicitly stated that many of the songs and poems were to keep up morale. Sam's "The Stone Troll" is said to have improved morale after he sang it. During the siege of Minas Tirith, there is a reference to Gondorian soldiers singing "amid the gloom".

Sam's Songs in the Tower

During his service in World War I,[7] Tolkien developed a great respect for the ordinary soldier.[8] He said: "My 'Sam Gamgee' is indeed a reflexion of the English soldier, of the privates and batmen [officers' servants] I knew in the 1914 war, and recognised as so far superior to myself" (Carpenter 81). In a 9th June 1941 letter to his second son Michael, then in the army, Tolkien pointed out that they were alike "[…] only in sharing a deep sympathy and feeling for the 'tommy', especially the plain soldier from the agricultural counties)" (*L* 54; Letter 45). A comparison of Sam as Frodo's batman with such officers' batmen in real life has been made elsewhere (Hooker 125-36). Tolkien said in a 1963 letter that Sam was "a more representative hobbit than any others that we have to see much of" and had consequently a "stronger ingredient" of

> a vulgarity – by which I do not mean a mere 'down-to-earthiness' – a mental myopia which is proud of itself, a smugness (in varying degrees) and cocksureness, and a readiness to measure and sum up all things from a limited experience, largely enshrined in sententious traditional 'wisdom'. (*L* 329; Letter 246)

He pointed out that the readers "only meet exceptional hobbits in close companionship". He asked his correspondent to "Imagine Sam without his education by Bilbo and his fascination with things Elvish!" (ibid.)

---

7 For a comprehensive account of his service in that war, see Garth, passim, in particular Chapters 7-10.
8 Henry (Harry) Patch, the last UK soldier to have survived fighting in the trenches on the Western Front in World War I, therefore the last "Tommy", died on 25th July 2009 at the age of 111.

Sam's song "In western lands" in the Tower of Cirith Ungol, and Frodo's response were, Tolkien admitted, partly inspired by the legend in which King Richard I of England, imprisoned when returning from the Third Crusade, was located by Blondel de Nesle, who went from castle to castle, singing one of that monarch's favourite songs, until he received an answer (Hammond and Scull 603-04). But it could also have been based on a soldier or soldiers in a situation of despair, singing to keep his or their spirits up. Sam did not *deliberately* sing in order to get a response from Frodo; it and other songs were in defiance of the overall situation. Whether something or someone prompted him to sing in this way is another matter entirely.

Why so Few Gondorian Songs?

On the question of why there are so few Gondorian songs, or from the other point of view so many hobbit ones, I feel there are two answers. The first, and obvious, is that the story of *The Lord of the Rings* is told from the perspective of some hobbits. The second is possibly because Tolkien was aware that Gondor would be far too "modern" for readers, compared to the Shire, a place safely located in the peaceful past.

The Perspective of Some Hobbits

The Lord of the Rings was presented by Tolkien as a "translation" of an account by hobbits of the War of the Ring, part of the *Red Book of Westmarch* (*LotR* 1; Prologue; ibid. 1003-04; Book 6, Ch. IX). The readers see matters through hobbit eyes. Tolkien made this also clear when he admitted in a 25th September 1954 letter to Naomi Mitchison, that making the Shire resemble a village in 1897 led him into inconsistencies in his portrayal of the hobbits, in particular "Some of the modernities found among them (I think especially of *umbrellas*)". They are "probably, I think certainly, a mistake, of the same order as their silly names"; both are tolerable only as "a deliberate 'anglicization' *to point the contrast between them and other peoples in the most familiar terms*". (my italics) He did not think people "of that sort and stage of life and development" could be both "very peaceable and very brave and tough 'at a pinch'". Experience in two wars "has confirmed me in that view" (*L* 196-97; Letter 154).

In a footnote Tolkien said that the "chief way" hobbits "differ from experience" was that they were not cruel, had no blood-sports, and had "by implication a feeling" for wild-creatures that "are not alas! very commonly found among the nearest contemporary parallels". (ibid.)

Gondor more "Modern"

In contrast to the Shire, which was set in the past, Gondor resembled the United Kingdom in both World Wars. This country experienced large numbers of the population swearing oaths of allegiance on joining the armed forces, putting on a uniform, and then subjecting themselves to military discipline. Other experiences included food rationing, and the evacuation of civilians from urban and military areas. (In the late summer of 1940, two women evacuees were billeted for a short time on the Tolkien household, ibid. 46; Letter 39).

In both World Wars, the United Kingdom was opposed by enemies of equal strength, who had the potential to inflict defeat. In World War II, more precisely in 1940, it also had to face the serious possibility of direct invasion. The situation Gondor was in during the War of the Ring was something that Tolkien knew would be familiar to different generations of readers of *The Lord of the Rings* when it was published, which happened in 1954-1955. The journalist John Simpson, born in 1944, spoke of how the world was when he first began working for the BBC in 1966:

> Survivors of the Boer War [1898-1902] were numbered in their thousands, and of the First World War in their hundreds of thousands. As for the Second World War, it was only a couple of decades back: every adult remembered it. (Simpson 29)

Conclusion

I believe that songs sung by UK servicemen in the two World Wars, particularly the first, may have influenced the portrayal of the hobbits of the Shire in terms of their songs and poems, which deal with material servicemen would have recognised. There were songs about everyday life dealing with food and (sometimes alcoholic) drink or body care and comfort as well as comic songs.

The humming and murmuring or chanting of songs and poems resembles the way in which many "Tommies" sang on the march. Such songs were intended to keep up their spirits, as is seen in hobbit and Gondorian situations, Sam singing in the Tower of Cirith Ungol being the best example.

While hobbits have no sense of patriotism, Gondorians seem to have one, at least to the extent of a song resembling a national anthem. Both, however, do not show any xenophobia (not even towards Sauron) and hardly curse. The first aspect was true of UK servicemen in general, if certainly not the second. In *The Lord of the Rings*, there are no songs dealing with satires on civilian and military superiors and military discipline, perhaps because the hobbits had no experience of such civilian and military structures until much later in the story; and the Gondorians seem to have had competent leaders.

The lack of Gondorian songs, save the "national anthem" may be due to Tolkien not wanting to make Gondor seem too "modern", or too similar to the United Kingdom at war in 1914-1918 and 1939-1945. It may also reflect his rejection of overblown patriotic rhetoric, which so many servicemen came to dislike, and which had nothing to do with genuine patriotism.

Just as Sam Gamgee was a specific tribute to the English soldier, the hobbit and Gondorian songs and poems may be a partial, general tribute by Tolkien to the "Tommies" of both World Wars, the first in which he fought and in which he began to form his concept of Middle-earth, the second in which he was writing *The Lord of the Rings*.

About the Author

Murray Smith was born and raised in Dublin, Ireland. A fan of J.R.R. Tolkien and his works since the age of twelve, when he began reading a copy of *The Hobbit*, found when moving house with his family, he joined the Tolkien Society in 2002. He was called to the Irish Bar in 1999, has written a number of articles on historical and legal topics, and has given lectures on Tolkien at conferences in the UK since 2004.

Tolkien References

TOLKIEN, J.R.R., *Farmer Giles of Ham and the Adventures of Tom Bombadil*, London: Unwin Paperbacks, 1982.

The Hobbit, London: Unwin Books, 1970.

The Letters of J.R.R.Tolkien, (ed. by Humphrey Carpenter with the assistance of Christopher Tolkien), London: HarperCollins, 1995.

The Lord of the Rings, London: HarperCollins, 1995.

References

ARTHUR, Max, *When This Bloody War is Over: Soldiers' Songs of the First World War*, London: Judy Piatkus Ltd., 2001.

BROPHY, John, and Eric Partridge, *The Daily Telegraph Dictionary of Tommies' Songs and Slang, 1914-18*, London: Frontline Books, 2008.

CARPENTER, Humphrey, *J.R.R. Tolkien: A Biography*, London: George Allen & Unwin Ltd., 1977.

DAVIES, Norman, *God's Playground: A History of Poland: II. 1795 to the Present*, Oxford: Oxford University Press, 2005.

GARTH, John, *Tolkien and the Great War: The Threshold of Middle-earth*, London: HarperCollins, 2003.

HAMMOND, Wayne G., and Christina Scull, *The Lord of the Rings: A Reader's Companion*, London: HarperCollins Publishers, 2005.

HELMS, Randel, *Myth, Magic and Meaning in Tolkien's World*, Frogmore, St. Alban's: Granada Publishing Ltd., 1976.

HOOKER, Mark T., "Frodo's Batman", *Tolkien Studies: An Annual Scholarly Review*, 1 (2004), 125-36.

LIEBOVITZ, Leil and Matthew Miller, *Lili Marlene: The Soldiers' Song of World War II*, New York, W.W. Norton & Company, Inc., 2009.

PALMER, Roy, *'What a Lovely War!' British Soldiers' Songs from the Boer War to the Present Day*, London: Michael Joseph, 1990.

ROBB, George, *British Culture and the First World War*, Houndmills, Basingstoke: Palgrave, 2002.

SIMPSON, John, *Strange Places, Questionable People*, London: Pan Books, 1999.

Part D

Interpretations of Tolkien's Music in Our World

Michael Cunningham

An Impenetrable Darkness: An Examination of the Influence of J.R.R. Tolkien on Black Metal Music

Black Metal is an extreme sub-genre of Heavy Metal, one that is defined by aggressive musicality, misanthropic aesthetics and, notably by being Norway's largest musical export. The dark spectrum of Black Metal, as an established musical form, began to take shape towards the close of the 1980s. It subsequently burst upon the greater public consciousness when in 1993 a member of the so called Black Metal inner circle was linked to a number of church arsons and murder, all of which culminated in Norway's largest criminal trial; one which concluded with the longest sentence ever handed down in the country's history. The associated scandal and media attention helped to fuel both the fire and the myth from which Black Metal would rise and assert itself. The individual at the centre of the trial was Varg Vikernes who created his music under the band name of *Burzum*. The word "Burzum", of course, being lifted from J.R.R. Tolkien's novel, *The Lord of the Rings* and in the book's "Black Speech" of Sauron, may be understood to mean "darkness". A considerable number of other bands in the Black Metal genre have also named their acts using aspects from the works of Tolkien: "Gorgoroth", "Balrog", "Nazgul" and "Isengard" are but some examples.

The artists themselves recognise, to varying degrees, the influence of Tolkien's works upon them. Many, such as members of the group "Balrog", cite a perceived correspondence between the iniquitous characters present in Tolkien's fiction and the ideology of Black Metal both in terms of its dark aesthetics and, at times, explicit anti-Christian sentiments: "Black Metal is about the dark side, and most people involved in it enjoy Tolkien's work [...]. It's even more brilliant than the Judeo-Christian mythology" (personal communication). This opinion is echoed by other Black Metal artists, who advocate Tolkien as being an early influence; even going further to say that they sensed their attitudes to society more in bearing with Sauron, the enemy in *The Lord of the Rings*, and his denizens rather than with the heroes and those who opposed evil within the context of Tolkien's narrative. In general, many of those within the Black Metal community, both artists and fans, voice an alienation from contemporary society and contempt for Christianity. They are the anti-heroes of this counter-culture. challenging societal conventions and presenting a seemingly immoral façade that is designed to shock.

Black Metal also contains many elements present in the concepts of elitism, Nietzschism, Satanism and nihilism which are expounded through attendant lyrics and artist interviews. Tolkien was both scholar and enthusiast in respect of the fields of Old Norse, Finnish and Anglo-Saxon cosmologies and related lore; as such it was inevitable that nuances of these would bleed into his tales. Indeed, many Black Metal artists discern in Tolkien's writings a resonance with their own past cultures together with an alternative world in which to immerse themselves. When some members of this same audience came to author their own musical projects they would look to Tolkien's demons and devils as a means to discriminate and formulate their resultant bands. By doing this they would also establish a subtle connection with Tolkien's fans within the extreme metal community. In *The Lord of the Rings* the heroes and those who fight against the warmongering of Sauron and his allies often call upon the lore and wisdom of their forefathers through song and verse. In comparison, Sauron's minions manage only terrible cries or the harsh, guttural argument of the Orcs. What this paper seeks to establish, with the input of some of the groups and artists themselves, to whom I extend my gratitude, is how Tolkien's literature came to influence, in varying degrees, a number of Black Metal artists. Could it be said that Black Metal is the true Mouth of Sauron?

Tolkien's literary sub-creation of Middle-earth was, in essence, constructed from music, and music would continue to play an important part, along with moments of prose and verse throughout Tolkien's *legendarium*, at times serving to enrich and relate the histories and myths of Middle-earth while adding back-story to the relevant narrative structure. Tolkien's posthumously published work *The Silmarillion* opens with the creation of the world, Arda, by Ilúvatar, the supreme creator god. The events of this creation are recounted in the chapter "Ainulindalë" (The Music of the Ainur), in which Ilúvatar made the Ainur, the lesser gods, and taught them both song and musical themes while each of the Ainur functioned only as a part, a single instrument in the celestial orchestra.

Subsequently, Ilúvatar brought all of the Ainur together and disclosed to them a superlative composition in which each of their respective parts formed the whole – a form that was unbeknown to the Ainur at that time, according to their natures. This great theme would be the manner by which the world itself was formed.

It was as this music flowed under the direction of Ilúvatar that one of the greatest of the Ainur, Melkor who was also known as Morgoth, sought to introduce his own will and thus composition into Ilúvatar's theme. Melkor's interference with the theme was such that he caused discord to spread throughout the music which, in turn, led to turmoil and eventual confrontation. A counter-theme, strident and intrusive, now raged with Ilúvatar's until the music suddenly ceased altogether. Ilúvatar did not rend the resultant theme or begin afresh; rather the theme was now considered finished, replete with Melkor's discordant notes which were, in essence, ultimately drawn from the will of Ilúvatar. The collective theme served to shape the world through the crystallization of the music, as the nuances peculiar to each of the Ainur, including Melkor, were added to the newborn Arda where they would become natural features and events. In terms of the music Bradford Lee Eden recognises that

> [...] as the reader is drawn into *The Silmarillion* that music is the ultimate power in the cosmological history of Middle-earth. [...] Tolkien slowly yet intentionally weaves cosmological and human / vocal music throughout his mythology, in individual stories and dramas[...] (Eden 188)

In the story, as envisioned by Tolkien, Melkor clearly assumes the role of adversary, a veritable agent of chaos, by seeking for the flame of creation and attempting to seize command of Ilúvatar's theme, and later Arda, rather than be subject to it. Through Melkor's active opposition the harsh face of nature may be seen to have been introduced in a seditious manner to the newly formed world of Arda. The natural elements of fire, ice and storm were now resident in the world and in constant friction; through their collisions destructive forces were unleashed yet these very forces would also have been creative through their fury; a chaotic landscape of destruction and regeneration. Melkor in his unbounded envy was desirous for ultimate domination over the works of Ilúvatar; thus he became the first Dark Lord, a Black Enemy of light, casting his long, brooding shadow over the face of creation.

In keeping with the aspect of a terrible nature unveiled, the very description Tolkien used to illustrate Melkor's descent upon Arda is enshrouded with an awesome visage, like that of an immense erupting volcano pouring fire upon the earth: "Clad in ice and crowned with smoke and fire; and the light of the eyes of Melkor was like a deadly flame that withers with heat and pierces with a deadly cold" (*S* 23).

This may convey the developing landscape of a world shaken and ravaged into form by malevolent forces through which Melkor railed against the light and new beauty of Arda in an attempt to scar his will upon it and corrupt it by drawing down darkness against the light. In summation Tolkien writes:

> [Morgoth] began with the desire of Light, but when he could not possess it for himself alone, he descended through fire and wrath into a great burning, down into darkness. And darkness he used most in his evil works upon Arda, and filled it with fear for all living things. (*S* 35)

From here on Tolkien continued to flesh out his sub-creation but, albeit for a few instances primarily contained within *The Silmarillion*, any voice of the Dark Powers and their servants became gradually reduced to guttural sounds or simply terrible cries and screams. On the other hand, the entrancing voices of elves and, to a lesser degree, men who enraptured their lore and wisdom through the form of hymn, verse and songs coloured with captivating melodies and eloquent prose took primacy throughout Tolkien's *legendarium*.

In later years Melkor was "thrust through the Door of Night beyond the Walls of the World, into the Timeless Void" (*S* 307). Nevertheless, he was succeeded in the form of his lieutenant Sauron, who had a part in his master's works only being "less evil than his master in that for long he served another and not himself. But in after years he rose like a shadow of Morgoth and a ghost of his malice, and walked behind him on the same ruinous path down the void." (*S* 35).[1] Remaining with *The Silmarillion* one reads in the chapter "The Tale of Beren and Lúthien" of a time when Felagund, a name of King Finrod

---

1 Tolkien wrote of "[…] the absolute Satanic rebellion and evil of Morgoth and his satellite Sauron[…]" in a letter dated November 1954 (*L* 202).

who was a Noldorian elf, contested with Sauron through what Tolkien termed "Songs of Power"[2]:

> [Sauron] chanted a song of wizardry,
> Of piercing, opening, of treachery,
> Revealing, uncovering, betraying.

Felagund retorts, seemingly with equal measure, and thus Tolkien alludes to the level of success of chant and counter-chant by employing contrasting natural devices as when Felagund seems to have the upper hand then:

> Softly in the gloom they heard the birds
> Singing afar in Nargothrond
> The sighing of the Sea beyond […]

Sauron's subsequent victory over Felagund is conversely revealed:

> The wolf howls. The ravens flee.
> The ice mutters in the mouths of the sea.
> The captives sad in Angband mourn.
> Thunder rumbles, the fires burn […] (S 205-06)

The text is enlightening in that it shows how Tolkien aligned Felagund, an elf who naturally opposed the Dark Lord, with the natural tranquillity evoked by birdsong accompanied by the gentle sound of the sea. Sauron, however, through his "Song of Power", may be seen to be equated with such things as treachery, enslavement, and destruction. The description of Sauron's victory may have much in common with the prose contained in Old Norse myths, which in themselves at times echoed the dark and bleak perception of existence and fate. Another song which may be attributed to the enemy is recounted by Tolkien in *The Hobbit* in the form of a Goblin song. Given that *The Hobbit* was written as a children's book, the mood is lighter than that found in *The Silmarillion*:

> Clap! Snap! The black crack!
> Grip, grab! Pinch, nab!

---

2 Tolkien's "Songs of Power" may have been influenced by an episode in the Finnish epic *The Kalevala* wherein the chapter entitled "The Singing Match" young Joukahainen is warned that if he enters Väinö-land that "There you will be sung / you'll be sung and chanted, face / into snow, head into drifts / fists into hard air / until your hands cannot turn / until your feet cannot move." Needless to say Joukahainen ignores this advice and comes up against old Väinämöinen of whom he falls foul to in the Singing Match. In the context of The Kalevala "sang" may be construed as "bewitched" often connoting magic (Lönnrot, *The Kalevala*, p. 23, n. 3:45 p. 668).

> And down down to Goblin-town
> You go, my lad!
>
> Clash, crash! Crush, smash!
> Hammer and tongs! Knocker and gongs!
> Pound, pound, far underground!
> Ho, ho! My lad!
>
> Swish, smack! Whip crack!
> Batter and beat! Yammer and bleat!
> Work, work! Nor dare to smirk,
> While Goblins quaff, and Goblins laugh,
> Round and round far underground
> Below, my lad! (*H* 70-71)

While the song voices more of a mischievous tone it nevertheless contains obvious overtones which clearly outline the subterranean location of "Goblin-town" and the rowdy, industrial environment experienced by its populace, whether resident by choice or by whip. Clearly, this den of Goblins is not a place of laughter and light-heartedness; instead it distantly echoes the military-industrial habitats that would have been home to the Orcs. These in turn are most vividly outlined in *The Lord of the Rings*, in the descriptions of Mordor and Saruman's pits in Isengard. By definition, the music of the Enemy in this instance appears dictated by its coarseness and the concentration of industry. Being a form of oral history and expression, song remains altogether absent from their lips of the corrupted races who gave succour and service to Middle-earth's Dark Powers within *The Lord of the Rings*.

Accepting the importance and recurring use of music Tolkien placed throughout his *legendarium* it may be said that he, naturally, developed a tone for the music that he evolved for his stories. Subsequently, Donald Swann, who composed music for a number of Tolkien's songs, reflected that when Tolkien first heard his composition for *"Namárië"* that, "He had heard it differently in his mind, he said, and hummed a Gregorian chant" (Tolkien and Swann, *The Road Goes Ever On* v-vi). Swann, as will become evident, was not alone in his wish to further embellish aspects of Tolkien's literary works through the medium of music. Certainly throughout the 1960s the popularity of Tolkien's writings had been steadily growing and eventually found a ready audience at a time of great cultural shifts in viewpoint and world events. Of course, this period saw "The

Summer of Love" and the flowering of attitudes more towards nature and the revision and renewal of old folk beliefs and ways. In such a climate Tolkien's writings found new relevance with a readership willing to explore the natural facets of Middle-earth and the seemingly anachronistic language used to evoke a sense of time and place.

As the 1960s drew to a close, musical acts such as *Gandalf*, a psychedelic rock outfit began to emerge, having become familiar with Tolkien's creations in so far as to use characters from his stories to distinguish themselves and their music, no doubt also seeking to exhibit a form of allegiance to Tolkien's narrative. From amongst such bands a group called *Led Zeppelin* would become one of the foremost Rock bands to draw from Tolkien by including in their song lyrics allusions to characters and places from Middle-earth. The obvious example is "Misty Mountain Hop", but "Ramble On" mentions both Gollum and Mordor while

> 'The Battle of Evermore' is a more expansive arrangement that was originally intended as a sort of Olde English instrumental, but Robert [Plant] had been reading about the Scottish border wars, and 'The Battle of Evermore' was written out of a modern descendant of the Anglo-Saxon battle sagas. (Davis 133)

This "saga" would also include references to Ringwraiths, Dragons, Runes and a Dark Lord; subjects that would be very familiar to readers of Tolkien.

On 12th January 1969 *Led Zeppelin* released their eponymous debut album which has long since been cited to have been the blueprint and impetus for the whole Heavy Rock and Metal genres which soon followed in its wake. The following year, and encouraged by the success of *Led Zeppelin*, another formative British group, *Black Sabbath*, would through their music add dark aesthetics, in the guise of satanic imagery and innuendo, together with low chord structures. Throughout the 1970s Heavy Metal and Progressive rock groups flourished, and the latter, who favoured complex instrumentation, themes, and song structures, would soon develop new arrangements to encapsulate their literary interests. The Canadian progressive rock group *Rush*, formed in 1973, found scope in their early works for songs which contained fantasy-tinged lyrics. Their second album "Fly by Night" contained the track, "Rivendell" which was a gentle acoustic fare that evoked much about contemporary society's perception of

Tolkien's Elves within the context of *The Lord of the Rings*, while also expressing so much about the appeal of the book itself.[3] For their third album, "Caress of Steel", a whole vinyl LP side is dedicated to the tale of a necromancer and the heroic journey of three adventurers who would oppose him. Naturally, fluctuations of societal attitudes in the mid 1970s were inevitably reflected in much of the music of the period. In due course the popularity of Progressive Rock and Heavy Metal began to fade somewhat into the background as it gave way to upstart angry punk sounds and harsh diatribes spat out by a seemingly disenfranchised youth.

It was not until the curtain was about to close on the 1970s that an assortment of young British musicians, inspired by the Heavy Rock and Metal groups of the late 1960s and 1970s, were seen to take up the flagging Heavy Metal banner. The music they came to play would be known as the New Wave of British Heavy Metal. This musical collective gave rise to bands with a more musically aggressive playing style, and from amongst this milieu would emerge a vitriolic trio known as *Venom*. This band would soon become renowned for creating what can best be described as a "raw" approach to playing which saw the utilization of screeching guitar parts, booming bass chords and a harsh, often shouted or growled vocalization of their songs. The three members of *Venom* played strongly on theatre as an integral part, not only of their performance but also of their stage personages – satanic imagery and lyrics abounded. Adopting stage names, the members of *Venom* would be better known as Chronos, Abaddon and Mantas; although this was nothing new, the four members of American Rock band KISS performed as "The Demon", "Star Child", "Cat Man" and "Space Ace", each persona defined stylistically under costume and make-up. Considered by some to be amateur and mawkish, *Venom* nevertheless produced a clamour that sounded very distinct. Together with their designed-to-shock imagery and fiery lyrics they soon found appeal

---

3 Rush's key lyric writer was Neil Peart, who continues to enjoy Tolkien along with vocalist Geddy Lee, and his lyrics especially for Rivendell reflect it as a place of sanctuary and respite, safe from the dangers of the outside world as the lyrics express: "You feel there's something calling you / You're wanting to return / to where the Misty Mountains rise and the friendly fires burn / A place you can escape the world / Where the Dark Lord cannot go / Peace of mind and sanctuary by loud waters flow." (Authors: Geddy Lee and Neil Peart. Core Music Publishing 1975. Anthem Entertainment Group. S.R.O. Productions Ltd. Toronto. Canada).

amongst sections of the Heavy Metal and Rock community and those that were seeking new fashions of rebellion.

Of all the albums to be released by *Venom* it was their second that would later be described as defining a new genre in extreme metal music. "Black Metal", released in 1982, would become the cornerstone for those it later inspired. The album art comprised of a goat's head replete with inverted pentagram gazing from the black cover together with stylized band and album name while the album's two vinyl sides were named "Black" and "Metal". It contained tracks such as "To Hell and Back", "Leave me in Hell" and "Countess Bathory", and while the album bathed in satanic theatre the artist's tongues appeared firmly in their respective cheeks, "'To create the intro [of the album track "Buried Alive"] we piled lots of earth on the stairwell at the studio and shovelled it down onto a microphone', recalls Abaddon. 'Needless to say, the studio manager was unimpressed – to say the least!'"[4]

As *Venom* busied themselves spreading their hellish disquiet in Britain, across the Atlantic Ocean a young Swede, Thomas Forsberg, was forging his own harsh style of extreme Heavy Metal under the moniker of *Bathory*. Forsberg also adopted a stage name, that of Quorthon, to complete the image. Now all that was required was the music. Bathory employed instrumentation that was primitive and cold in execution and that was further blackened with vocals that were high-pitched – an almost barbed wire falsetto. As Bathory also developed upon the shock value of overt satanic imagery, the aesthetic and the musical aggression of early albums would eventually give way to Quorthon's growing interest and expression of the Old Norse cosmology and myths through the music. The Bathory albums, "Blood Fire Death" and "Hammerheart" not only found Quorthon singing of Old Norse and Viking themes but also signalled a change in the music; it became more epic in scale and atmospheric in arrangement. As such the pure aggressive musicality that featured heavily on preceding albums was lessened to a certain degree.

---

[4] Liner notes for *Venom*: Black Metal, CD CMRCD472. *Venom* also considered the category in which their sound may have comfortably resided: "Our music is Power Metal, Venom Metal, Black Metal, not Heavy Metal cos that's for the chicks."

In 1984 a group of teenagers calling themselves *Mayhem* emerged onto the Norwegian music scene. Within Mayhem's line-up was one Øystein Aarseth in whom the fledgling genre would recognise both an enfant terrible and, to some, a martyr. Within and without the confines of extreme music his condoning of the church arsons, aggressive, unpredictable nature and murder would catapult Black Metal into public and media glare. Aarseth also established Helvete[5], a somewhat modest record shop in Oslo's East End that specialized in selling and acquiring both well known and underground extreme metal releases. The dungeon-like interior of Helvete also doubled as a meeting place for like-minded individuals. Aarseth also sought to control a Black Metal inner circle of fans and friends who frequented the shop creating something akin to a hierarchal structure; the uppermost tier of which was made up of those being in Aarseth's confidence. "Deathlike Silence Productions" was the record label created by an industrious Aarseth. The label permitted young artists starting off in the local metal scene to experiment with, and record, their music without the impositions or demands of larger, established labels. Of these young artists one, a close friend of Aarseth, was Christian Vikernes, who soon changed his name to Varg Vikernes in order to eradicate the irony he, no doubt, anticipated when he played his music that contained a strong anti-Christian theme.[6] Vikerenes would also adopt the stage name, Count Grishnackh, taken in part after one of Tolkien's Orcs.[7] The name Vikerenes chose for his solo act was *Burzum*, the word denoting "darkness", also taken from Tolkien's *The Lord of the Rings*. "Burzum", in the context of Tolkien's writing, is a word from the "Black Speech" and is found on the inscription that was revealed in the narrative to be hidden upon the One Ring.[8] In 1992 Vikernes released his eponymous debut album, "Burzum", on the Deathlike Silence Label. Containing the brief instrumental track, "The Crying Orc" as well as "Dungeons of Darkness" amongst its numbers it bristled with subtle references to Tolkien. Vikerenes followed this with "Det Som Engang Var" (That Which Once Was) that contained the track "En

---

5 From the Norwegian for "Hell".
6 "Varg" is an Old Norse term for wolf and may also be associated with an "outlaw" in Viking times. Cf. Tolkien's Wargs.
7 Grishnákh was a captain of the Mordor Orcs who captured the Hobbits Merry and Pippin in *The Lord of the Rings*.
8 The section of the One Ring's inscription pertaining to this is: "Ash nazg durbatulûk, ash nazg thrakatulûk, agh *burzum*-ishi krimpatul" which roughly translates to: "One ring to rule them all, one ring to find them, one ring to bring them all, and in the *darkness* bind them." (*LotR* 64, 271)

Ring til å Herske" (One Ring to Rule). An EP was subsequently released in 1993 called "Aske" (Ashes) which opened with the track "Stemmen Fra Tårnet" (Voice from the Tower). The Tolkien associations with Vikernes' music, while rarely explicitly obvious, nevertheless may be seen as a device which permitted him the foundation from which he then constructed an ideology that evolved in concert with *Burzum*. "*Burzum* had an occult concept, but it is more correct to say it was a magical concept, or a concept built on fantasy magic. Everything with *Burzum* was out-of-this-world, even the name." [9]

However, while not overtly prolific in the extreme metal community, the 1990s would see a number of Tolkien's literary characters and locations from Middle-earth appear as either the title of a band or song, even a track themed wholly around an aspect from Tolkien's works. Yet many of those bands were not completely Tolkien themed in the sense of their overall conveyance of Middle-earth but rather employed infrequent and subtle references. Ultimately it would be Scandinavia from where many of these bands would originate and flourish. Today the region is recognized as the "epicentre" for Black Metal bands; many of whom incorporated elements of their native landscape together with a rich mythological past that contained gods, giants, magic along with actual artefacts such as runes, runic inscriptions and, of course, the Viking legacy. The fictional cosmos of Tolkien also drew from Old English and Old Norse epics and sagas such as the *Eddas* and the Old English *Beowulf* as well as the Finnish *Kalevala*; the influence of such historical works in Tolkien's fiction would have found a degree of resonance with many Black Metal artists who regaled north-western Europe's pre-Christian past. The increasing popularity of Tolkien's works in the late 1960s and through the 1970s saw not only an influence on music but also on the creation of a wholly new gaming system, primarily one that would become known as the Fantasy Role-Playing Game of which the first gaming system *Dungeons and Dragons* would become the flagship of the genre. As the Fantasy Role-Playing Game became more popular and accessible in the 1980s it would not remain restricted to America, where it originated, but would soon migrate to Scandinavia where a number of teenager players eventually found a new medium of expression for their fantasy worlds within the realms of extreme music. Leif Nagell, whose early

---

9 A Burzum Story: Part I – The Origin and Meaning (accessed 19/05/2007).

Black Metal project was called *Isengard*, happily relates that in his youth, "I read the Lord of the Rings as a kid and played a board game of Middle-earth a lot – I loved that game, and ultimately it had quite an impact on me." (personal communication)

Conceived in the early 1970s, the Role-Playing Game defined itself primarily by drawing on a great wealth of inspiration and structure from the genre of Fantasy literature. The most famous, and still extant, gaming system of this nature, *Dungeons and Dragons*, was developed by E. Gary Gygax and David Arneson and published by Tactical Studies Rules (TSR). Succinctly, the function of the Role-Playing Game was to allow players to create their own fantasy characters, or avatars, through which they could explore and interact with pre-constructed fantasy landscapes and events therein, all regulated by a "Gamesmaster": basically, a referee in charge of plot, rules and fair play. The Role-Playing Game itself remains extremely popular to this day and over its history a great many variants especially on the themes of Fantasy have been developed. The influence of Tolkien on these games and their developers is self-evident. *The Lord of the Rings* would have been well known to many of those who played and contributed to the development of such games. The 1980s would also see the release of an animated version of the first three books of *The Lord of the Rings* which, doubtless, also contributed in reaching an audience, of whom many may not have previously possessed an interest or indeed, knowledge of Tolkien's works. Silenius of the Epic Black Metal band *Summoning* explains,

> One day I watched the Lord of the Ring[s] cartoon of Ralph Bakhshi and Frank Frazetta. It was quite interesting for me but nothing special in that time. Afterwards a friend of mine told me how the story would end. Because of this point I never wanted to read the Lord of the Rings because I already knew the basics of this tale and I continued to read other fantasy literature but more and more realised that whenever I was reading a book it nearly always was advertised by being similar to Tolkien. [...] I borrowed a copy of The Lord of the Rings and since that time I was captured by [the] incredible imagination of [Tolkien] and since then I bought everything from and about Tolkien. (personal communication)

It was also during this period that a new gaming system was being developed; one that was concentrated purely within the sphere of Middle-earth. *The Middle-earth Role-Playing Game (MERP)*, created by Iron Crown Enterprises, operated with rules independent to those of the more popular Role-Playing Games and allowed players to immerse themselves wholly within Tolkien's Middle-earth; featuring characters and locations from the books as well as creating new ones. The game developers also expanded Tolkien's maps of Middle-earth thus greatly enlarging the scope of Middle-earth's geography and peoples to their own vision. The *Middle-earth Role-Playing* system, while taking a few liberties, nevertheless cited its pursuit in the creation of an almost forensically accurate representation of Tolkien's sub-creation, going so far as to provide a disclaimer that:

> Each [MERP gaming sourcebook] is based on extensive research and attempts to meet the high standards associated with the Tolkien legacy. Rational linguistic, cultural, and geological data are employed. […] [Iron Crown Enterprises] does not intend it to be the sole or proper view; instead, we hope to give the reader the thrust of the creative processes and the character of the given area. Remember that the ultimate sources of information are the works of Professor J.R.R. Tolkien.'[10]

Even though the largest distribution of the game was printed and distributed in English, the United States version proved very popular in Europe. This subsequently saw the release of a Swedish and Finnish version of the game entitled: "Sagan om Ringen: Rouspelot" and "Keski-Maa Roolipeli" respectively. What the *Middle Earth Role-Playing Game* ultimately achieved was the creation of a further dimension to Tolkien's *legendarium* in which an individual could leave the page, not only escaping to Middle-earth but existing within it.

During their formative years many teenagers strive to find a means of expression and definition for the personas they will develop and carry forward into adulthood. Naturally, those teenagers of Scandinavia were no different. In some cases the Role-Playing Game would serve to inform not only their music but the character and ideology through which they would fashion it. Leif Nagell, who was a young Norwegian during the late 1980s, developed a musical project which he called *Isengard* after the walled tower of Saruman in *The Lord of the Rings*. The aesthetics of it would be taken from the Middle-earth Gaming system; Nagell, who would use the stage name of Fenriz, used, as part of Isengard's logo, the image of a vampire which the game's developers employed in both their Role-Playing Game and *Fellowship of the Ring* boardgame, also developed by Iron Crown Enterprises. Nagell recorded three demos under the moniker

---

10 Rangers of the North module, Iron Crown Enterprises, p. 2, 1985.

of Isengard: "Spectres over Gorgoroth", "Horizons" and "Vanderen". These recordings contained some elements relative to Tolkien's works in both title and tracks; dark forests, trolls and, of course, the hellish plateau of "Gorgoroth" are all present. What is also evident is that though Nagell retained the title of Isengard for a final album in 1995, entitled "Høstmørke", this last album signalled a move away from associations with Tolkien's works in the context of Nagell's attitude towards his music and the ideologies he expressed through such; rather, "Høstmørke" drew from Old Norse mythology combined with a fervent anti-Christian undercurrent. The use of Tolkien's more maligned characters and locations had served to inform the evolution of Nagell's Isengard project yet once the image was created the subsequent music was never going to be bound purely to Middle-earth, instead it would follow a more anti-establishmentarian direction in accordance with the premise of extreme metal, or more correctly: Black Metal. Possibly, the use of Tolkien's works primarily contributed a familiar reference from which was established an aesthetic that would be easily recognisable to those sharing a passion for both Tolkien and extreme music. At the same time it would alienate, to a degree, those who had not read Tolkien or played the *Middle-earth Role-Playing game*. As Nagell observes when reflecting upon Isengard: "I'd say [Isengard] could have very well existed without Tolkien, I just needed that FRAME for it, and I already chose it in Summer 1989 when I did the first demo. Then I actually kept this "concept" into the first solo album which came in '93 or '94" (personal communication).

The influence of role-playing games gradually becomes clear amongst a number of artists within the extreme metal genre. Johnny Hedlund of *Unleashed* explains that their first song "The Dark One", which was written in 1989, was "[h]eavily inspired by the works of Mr. Tolkien, especially then the role playing games I played during the [1980s] […] Middle Earth". (personal communication) Varg Vikernes of *Burzum*, writing in 2004 during his incarceration, enthuses that

> In 1988 or 1989 […] I used to play RPGs (Role-Playing Games) […] like AD&D ("Advanced Dungeons and Dragons") and MERP ("Middle-Earth Role-Playing") with GM ("Game Master") rules, and was very much influenced by the fantastic world of Middle-Earth. One of our songs was because of that named "Uruk-Hai", and we soon changed the name of the whole band to Uruk-Hai. I don't remember the lyrics of that song, but I don't think it was very deep or particularly advanced (the chorus was: "Uruk-Hai! You will die", or something like that […]). Now, "Uruk-Hai" is as most *Burzum* fans should

know the name of the "High-Orcs" of Sauron, and it translates as "Orc-Race", from Black Speech, the language of Mordor.[11]

The aesthetic direction of Vikernes' project, *Burzum*, was at first somewhat dictated by references to Tolkien and Role-Playing Games,

> The artwork of the two first records are inspired by an AD&D [Advanced Dungeons and Dragons] (1st edition) module called "The Temple Of Elemental Evil", and the artwork on the third and fourth album is inspired by traditional Scandinavian fairy tales. (ibid.)

Whereas *The Lord of the Rings* may be seen to convey a story from the aspect of those who opposed and fought against Sauron and his minions, for Vikernes and others in the Black Metal community it would be the Dark Lord who provided the creative sustenance. Vikernes continues:

> In my teenage interpretation I pretty much saw the Hobbits as children or simply boring. The dwarves […] were pretty boring. […] The elves were fascinating, beautiful and especially their immortality and closeness to nature was cool, but they were kind of dull and they fought for the wrong side. Instead I felt a natural attraction to Sauron, who was the person who gave the world adventure, adversity and challenges in the first place. His One Eye was like Óðinn, the One Ring was like Óðinn's ring, Draupnir [the dripper], and Barad-Dur was like the tower or throne of Óðinn, called Hliðskjálf [tower of the gate]. His Uruk-Hai and Olog-Hai ("Troll-Race") were like Viking berserkers, the Warges (sic) were like Óðinnic werewolves, and so forth. I could easily identify with the fury of the "dark forces", and enjoyed their existence very much because they were making a boring and peaceful world dangerous and exciting.' (ibid.)

To some degree Vikernes' thoughts are far from unique, especially within Black Metal. Martin Gestranius of Black Metal band *Cruor Deum* included the tracks "By the hand of no Mortal Man" and "Stabbed by a Morgul Blade" on his first full length album, "Recubo Mos to Order – Lies Shall Command". Both tracks comfortably embellish the mood of the album with the latter track serving almost as a paean to the Witchking. Vikernes makes several assumptions which are of interest: firstly, that Sauron engenders chaos amongst the ordered world of Middle-earth, thus creating a friction that upsets what may be seen as mundane repetitiveness. Through his machinations, Sauron sets in motion an environment of conflict where heroes and anti-heroes are compelled to exist amidst shifting allegiances and the rise and fall of nations. To this extent the role

---

11 A Burzum Story: Part I – The Origin and Meaning (accessed 19/05/2007).

of the adversary embodied by Sauron, in the context of Tolkien's writings, may find resonance to the worldview of some young people who feel disenfranchised and disengaged from society and who thus seek to upset and oppose societal conventions by setting themselves apart. It is also interesting that Gestranius finds the "dark side" of Tolkien's stories attractive, possibly because it may be perceived as presenting an oppositional reflection of contemporary society; a non-conformist stance against conventional norms and attitudes. Secondly, Vikernes interprets the allies of Sauron as those figures from the pre-Christian Viking mythological tales such as werewolves and gods, going further to also associate the Vikings, vilified by Judeo-Christianity, to Tolkien's narrative; thus by extension he sees these heathen characters also maligned by society:

> I grew up reading the traditional Scandinavian fairy tales, where the [p]agan gods are presented as "evil" creatures as "trolls" and "goblins", and we all know the inquisition turned Freyr [...] into "Satan". Tolkien was no better. He had turned Óðinn into Sauron and my [p]agan forefathers into the fighting Uruk-Hai. To me the "dark forces" attacking Gondor were like the Vikings attacking Charlemagne's Christian France, the "dark forces" attacking Rohan were like the Vikings attacking the Christian England.[12]

At later stages Vikernes, to an extent, disassociates his use of Tolkien's work and attempts to instil a more considered rationale in his music that recognizes the essence of Old Norse saga and myth with which Tolkien was extremely familiar and which had inspired much of his fictional writing. Vikernes appeared worried that *Burzum* would be seen primarily as a musical creation purely for fans of Tolkien's works and so not taken seriously, although he submits "*Burzum* was an attempt to create (or 'recreate' if you like) an imaginary past, a world of fantasy." (ibid.) Therefore he began to draw more on the Old Norse aspects of his "forefathers" as the stronger element in his music where Tolkien is recognized as providing the spark of influence, to reference Fenriz, the "frame for it". Vikernes' view of the usurpation of the gods of the heathen Vikings by the Judeo-Christian church is, to some degree, shared by the *Balrog*:

---

12 A Burzum Story: Part I – The Origin and Meaning (accessed 19/05/2007) Cf. Tolkien's consideration upon the process of conversion and its effects upon indigenous lore: "One does not have to wait until all the native traditions of the older world have been replaced or forgotten; for the minds which still retain them are changed, and the memories viewed in a different perspective: at once they become more ancient and remote, and in a sense darker." (*MC* 21) The "remote" darkness into which much of the old traditions fell may have assisted the demonization of the heathen gods and mythological figures into the foe both in Christian doctrine and the Fairy Tale.

> I guess what Tolkien [would] describe as 'evil' in his piece of art is rather coherent with the images that have been used and abused by Christianity to give a face to the antithesis of what is good. Black Metal is about the dark side, and most people involved in it enjoy Tolkien's work, especially because his vision of Mordor and all the chaotic distorted entities that come with it is the most [beautiful] that was ever given. It's even more brilliant than the Judeo-Christian mythology.' (personal communication)

In a sense, for many of those involved in Black Metal, Tolkien's writings supplanted the organized religion they grew up knowing and so sought to reject. Yet the fact that Tolkien's narrative holds echoes from the Old Norse and pre-Christian myths continued to appeal. Martin Gestranius of *Cruor Deum* considers that,

> *The Lord of The Rings* is a very dark story, and when considering the "dark forces", I don't think evilness has ever been portrayed, by anyone else, as such a powerful force. Perhaps some [Black Metal] bands associate those creations of Tolkien with religion nowadays. Personally, I've created songs which have contained lyrics inspired by the story of the One Ring, although the main "plot" was about the Witchking. I found him to be a superior character to all those mentioned in the story. (personal communication)

This attitude is also shared by Black Metal band Gothmog:

> I think that's because Tolkien's main topic of each of his books is the eternal struggle between good and evil, which is probably one of the main [Black Metal] topics. [...t]he empathy with [Black Metal] is evident, the epic[ness] of his stories, the battles, the heroes [...] and Tolkien's own Satan, that is Morgoth and his captain Sauron. That's pure darkness and evil, pure black!!! [...] His books really suits with epic and dark music. (personal communication)

Vikernes later explained the reason he was so much enamoured by *The Lord of the Rings* was "because of the veil of hidden mythology" (Moyhnihan and Søderlind 150), the "hidden mythology" alluded to being specifically that of the heathen Old Norse. Indeed, Vikernes even ruminated over the word "burzum" in an attempt to subjugate it to fit his philosophy, "As most Tolkien fans should know 'burzum' is one of the words written in the Black Speech on the One Ring of Sauron. [...] The 'darkness' of the Christians was of course my 'light'." (ibid.) Conceptually to Vikernes this allowed him to retain the name *Burzum*, under which his music was produced and marketed, though he now aligned it more as an oppositional expression against Christianity. Through a somewhat less-informed and vitriolic publication Vikernes had earlier reasoned that the Judeo-Christian "darkness" was in fact the heathen "light" and that the name *Burzum*

> [...] was a way to 'camouflage' the heathendom by using a name [*Burzum*] that had to be interpreted in order to see the connection with heathendom. This was done in order to have the most cryptic and esoteric name possible. Only the most well informed would understand the connection.[13]

Again, Balrog would surmise that

> [...] the northern mythology has been particularly lost and forgotten during the [C]hristianization of [S]candinavia, and Tolkien gave it a new birth, making it equal to Latin or Greek mythology, with even more cultural details, when you read [The Lord of the Rings], every single stone has a story, every character has his own dialect, his own customs. (personal communication)

If allowed, then by default Tolkien's attempt to construct a mythology for England by re-imagining the old lore and tales of north western Europe's pre-Christian times had condensed and exposed the essence of that lore to a new readership who sought to rediscover its source. The captivating mystery reflected by characters such as Tolkien's Nazgul would also commend a sense of admiration in regards to their portrayal, indeed the whole concept of "evil" in Tolkien's *The Lord of the Rings* has been recognised not least by *Cruor Deum* who, when mulling over the darker facets of Middle-earth believe that they "[...] don't think evilness has ever been portrayed, by anyone else, as such a powerful force" (personal communication). It may be that Tolkien was able to retrieve fragments of primal human fears that had subsequently fed into the folklore and mythology of north western Europe. Such fragments found form, of sorts, in the guise of those characters Tolkien created to oppose the plight of good within the context of Middle-earth.

One of the foremost defining facets of Black Metal is Satanism, either expressed vehemently or furtively through lyrics or image, providing a vehicle for explicit opposition to Christianity. Many Black Metal groups also identify with the world that Tolkien created, insofar as they would deem his Sauron as Satan and the Forces of the Free Peoples as representative of Christianity. Thus the subsequent dissolution of the heathen religions that existed in Scandinavia and northern Europe were viewed as akin to the final overthrow of Sauron. Yet

---

13 Vargsmål

supporting the losing side is not a disadvantage either it seems as Vikernes cites "[...] the Vikings eventually lost their war as well, just like Sauron and the orcs did – and I didn't mind supporting the [losing side]." (ibid.) Inevitably, while Tolkien's Army of the West would eventually overthrow great evil it would be Sauron's denizens who would generate more of an interest amongst those readers within the Black Metal genre as *Cruor Deum* continue, "I find the dark side very interesting. It's powerful, and it's fulfilling. Nobody r e a l l y took Frodo's side in Lord of the Rings, everyone probably felt stronger for the evil forces" (personal communication). British journalist Gavin Baddeley interviewed Vikernes in 1993, and when asked about the subject of his "Satanic theology" (at that time Vikernes still saw himself as a Satanist) Vikernes responded tersely, "There's a lot of inspiration from Mordor in the Tolkien stuff. I don't believe in Tolkien's world, but it has a lot of connections with the real thing. There are major parallels between Hell and Mordor" (Baddeley 206). When Baddeley asked him if he considered himself a soldier of Sauron Vikernes replied, "I don't want to use words like Mordor because it could be dismissed as a joke. Mordor is just one word for Hell. Call it whatever you like. Like Satan, you can call Him Sauron if you want. I don't care. He's still my Lord." (ibid.)

It is a given that *Venom* are in many quarters credited for laying down the building blocks from which Black Metal eventually took form, but the attitudes and personalities of figures such as Aarseth and Vikernes injected more intense and maligned nuances. To the genre would now gradually be added an ideology that, in turn, informed the music and subsequent theatre through which it would be communicated. Some in the Norwegian extreme metal fraternity had come to view early acts such as *Venom* as being too showbiz and mainstream, rather than embracing a wholly anti-establishmentarian and dark, aggressive posture. Black Metal was quickly becoming an alternative lifestyle for the performers and fans involved and they began to seek ways to give character to their developing alter egos.

Kim Bendix Petersen, a Dutchman, would become famous during the 1980s as the falsetto vocalist known as King Diamond, fronting the extreme metal band *Mercyful Fate*. The stage persona of King Diamond is at once recognizable by the fact that his face is painted using black and white make-up to depict inverted crosses and even bat-like wings and shades. To some degree this borrows from stage images that had been previously employed by bands such as KISS, Alice Cooper, Celtic Frost and Slayer, all of whom used face-paint to varying degrees during some of their performances. Within the realm of Black Metal this style of face-paint was adopted but became better known within the genre as "corpse-paint". Dead, the morose singer of *Mayhem* who took his own life, was one of the first Black Metal artists to introduce the style of corpse-paint now commonly seen in the genre. Of course, Aarseth embraced this as a means of allowing his *dramatis personæ*, which, ironically, was not always restricted to the stage, to manifest itself. Known as "Euronymous", he had a number of promotional photos "[...] taken shortly after the opening of Helvete [...] show [Aarseth] cloaked in a black cape, candle or sword in hand, his face austerely decorated in corpse-paint, obscuring his small dark goatee under white make-up." (Moynihan and Søderlind 75) The corpse-paint not only projected a macabre mask onto the artist's faces but also dehumanized them; framed usually with long, lank black hair their faces seemed to express a demonic corruption of a more familiar, human off-stage appearance. They could almost have said to have become Orkish, much in the manner by which Felagund, of Tolkien's early legendarium, had devised in order to disguise his comrades as Orcs:

> The poisoned spears, the bows of horn,
> The crooked swords their foes had borne
> They took; and loathing each him clad
> In Angband's raiment foul and sad.
> They smeared their hands and faces fair
> With pigment dark; the matted hair
> All lank and black from goblin head [...] (*LB* 226)

"Raiment foul and sad" is an apt description of the costume theatre employed by a number of Black Metal bands to create an intense and ultimately evil atmosphere of darkness that serves to give flesh to the tone of the guitars, machine-gunning drumbeats and sinister vocal delivery of the songs. The latter harsh, growled vocals when in concert with the dehumanising concept of the corpse-paint are an integral part of the Black Metal template. When Tolkien conceived of Orc speech he wrote that when the Orcs were first bred they

> took what they could of other tongues and perverted it to their own liking; yet they made only brutal jargons, scarcely sufficient even for their own needs, unless it were for curses and abuse. [...] Orcs and Trolls spoke as they would,

without love of words or things. [...] Much of the same sort of talk can be heard among the orc-minded; dreary and repetitive with hatred and contempt, too long removed from good to retain even verbal vigour, save in the ears of those whom only the squalid sounds strong. (*LotR* 1165-68)

It would be unfair and disingenuous to cite the above as an accurate description of Black Metal vocals but, rather it is the very nature of the corrupted sounds voiced through harsh and guttural deliveries that, in part, serve to facilitate the counter-cultural and adversarial countenance behind the philosophy of Black Metal. All these facets: the corpse-paint, dark satanic theatre and anti-human vocals coalesce to create an aural atmosphere of furious ritual in which Black Metal thrives and is recognised.

For all the attendant controversy and notoriety surrounding, and sometimes encouraged by Black Metal, it is nothing if not diverse and forward looking. From its inception in the late 1980s through the rigours of colliding egos and criminality in the 1990s to the present the genre is now enjoying a renaissance of sorts through the growth of a variety of sub-genres: "Viking"; "Ambient"; "Folk"; "Epic" and "Symphonic" prefixes, to name a few, are now increasingly becoming more common as the genre expands to meet a wealth of experimentation and diversity to which it frequently becomes exposed as new artists and ideas are absorbed into the Black Metal fraternity. Black Metal has also overlapped into other styles of extreme music such as Death and Thrash Metal as artists migrate between bands taking individual playing styles with them; thus enjoying a generally positive reciprocation of musical skills. The attendant components of highly polished production values and artists ready to adopt or diversify fresh sounds and arrangements have guided the genre towards becoming the premier embodiment of extreme music.

Many of the bands whose primary conception was credited to a direct influence from Tolkien have since revised, to an extent, their attitudes as to how they wish their music to represent both themselves and their respective ideologies. Some artists have chosen to reflect instead upon their own cultural histories such as the Celtic Black Metal band *Cruachan* which began musically from very overt Tolkien influences, as Keith Fay of the band recalls,

> [...] at the beginning in 1993 we were actually called Minas Tirith, and sang exclusively about Tolkien based themes. As we progressed we decided

that our own culture and history was more important for the concept of the band and we moved toward writing lyrics and basing the image of the band around cultural and mythological themes. Having said that, we never moved completely away from Tolkien and I have wrote songs about Middle Earth and its history right up to our last album 'The Morrigan's Call', there are two songs featured on there titled 'Shelob' and 'Ungoliant'. (personal communication)

Given that a number of bands who were initially compelled to write music around themes Tolkien created have since gone on to mine their own cultural histories, nevertheless a number, as evinced by Cruachan, who themselves have not wholly abandoned Tolkien's shadow, have in fact returned to Tolkien's narrative in later recordings. This is much the same as *Unleashed* who in 2006 included the track, "We Must Join With Him" on their album, "Midvinterblot". The lyrics are unquestionably a call to arms, to join with Sauron:

> His gaze goes through
> Cloud and shadow
> Earth and through flesh
> The Lord of Mordor sees it all
> Gathering all evil without rest
> We must join with him
> We must join with Sauron
> Or we have chosen death.[14]

In a sense the song above could almost be said to have grasped the opining of those who did indeed choose to follow Sauron; for Orc, Easterling or Southrons the seat of command at the end of the War of the Ring would have been ruled from Mordor, had not the One Ring been destroyed. Of Course, Unleashed are primarily a Viking Metal band whose playing style is Death Metal but, nevertheless they too recognise the parallels between the worlds of Old Norse and Tolkien's Middle-earth:

> Tolkien was heavily influenced by Norse mythology. Unleashed is a band that promotes the Viking values and traditions so it is easy to find empathy and inspiration among the great creations of Tolkien. The atmosphere of his works also fit very well to the atmosphere in Death Metal music, as it's core [playing] is horror-like. As is much of Tolkien's darker characters and places. (personal communication)

---

14 Lyrics reproduced with permission of Johnny Hedlund of Unleashed.

It is clear that for a number of extreme metal bands Tolkien's narrative provided recognisable characters and landscapes that, by their nature, provided an instant aesthetic for how the bands wished to portray their own idioms. *Gorgoroth*, a Black Metal band which continues to be steeped in notoriety, took its name from Mordor's great plain, yet the band has always remained purely Satanic in both ideology and music. Tolkien's Gorgoroth provides only the initial atmosphere the band's creator wished to establish while betraying further evidence of Tolkien's influence within the extreme metal community. The ash-choked landscape of Mordor in itself was a hell, of sorts, in which dark shapes and shadows moved and shifted in disparate machinations, rather than being merely populated with tortured souls. For many youths who would progress into extreme metal, Tolkien's shadowland permitted a contemporary reference without any requirement to quarry the Judeo-Christian mythology for diabolical terms, as the artists were vehemently opposed to Christianity; rather, not only could individuals express their admiration for Tolkien but they could instil their bands with a premeditated ideological direction as well as providing a subtle nod to fellow fans of Tolkien. "Only people who had a special interest in Tolkien's world would know, and that was kind of cool – or so I thought. It enabled the listeners to feel special and to feel that *Burzum* was made especially for them (and it was)", considered Vikernes.[15]

As the genre of Black Metal evolves and expands there has been a significant move by a number of artists to incorporate a more cinematic ambience to their music. While remaining well within the stable of Black Metal, this aspect has been developed by book-ending music tracks with pre-recorded sounds of either constructed "battle-noise" employing sounds such as clashing swords, hoof beats or simply, natural sounds which may include running water or the wind. These sounds are sometimes referred to as "field-recordings" and help to establish atmosphere and even a sense of place which add another dimension to the music itself. *Summoning*, for example, is a band that has continually evolved a sound which marries elements of Black Metal and the Cinema soundtrack to produce an aural atmosphere of sweeping and epic qualities within the framing of Middle-earth. As Silenius of Summoning explains,

---

15 A Burzum Story Part I – The Origin and Meaning (accessed 19/05/2007).

Summoning's music is a mixture between melodically Black Metal music in the old way (similar to the music of Bathory in their Viking phase) and orchestral soundtrack music. [It] may be compared to some soundtracks like the first Conan movie or music from Vangelis of the "Conquest of Paradise" [album]. (personal communication)

Tolkien's narrative, it seems, provides a rich source of inspiration, not only for the inception of a band's musical framing but also for the atmosphere in which the music is wrapped. When referencing Tolkien in a musical context artists are cognizant of the "real-world" history it imbues and are mindful of how the compositions must sound. *Balrog* explains, "It may have influenced the music in some songs where I tried to make it sound epic, medieval, and I always think about Tolkien's universe when I'm looking for a way to describe that kind of atmosphere" (personal communication).

On reflection it can be seen that a number of factors led to the evocation of Tolkien's fiction within the genre and indeed were to some degree present at the inception of several formative Black Metal bands, establishing a trend. The essence of the pre-Christian myths, folklore and tales of north-western Europe, which were explored by Tolkien to a varying extent through his writing, offered young musicians an archetypal framework within which to create and mould a vehicle by which they could express themselves and any attendant beliefs in a musical context. The continued attraction of Tolkien's darker characters such as Morgoth, Sauron and their subjects, such as the Nazgul, in the extreme metal community, personified the mystery and menace sought by an artist and thus translated to the stage in the guise of corpse-paint, black Satanic theatre and the wolf-like growls of the vocals. Naturally, Black Metal with its ideology, aggressive attitudes and harsh music would find some of its patrons drawn towards Tolkien's works to distinguish their fledgling bands and inject some substance as they perceived Tolkien to be inspired by a history common to them too. *Gothmog* feel that,

It is absolutely evident that Tolkien bases some of the cultures reflected in his books [on Anglo-Saxon tales]. Even some of the languages he invented, the way of life of some races, the [epic scale]. That probably sets an empathy with [people from a Northern European descent], who are the sons of that culture and [who] might love and feel [an identification] with Tolkien's imagination. [Tolkien] is such an inspiration. His books [are really suited to] epic and dark music. (personal communication)

As literature such as Tolkien's found its way into popular culture it was inevitable that it should also be represented in contemporary music, which in itself is almost a barometer of societal moods and stresses. As I have shown, there is a chronology of influence which has led to Tolkien's narratives eventually being absorbed into Black Metal where his most terrible characters have become veritable icons, in turn, providing a ready expression for individuals seeking a means to infuse a drama of counter-cultural performances within their music. As such Tolkien has become an undeniable and compelling element of the Black Metal oeuvre.

About the Author

Michael Cunningham is an archaeologist living and working in Ireland. He is a member of the UK Tolkien Society and has contributed articles, reviews and interviews to a number of Tolkien-centred publications.

Tolkien References

TOLKIEN, J.R.R., *The Annotated Hobbit*, (annotated by Douglas A. Anderson), London: Unwin Hyman Ltd, 1989.

The Lays of Beleriand, Vol. 3 of The History of Middle-earth, (ed. by Christopher Tolkien), London: HarperCollins, 2002.

The Letters of J.R.R. Tolkien, (ed. by Humphrey Carpenter with the assistance of Christopher Tolkien), London: Unwin Hyman Ltd., 1990.

The Lord of the Rings, London: HarperCollins, 1991.

The Monsters and the Critics and Other Essays, (ed. by Christopher Tolkien), London: HarperCollins, 1997.

The Silmarillion, (ed. by Christopher Tolkien), London: Unwin, 1983.

References

BADDELEY, Gavin, *Lucifer Rising: Sin, Devil Worship and Rock 'n' Roll*, London: Plexus, 2006.

DAVIS, Stephen, *Hammer of the Gods*, London: Pan Books, 1995.

EDEN, Bradford Lee, "The 'Music of the Spheres': Relationships Between Tolkien's *Silmarillion* and Medieval Cosmological and Religious Theory", In: Jane Chance (ed.), *Tolkien the Medievalist*, London and New York: Routledge, 2003, 183-93.

LÖNNROT, Elias, *The Kalevala*, (transl. from the Finnish with introductory notes by Keith Bosley), Oxford: OUP, 1999.

MOYNIHAN, Michael and Didrik Søderlind, *Lords of Chaos: The Blood Rise of the Satanic Metal Underground*, California: Feral House, 1998.

VIKERNES, Varg, A Burzum Story, 1991-2009, http://www.burzum.org/eng/library/a_burzum_story01.shtml, Vargsmål, Cymophane Productions, 1997.

Paul Smith

Microphones in Middle-earth: Music in the BBC Radio Play

Introduction

I've been a fan of *The Lord of the Rings* since I was eight, a countertenor singer since I was 19, and an actor lucky enough to perform adaptations of the Radio Plays in front of an audience including Brian Sibley, the man who co-adapted this version of Tolkien's masterpiece for the radio with Michael Bakewell. I admit to a certain satisfaction from causing a few raised eyebrows in the audience when Gimli the Dwarf's gruff, Yorkshire tones suddenly leaped two octaves up to sing the Eagle's Celebration at the Field of Cormallen.

As someone who has experienced the music of the plays from inside as well as out, as singer, fan and actor, I attempt to analyse the music from both a musical and a literary point of view – how it came to be, why it has the structural elements it does, and who performed it.

Genesis of the Radio Play and its Music

The history of the music cannot, of course, be separated from the history of the radio play and its genesis in 1979-1980.

Tolkien himself considered the book "quite unsuitable for dramatisation" (*L* 228). In fact, according to Brian Sibley, "[Tolkien] subsequently referred to [previous] BBC's efforts, not as a dramatisation, but as a *sillification!*"[1]

However, Richard Imison, head of the BBC's Script Unit, was determined to bring *The Lord of the Rings* to the radio with full production values, and once the rights had been obtained and the scripts had been approved by Christopher Tolkien (curator of the Tolkien estate following Tolkien's own death in 1973), the dramatisation was clearly off the ground. A number of distinguished com-

---

1 http://www.fantasybookreview.co.uk/blog/the-making-of-the-rings/

posers, popular and classical, were considered as candidates to write the music, including Sir Malcolm Arnold, who declined when approached.

By the time Stephen Oliver (1950-1992) agreed to write the music, his music for the Royal Shakespeare Company's epic production of *Nicholas Nickleby* (available on DVD) was already well known and highly praised; however, this was not the driver for choosing him. First, Sir Malcolm Arnold's agent suggested Oliver as an alternative. Then, in a fortuitous coincidence, Brian Sibley had a recording of the music Oliver had written for an open-air production of *Alice through the Looking Glass*; the "pastoral" quality of it attracted Sibley's, and then director Jane Morgan's, attention.

"Essentially English" Music – What Does This Mean?

Tolkien himself said "[England] had no stories of its own, [...] not of the quality that I sought, and found [...] in legends of other lands" (*L* 144). The Middle-earth legendarium, and Tolkien's other stories, reflect his concepts of English society and pastoralism, which are often summed up in the one short phrase, "a mythology for England." The BBC production team had sensed this and director Jane Morgan noted that "everyone was agreed that [the music of the play] must sound essentially English" (radio play sleeve notes).

It is hence worth taking some time to explore the concept of "Englishness" in music, and then to see how Oliver applies "essentially English" ideas and motifs to his own creation.

When music lovers think of music that "sounds English", they often cite the early 20th-century Pastoral School of English composers such as Vaughan Williams (epitomised by the Fifth Symphony, *The Lark Ascending*, or the *Tallis Fantasia*), Finzi, Moeran and Delius, as well as the contemporary setters of pastoral verse (e.g. *A Shropshire Lad*) such as Quilter, Butterworth and Gurney. Much of this music can be characterised by generally quiet dynamics, consonant harmony, simple melodic contours, and often a "rocking" accompaniment in 6/8 or similar compound time signatures. It aims to evoke a particular atmosphere of place – "landscape in music".

As the musicologist Tim Foxon puts it,

> "These works reflect, in their totality, a retreat from the tedium, complexity, or iniquity of society. [...] The English pastoral style undoubtedly utilises many characteristics of the pastoral topic of European Classical and Romantic music [cf. Beethoven's *Pastoral Symphony*, Vivaldi's *Four Seasons*], but is particularly associated with the musical language of folksong." (Foxon)

Several important features characterise folksong and music derived from it – phrase lengths that match common English verse forms (the Common Metre and Long Metre of hymnbooks, with lines of four or five iambic feet); modal or pentatonic harmonies, particularly the minor-sounding Dorian, the "questioning" Phrygian, or the major-sounding Mixo-Lydian scales, used in church music since the 15th century; and an essentially monophonic texture which reflects perceived rural "simplicity" – the shepherd's pipe, if you will.

Consideration of the role these devices play in the "Englishness" of music leads us to highlight a particularly important aspect of Oliver's compositions; his settings take inspiration from the *whole* history of English music, from the modal harmonies and polyphonic invention of the Elizabethans and Jacobeans, through the structural devices and floridity of the English Baroque to the English Pastoral School and even the highly individual textures of Britten.

We will now use this concept of "Englishness" to move to an exploration of the types of music used to evoke particular aspects of the drama, characters and places of *Lord of the Rings*.

Drama, Characters and Places

The role music plays dramaturgically in radio and films is perforce different; the medium of radio invites the listener to use the mind's eye, while the television offers pictures for direct consumption. There are moments in the radio plays where the music is the central means by which the drama is propelled forward and is the primary driver for the picture painted in the listener's mind. "The Ride of the Rohirrim" and "Battle of the Pelennor Fields" are the obvious examples, but this can also be applied to the "March of the Ents" and, perhaps, "Bilbo's Last Song".

Unusually, the background music was recorded before the drama. This required the characters, especially the narrator (Gerard Murphy), to react to the music rather than the music to the characters (as is the case in the films). This gives the music the chance to lead the drama by providing the framework for the characters' interaction.

Music does not, generally speaking, play such a central role in the films, but there is one very clear nod to the radio play's treatment of action, particularly the Battle of the Pelennor Fields. This is when director Peter Jackson places the doomed charge of Faramir and the knights of Gondor into Sauron's orc army against the background of Pippin singing to Denethor in the Hall of Minas Tirith ("Home is behind, the world ahead" – Tolkien's poem in *Fellowship of the Ring*). The music overrides all; the slaughter takes place in apparent silence. Billy Boyd, the Scottish actor playing Pippin, is an accomplished musician and sings and ornaments his own tune in a manner clearly influenced by Celtic folk style. In Boyd's own words, he wrote "a song he might have heard his grandfather sing" (RotK EE DVD Commentary). Boyd's choice of the Dorian mode for this piece is surely intentional, adding to its folksong-like quality.

Nevertheless, the Peter Jackson films have very few moments where the drama is primarily moved forward by verse or song; even the "Lay of Leithian" is mentioned only in an aside, and perhaps the only true such moments are the charge mentioned above, the burial of Théodred, and the crowning of Aragorn as King Elessar. These are all relatively short moments when compared to Jackson's massive set-piece battles of Helm's Deep and the Pelennor Fields, or the Ents destroying Isengard.

As for place and character, the concept of "landscape in music" mentioned earlier plays a crucial role in the listener's shaping of Middle-earth. Oliver's stylistic choices are critical to the pictures painted in our imaginations. As we shall see when we look at the organisation of the pieces, the style of music chosen purposely evokes a specific type of landscape, especially to a listener familiar with the genres and styles that are being used. The use of styles also allows us to group each piece of music into one of several stylistic categories corresponding to key characters and places within Middle-earth.

Middle-earth

The theme to the series, called simply "The Lord of the Rings", is the piece most casual listeners will remember. After a single introductory note of foreboding, which is the last we hear in this piece of the horn, a slitheringly chromatic string figure resolves into a theme based on two three-note phrases, answered by a motif of a falling fifth, backed by a chugging bass evoking treading feet. This undergoes various episodes of development, all of which tend to ascend in tessitura from the initial statement, and occasionally range through some remote keys; music which symbolises questing and striving to a goal, which is reached harmonically with a resolution into a triumphant final major chord.

The setting of "Seek for the Sword that was Broken", the rhyme Boromir (and Faramir) hears in his dream that sends him to Rivendell, is a simple hymn for solo treble against a cello drone, with an appropriate clash on the word "doom" in "that Doom is near at hand". This is fully in keeping with the "voice, remote but clear" (*FotR* 320) described in the text and the simplicity of the rhyme that voice recites.

At the Field of Cormallen, the Eagle Gwaihir comes out of the West crying for the folk of Gondor to celebrate the victory over Sauron. Stephen Oliver transforms this into "Gwaihir's Song", a dramatic (and taxing!) counter-tenor aria, relatively brief but full of changes of character from the florid declarations of "Sing all ye people" to the calmness of "And the tree that was withered shall be renewed", backed by strumming harp chords, piano octaves, rattling percussion, and rolling timpani. Oliver uses the upper register of the male alto voice, particularly David James' piercing top notes, to evoke the otherness of the Eagle. Dramaturgically, the short episodes of the aria move the action forward by framing the discovery of the sapling on Mindolluin and the acclamation of Aragorn as Elessar. There is a certain inspiration from Baroque *recitativo accompagnato*, but of all the music in the play this is probably the piece that gives the greatest hints of Oliver's own individual style.

Elves

Oliver's three pieces, "O Elbereth Gilthoniel", "O Lorien", and "In Caras Galadhon", intended to evoke an Elven atmosphere, are noticeably "early" in character, ranging from late Renaissance to High Baroque. They are also "background" music; during these pieces, the actors or the narrator are usually moving the action forward.

Of these, "O Elbereth Gilthoniel", the hymn to the Vala Elbereth sung while the Fellowship meets Galadriel and Celeborn in Lorien, is the most virtuosic and is clearly inspired by the Italian duets of Handel, Vivaldi or Pergolesi. It is a mini-cantata for soprano and alto, full of traditional Baroque musical rhetoric such as resolving suspensions, semiquaver runs, inverted phrases, and musical dialogue between the soloists – but with a decidedly non-Baroque percussion accompaniment reminiscent of Britten's "fairy" music in *A Midsummer Night's Dream* (e.g. "I know a bank").

"O Lorien", Galadriel's farewell to the Fellowship as they leave Lothlorien, is set as a ground-bass, a popular device of early Baroque composers. Both this ostinato bass and, in places, the melody, have marked similarities to Purcell's "Evening Hymn" ("Now that the sun hath veiled his light"). The constant, repetitive movement of the ground bass suggests an unchanging eternity well suited to Lorien's status as the home of immortal Elves. However, Purcell uses ground-bass arias to bring dramatic closure (another example being "Dido's Lament" – "When I am laid in earth") in *Dido and Aeneas.* And so here, as the Fellowship drifts down the Anduin away from Lorien, Oliver uses the ground bass to frame Galadriel's farewell both to them and to the certainty of her exiled life.

Given that these words are spoken by Galadriel herself, whom Tolkien himself described as having a deep speaking voice, it is interesting that this solo is assigned to a counter-tenor rather than a contralto; perhaps, since the music plays in the background of the narration, an evocation of other-worldliness associated with the male alto voice was considered to be more important.

"In Caras Galadhon", played while the Fellowship reflects on the beauty of Lorien and Galadriel, is a brief contrapuntal fantasia featuring harp and, rather incongruously but effectively, xylophone, sharing the same musical material. There are echoes here not only of the early 17th century – Orlando Gibbons' instrumental works and Byrd's keyboard music – but, again, of Britten. So, once again, we have the "early" character of Elven music set against more modern instruments and inspiration.

The setting of "The Healing of the Shire" is also Elven; by his use of the little box of Lorien earth, Sam partakes of Galadriel's elf-magic to restore the Shire in 1420. Oliver reflects this musically by using the same ground-bass and much of the same music as was used in "O Lorien", over which he builds shimmering arpeggios to suggest the scattering of the earth and awakening nature.

Hobbits and the Shire

Oliver's music to be sung by Hobbits, or set to Hobbit poetry, contains the simplest, yet most memorable, folksong-like melodies.

"The Road goes Ever On" is, of course, a recurrent theme for questing hobbits – first heard in *The Hobbit*, then repeated when Bilbo visits Rivendell in *The Fellowship of the Ring*, then again by Frodo on leaving the Shire, and finally by an older, weary Bilbo when the hobbits meet him again after the conclusion of the Quest. It is Frodo's version that Ian Holm sings in the radio play; the fairly four-square melody is backed by lush, modal string orchestrations clearly English Pastoral in inspiration. The melody is then transformed when the violin takes a winding journey through the landscape of the Shire and onwards – in the same key as, and with clear melodic and developmental similarities to, Vaughan Williams' *The Lark Ascending*.

In its haunting melodic beauty and all-too-short duration, "Gil-galad was an Elvenking", sung by Bill Nighy as Sam Gamgee during the journey to Weathertop, is for me the gem of the entire collection. The melody is once again Dorian, with a brief harmonic twist when the second of the scale flattens, suggesting the Phrygian mode, at "Of him the harpers sadly sing" and has a timeless simplicity.

Manuscript from "Gil-galad was an Elvenking" – from Brian Sibley's blog[2]

"Bilbo's Last Song" features gently stroked chords over a rocking melody which only leaves its relatively narrow vocal compass when it reaches the top G at the apex of its final phrase, supported by the strings. Oliver chooses to set this for treble rather than an adult male voice to emphasise the link with the divine and the universality of the experience of passing, as the Last Ship crosses the Sea and Bilbo reaches Elvenhome.

And yet, simple Hobbit faith is evoked most powerfully by Sam, unaccompanied, singing the simple, modal (again) melody of "In Western Lands beneath the Sun". This is given to Bill Nighy, the actor playing Sam. Both musically and dramaturgically, this has strong echoes of soldiers singing folksongs in the trenches – "I will not say the Day is done, nor bid the stars farewell." – and of the Pastoral School's settings of folksong to recall lost innocence. George Butterworth's settings of A.E. Housman's *A Shropshire Lad,* with memories of a pastoral ideal blighted by war and death, and Britten's *War Requiem,* for the folksongs in the trenches, are particularly relevant musical references.

---

2 http://briansibleytheworks.blogspot.com/2008/01/this-page-is-still-under-construction_23.html

Ents

The settings for the Ents, like those for the Hobbits, show clear inspiration from the compositional techniques used by the English Pastoral School.

"The Tree-lords" is Oliver's conflation of all Treebeard's rhymes. "Learn now the lore of living creatures" has short phrases over strumming string chords, bardic and oral in nature rather like the music of the Rohirrim explored below. There is a beautifully set up opposition between the Ent's invitations, phrased in primitive modal folksong melody, for "When spring unfolds the beechen leaf", and the more complex, Finzi-like flowing reply from the Entwife, fitting her less wild, more "civilised" character.

The "March of the Ents" ("To Isengard we come, with doom we come") sets plodding string chords over a distinctly sea shanty-like melody with an irresistible forward momentum, only interrupted by a brief departure from the home key approximately halfway through the piece.

Rohan

The "Lament for the Fallen" features long French horn calls over softly moving strings to commemorate those who have fallen in the Quest of the Ring and develops into Théoden's funeral eulogy. So, the horn reminds us both of Boromir and of Théoden, though in the drama itself this music plays specifically at Boromir's death. For me, the bitter-sweet nature of this music is most reminiscent of Finzi's vocal music.

One would expect the French horn used in the "Lament for the Fallen" to be prominent in the orchestration of battle scenes, to mirror the "great horns of the North wildly blowing" (*RotK* 1085). In the sleeve notes to the series, Jane Morgan, the director, said "I was anxious to avoid effects that were too literal." So, for Oliver, this would be too literal a parallel. Instead, the music featuring the Rohirrim is driven by the words' retrospective nature; these are deeds of legend and they are commented on from a vantage point somewhere in the Fourth Age. Hence, Oliver creates an aural picture of a bard in a mead-hall of Rohan, using short-phrased closely related melodic units in both the bard's pieces.

"Forth rode the King" sets anapaestic string hoofbeats against a galloping, chant-like melody for the baritone which eventually (at 2:03) undergoes a superb, almost Purcellian moment of harmonic inversion to return to the main "Lord of the Rings" theme.

For the "Battle of the Pelennor Fields", strumming strings and brief harp interventions back the Rohirric bard and the simple harmonic structure builds to the final, terrible line, sung by Oz Clarke with subdued dignity – "Red fell the dew in Rammas Echor".

Oliver gets closest to a sustained exploration of motion in his miniature tone-poem "Shadowfax", evoking the Prince of the Mearas through rapid hoofbeats and string trills backing sharply arched figures which gradually extend their short phrases to the apex of each musical statement, then to fall rapidly down the scale in a release of energy. With this shimmering musicality for the finest horse in Middle-earth, is it cheeky to wonder what Oliver would have composed for Bill the Pony?

What, no Dwarves?

There are no direct musical evocations of Dwarves, despite Tolkien's own references to their musicality in *The Hobbit* and *The Lord of the Rings*. Exactly why a musical characterisation of Dwarves is missing is a matter for some debate, but it may have to do with there being only one prominent Dwarven character in the radio play – the gruff Gimli of Douglas Livingstone – and perhaps the singers themselves had voices that were, ironically, too mellifluous. So, where Howard Shore, the film composer, gives powerful musical evocation of Dwarvenness when the Fellowship moves through the Halls of Moria, and expresses the Fellowship's agitation during the battle of the Bridge of Khazad-dûm, the radio play's treatment of these high points in the drama relies completely on sound effects.

Performers – Singers and Musicians

Just as the actors represented the cream of the Royal Shakespeare Company – Sir Michael Hordern, John Le Mesurier, Ian Holm, Bill Nighy, and so on – the BBC did not skimp on the calibre of musicians put at Stephen Oliver's disposal. This becomes evident from looking at their careers subsequent to the recording, and is proof, if any were needed, of just how seriously the BBC took their commitment to excellence in all aspects of the production.

For pieces where the actors themselves are not called on to sing (e.g. "In Western lands beneath the Sun"), the BBC employed three soloists, the young treble Matthew Vine, the counter-tenor David James, and the baritone Oz Clarke, as well as the London choir The Ambrosian Singers. While Stephen Oliver conducted the instrumental music, the experienced choral conductor Barry Rose was called on to direct the singers.

Matthew Vine went to Christ Church College, Oxford, as a Choral Scholar and is now a leading professional tenor. He is known throughout the London early music scene for his unerring sight-reading ability and is a regular member of leading ensembles like The Sixteen and the Tallis Scholars. Vine's perspective on the whole process of recordings is refreshingly direct and reflects an experienced boy chorister's ability just to turn up and perform:

> I turned up as a 12 year old kid and found myself in a recording studio with David James and Oz Clarke and we got the dots [notes] and sang them. We did each piece about 5 times, then Barry Rose bought me a nice supper on the way home! (personal correspondence)

David James became the counter-tenor in the four-voice group The Hilliard Ensemble – a post he still holds – and a well known soloist in Bach *Passions*, Handel *Messiahs* and the like up and down the UK.

Oz Clarke, who had been a bass choral scholar at Magdalen College, Oxford, later found wine and women more to his palate than song, and he has become probably the most famous of the three solo singers outside musical circles in his modern career as a wine critic and TV personality.

Barry Rose OBE has been active in the British cathedral music scene for many years; as Director of Music at St. Paul's Cathedral, a post he first occupied in 1974, he conducted at the wedding of Prince Charles to Lady Diana Spencer. From 1988 to 1997, he was Director of Music at my own local Cathedral and Abbey Church of Saint Alban, and in 1998 he was awarded an OBE for his services to cathedral music.

Hence, Oliver's music had performers amply capable of doing full justice to its merits, who provide an inspiring model for any future performances.

Conclusions

We have seen how the music was given high production values, as befits a score which plays a central part in the drama. We have also found that Oliver treats various aspects of Middle-earth by assigning them their own particular stylistic frame of reference, in particular by using influences from different musical periods to create associations between specific styles of music and specific types of characters. The styles used nearly all borrow some element of "Englishness" which musically aware listeners will recognise.

This leads us to wonder what this music reveals of Oliver's *own* style. Without a greater experience of his other music, I cannot say, but the level of richness and invention in this music alone suggests that his wider catalogue is worth exploring. This includes a number of operas (such as *Beauty and the Beast* (1984) and *Timon of Athens*, his final work, produced by the English National Opera in 1991) and film music for *Nicholas Nickleby* (1982) and a number of Shakespeare plays directed by Elijah Moshinsky (1981).

Unfortunately, the rights to the radio play music remain with the Oliver Estate and the BBC and there are currently no plans to release it in sheet music format, apart from the theme, published by Novello, which is a bestseller. All performances so far have required special permission from the BBC.

I earnestly hope they will publish the music to enable a wider public to enjoy it in its own right, as they have with Donald Swann's settings in *The Road goes Ever On*.

About the Author

Paul Smith is an IT professional and freelance counter-tenor, who in his spare time is a writer, actor, poet and comedian. He has been a Tolkien fan since the age of 8 and a singer since the age of 19. He has acted in three performances of the *Lord of the Rings* radio play, taking roles as various characters (often in the same performance) as Gimli, Denethor, Bilbo, Gollum, the Eagle, Elrond, Snaga and an Ent.

Discography

BRITTEN, *A Midsummer Night's Dream*, Asawa/Davis/LSO, Philips

    War Requiem, Vishnevskaya/Pears/Fischer-Dieskau/LSO/Britten, Decca

BUTTERWORTH, *A Shropshire Lad*, Rolfe-Johnson/Johnson, Hyperion CDD 22044

BYRD, *Keyboard Music*, Moroney, Hyperion CDA 66558

DELIUS, *Brigg Fair*, Richard Hickox/Northern Sinfonia Of England, EMI CDC7499322

FINZI, *Choral Music*, Finzi Singers/Spicer, Chandos CHAN 8936

GIBBONS, *Anthems*, Blaze/Varcoe/Winchester Cathedral/Hill, Hyperion CDH 55228

HANDEL, *Italian Duets*, Fisher/Bowman/King's Consort, Hyperion CDH 55262

    Acis and Galatea, McFadden/Ainsley/King's Consort, Hyperion CDA 66361/2

    Chandos Anthems, Collegium Musicum 90/Standage, Chandos 241-15

PERGOLESI, *Stabat Mater*, Fisher/Chance/King's Consort, Hyperion CDA 66294

PURCELL, *Victorious Love*, Sampson/Cummings, BIS BIS SACD 1536

    The Fairy Queen, The Sixteen/Christophers, Coro

    Dido and Aeneas, Graham/Haim/Le Concert d'Astrée, Virgin Veritas 45605

VAUGHAN WILLIAMS, *Fantasia on a Theme by Thomas Tallis* and *The Lark Ascending*, Academy of St Martin in the Fields/Marriner, Argo

Tolkien References

TOLKIEN, J.R.R., *The Fellowship of the Ring*, London: HarperCollins, 2007.

    The Letters of J.R.R. Tolkien, (ed. by Humphrey Carpenter with the assistance of Christopher Tolkien), London: HarperCollins, 1995.

    The Return of the King, London: HarperCollins, 2007.

References

Foxon, Tim, "What is English Pastoral Music?", 2005 http://www.musicalresources.co.uk/WhatisEnglishPastoralMusic.php

Sibley, Brian, http://www.fantasybookreview.co.uk/blog/the-making-of-the-rings/

http://briansibleytheworks.blogspot.com/2008/01/this-page-is-still-under-construction_23.html

Mira Sommer

Elven Music in Our Times

Elves and Music – An Introduction

"Elvish singing is not a thing to miss, in June under the stars, not if you care for such things" (*H* 57). It is not only the beauty of Elvish song that is praised in *The Hobbit*. The importance of music is already expressed in this first of Tolkien's published works.

Middle-earth was created by the music of the Ainur. Thus it is no wonder that music plays an important role, especially for the Elves. Tolkien thought about the music of the Elves a long time before the final version of his mythology was published. An example is an early sketch that resembles Eärendil's story called "Ælfwine":

> Then came there music very gently over the waters and it was laden with unimagined longing [...]. And one said: 'It is the harps that are thrumming, and the songs they are singing of fair things; and the windows that look upon the sea are full of light.' And another said: 'Their stringéd violins complain the ancient woes of the immortal folk of Earth, but there is a joy therein.' 'Ah, me,' said Ælfwine, 'I hear the horns of the Fairies shimmering in magic woods [...].' (*LT2* 327)

But how do composers today imagine such music? How do modern musicians interpret the culture of the Elves? And how great is the part which the Elvish languages play in the timbre and tone of the music?

The Fellowship of the Ring: Soundtrack vs. Book – Different Depictions of the Elves

Prologue

The first Elvish sounds reach the ear of the listeners right at the beginning, in the prologue of Peter Jackson's film *The Fellowship of the Ring*. Not only can Galadriel's voice be heard reciting J.R.R. Tolkien's poem "Namarië", but also "a choral rendering of the Elvish Lothlórien Theme" (Adams, *Annotated Scores FotR* 2). The text of this hymn was written by J.R.R. Tolkien and adapted by Philippa Boyens. David Salo then translated it into Sindarin, one of the Elvish languages that Tolkien originally created.

Man ammen toltha i dann hen Amarth?	(Who brings to us this token of Doom?)
I anann darthant dam morn	(That which has stood so long against the darkness)
Si dannatha.	(Will now fall.) (ibid. 15)

The text of this song is an anticipation of the events that are about to unfold. It gives a glimpse of the future, the ring, its bearer, and the fate of all the inhabitants of Middle-earth. It is also a first indication of Galadriel's ability to foresee the future. "In style it's the most Eastern and exotic of all the Elves' music. The writing is [...] mysterious and aloof" (Adams, *Complete Recordings* 16). On the soundtrack, the theme recurs in Lothlórien. The refrain, with Boyens' text as translated by Salo, and "Namarië" are then performed in Quenya by Galadriel.

Hymn to Elbereth Gilthoniel

The hobbits' first direct encounter with Elves occurs (in the book as well as the film) on their journey though the Old Forest. The Elves' trek westward is accompanied by the song "The Passing of the Elves/The Elvish Lament", which is sung by the Elves on their journey. The song's musical version in the film (on-screen-music) was produced by Plan 9.

> Plan 9 first collaborated with Peter Jackson on 1995's Forgotten Silver. In *The Lord of the Rings* films, they specialized in diagetic, or on-screen music, including the hobbits' party music ('Flaming Red Hair') and the Wood-elves' song ('The Elvish Lament'). (Adams, *AS:FotR* 29)

This Elvish lament was originally written in Sindarin by Tolkien. It is incorporated into the film in an expanded version by Salo:

Fanuilos heryn aglar	(Snow-white! Snow-white! O Lady clear!)
Rîn athar annún-aearath,	(O Queen beyond the Western Seas!)
Calad ammen i reniar	(O Light to us that wander there)
Mi 'aladhremmin ennorath!	(Amid the world of woven trees!)
A Elbereth Gilthoniel	(Gilthoniel! O Elbereth!)

I chîn a thûl lin míriel (Clear are thy eyes and bright is breath)
[...] Ngilith or annún-aearath. (Thy starlight on the Western Seas.)
(ibid. 16)

In the book this song is sung in Elrond's house. It praises Elbereth, the Lady of the Stars. "He stood still enchanted, while the sweet syllables of the Elvish song fell like clear jewels of blended word and melody" (*FotR* 312). The original text in Tolkien is:

A Elbereth Gilthoniel,
silivren penna míriel
o menel aglar elenath!
Na-chaered palan-díriel
o galadhremmin ennorath,
Fanuilos, le linnathon
nef aer, sí nef aeron! (ibid. 311)

The translation:

O Elbereth Starkindler,
white-glittering, slanting down sparkling like a jewel,
the glory of the starry host!
Having gazed far away
from the tree-woven lands of Middle-earth,
to thee, Everwhite, I will sing,
on this side of the Sea, here on this side of the Ocean![1]

Both versions follow a clear metre. In the original we find *aa ba b cd*. In the soundtrack version we have *abab cc dd efef cc gg*. The song describes the beauty and the Elves' longing for the stars, under whose twilight they were born into the world, and a yearning for the Undying Lands which lie at the end of the ocean. The Lady of the Stars, also called Fanuilos, Elentári and Gilthoniel by the Elves, is the spouse of Manwë, king of the Undying Lands (Valinor), and the Queen of the godlike Valar. Her element is fire as she kindles the stars and puts the sun and the moon into their orbit (cf. Day 271). The song as sung *a capella* in the film takes on the character of a sad "walking song".

---

1 http://en.wikipedia.org/wiki/A_Elbereth_Gilthoniel

Song of Lúthien

"As he and the hobbits make camp at night, the Ranger sings 'The Song of Lúthien' into the night. Here the a cappella melody was composed and performed by Viggo Mortensen" (Adams *AS:FotR* 6). The original text was written by Tolkien, the translation into Sindarin by Salo:

Tinúviel elvanui	(Tinúviel the elven fair,)
Elleth alfirin edhelhael	(Immortal maiden elven-wise,)
hon ring finnil fuinui	(About him cast her shadowy hair)
A renc gelebrin thiliol.	(And arms like silver glimmering.)
(ibid. 17)	

The song is a reference to the love story of Beren and Lúthien from *The Silmarillion*. Just like Lúthien, Arwen is in danger of losing her immortality because she falls in love with the mortal Aragorn. In the song Aragorn sings about Tinúviel's shadowy hair and her silver-glimmering arms. He describes not only her Elvish beauty in these lines but also her love and care for Beren, as her hair hides him from the enemy and her arms embrace him with fervour. The song originates in "The Lay of Leithian". The lay consists of 4,222 iambic four-footed verses in couplets and is divided into 14 chants.[2] In the book, Aragorn sings the song of Tinúviel in the Common Speech (Westron) at Weathertop (cf. *FotR* 252 ff.). Viggo Mortensen's sentimental, haunting melody gives the song an authentic note and makes the love story more tangible (and audible) for the spectators even before they see Arwen for the first time. Arwen's theme debuts in the song "Give up the Halfling", here still with a textual reference to Lúthien Tinúviel of whom Aragorn sang shortly before.

Arwen's Theme

Arwen encounters Aragorn and the hobbits in the forest. In introducing Arwen's theme, Shore stresses the dulcet tones of female voices—the characteristic choral sound of the elves. Arwen picks up Frodo and, with Ringwraiths in pursuit, makes for Rivendell with all her might. She defeats the Black Riders at the Ford of Bruinen, but the ride has taken its toll on Frodo. Arwen offers him a

---

2 cf. http://ardapedia.herr-der-ringe-film.de/index.php/Lay_of_Leithian. "The Lay of Leithian" deals with the deeds of Beren and Lúthien "the Fay". The title "Lay of Leithian" cannot be distinctly interpreted. One possible meaning is "The Song of England"; a second interpretation bestows the lay with the subtitle "Release from Bondage".

blessing and the score returns to its Elvish vein, repeating Arwen's theme then echoing her words in female chorus. (Adams *AS:FotR* 7)

The text for this song, which is called "Arwen's Prayer", was written by Philippa Boyens: "What Grace is given me, let it pass to him. Let him be spared. Mighty Valar, save him" (ibid. 17). She here refers directly to the Valar, the gods of Middle-earth, that are entreated to protect Frodo against the power of the Ringwraiths.

> Musically, Arwen is often referred as a citizen of Rivendell. The same seven note rising and falling patterns from the beautiful Elf village introduce her presence in the course of the second and third film. [...] As she emerges in the forest, a female chorus intones a set of angelic stanzas in a sweetly optimistic variant on Rivendell's palette of musical colors. (Adams, *Complete Recordings* 17)

As Arwen seems to be more rebellious and set apart from her people, she gets her own distinct melody.

| Tinúviel elvanui | (Tinúviel [the] elven-fair) |
| Elleth alfirin | (Immortal maiden) (Adams *AS:FotR* 17) |

The same text that Aragorn has sung before is now repeated by a female choir and merges with the melody of Arwen's theme, sung by a mixed choir. Arwen is the most beautiful representative of her people, only one of the many parallels to Lúthien. They also both have sobriquets related to the dusk: Tinúviel (daughter of the starry twilight, nightingale) and Undómiel (daughter of twilight, evening star).[3] Elvish words with their clear tone generally lend themselves to intonation and song. The syllables are well suited for different interpretations and lengths in melodic articulation. The slower, quieter, and more solemn melodies harmonise especially with strings and flutes and thus build epic, dramatic, and at the same time magical layers of sound. Waves seem to break on a beach and winds rustle through trees in Arwen's melody, underscoring her noble, non-human heritage and her closeness to nature. This is especially evident in "Give up the Halfling" on disk two of *The Complete Recordings (Fellowship of the Ring)*.

---

3 cf. http://ardapedia.herr-der-ringe-film.de/index.php/Arwen

Rivendell

> Safely deposited in Rivendell, the score relaxes a moment to commingle music from the hobbit and Elf societies. The iridescent Rivendell theme enters, with all the beauty and finality that it imparts. 'It's music for the end of a civilization,' Shore reminds us. The female choir now sings 'Hymn to Elbereth,' in reference to the Elves' Queen of the Stars. (Adams *AS:FotR* 8)

Here the "Hymn to Elbereth", which was heard earlier in a modified version in "Passing of the Elves", is repeated by a female choir in the way Tolkien originally envisioned the song. A link to the elegy of the Woodelves that are fading into the West is established. The former song has a stronger focus on parting, whereas the theme of the Elves of Rivendell is grander and also full of hope. The Rivendell theme also supports the power and homeliness of Elrond's house which is set securely in the middle of a valley, seamlessly fitting into nature.

> The Elves of Rivendell are more open to outsiders than other Elven societies […]. Here […] familiar orchestral instruments flourish in layers of writing that places an acclivous figure for female chorus and a series of arcing arpeggios amidst glinting chimes, harps and string harmonics. (Adams, *Complete Recordings* 15)

The sound of harps and strings seems to sprout like flowers in the valley which is the last place of real rest the Fellowship encounters before its great quest begins, and in which that quest originates.

Aníron (Aragorn and Arwen's Theme)

The song by Enya is the second she contributed to the trilogy. "In Fellowship, Enya wrote and performed 'Aníron' and 'May it Be'" (Adams *AS:FotR* 27). Roma Ryan furnished "Aníron" with its Elvish lyrics. "The 'Aníron' theme marks a rare inclusion of a non-Shore melody in *The Lord of the Rings* score, although it was he who championed Enya's inclusion. 'I imagined her voice for this scene, […]'" Shore recalls (ibid. 8).

Ai! Aníron Undómiel	(Ah! I desire Evenstar)
Tiro! Êl eria e mór.	(Look! A star rises out of the darkness.)
I 'lîr en êl luitha 'uren.	(The song of the star enchants my heart.)
(ibid. 18)	

Here the Evenstar is mentioned for the first time, whereas previously the Arwen theme was always linked to her as Tinúviel. An altogether new melody emerges from the already established themes of the score. It underlines the gentle love between Aragorn and Arwen which is likened to the yearning for the evening star, which is just as bright and full of hope but glimmering out of reach on the far horizon. With her unique voice, Enya gives the syllables a whole new tone and rhythm which represents Elves, Men and love. The end titles of "The Fellowship" feature Enya's composition "May it be". The refrain is in Quenya: "Mornie utúlië" (darkness has come) and "Mornie alantië" (darkness has fallen) – a reference to the ancient language of the Elves which has even made it into the charts (cf. ibid. 14).

Gilraen's Memorial

Darker and more mystical than the previous Elvish themes is the song of Gilraen, Aragorn's mother.

> Sung by alto Hilary Summers, 'Gilraen's Song' marks the first use of the Diminishment of the Elves, the melody that represents the Elvish concept of death and finality, but which will be more thoroughly explored in *The Two Towers*. Aragorn's visit to his mother's grave, offers a literal finality, but also calls Aragorn's future into question. Will he face the weight his heritage carries? If so, what will be the cost? (ibid. 9)

Tolo na rengy nin,	(Come into my arms,)
Beriathon	(Let me hold you safe)
A núriel annant	(But still you run)
Trin aduial,	(Through the twilight,)
Ne dúath roeg dagech	(Lost in your play)
Ne theilien.	(Slaying demons in the shadows.)
[...] Le iôn adar lín,	(You are your father's son,)
û iôn naneth lín.	(Not your mother's child.) (ibid. 18)

The song of Aragorn's mother speaks of love and protection. She proudly observes her son and how his father lives on in him. The text and translation are by Boyens and Salo. The Sindarin language again determines the mystical Elvish tone which appears far too dolorous and seems to get lost in the vastness of the night when Aragorn leaves his mark of respect at his mother's grave. Just like her son, Gilraen had a special and deep relationship with the Elves that is reflected in the melody. In order to give Gilraen a unique voice, a special soloist was chosen for the song. "Hilary Summers has the distinction of being the only alto soloist used in *The Lord of the Rings* films. 'I wanted an alto voice for Gilraen,' recalls Shore. 'I thought that a low female voice would be a great sound'" (ibid. 27). The "Diminishment of the Elves" theme is also given a voice through the melodic structure of the song. It incorporates an Elvish concept of finality. Their disappearance from Middle-earth and their concept of death are dealt with in this motif.

> Like other Elf music, there are chromatically-fueled Eastern flavors at the edges of the phrase, […] a uniquely dark color in the Elf music representing one of the few uncertainties in the culture. The melody […] ends on a single chromatically unstable pitch. (Adams, *Complete Recordings* 17)

The "Diminishment of the Elves" theme can be heard not only once in *The Fellowship* but also in *The Two Towers*.

Caras Galadhon and Galadriel's Mirror

> The Lothlórien motif from the prologue returns.
> The Fellowship ventures into Lothlórien and so the mystical theme of these Elves returns, featuring soprano Miriam Stockley, female chorus, monochord and a prominent sarangi solo. 'Lothlórien is more exotic,' explains Shore. 'Rivendell is about learning and knowledge, but this is different.' The Lothlórien music stretches into sustained, arrhythmic shapes that sound neither dangerous nor comforting, but create a sense of unanswered anticipation. After a phrase from the ney flute, a rolling tam-tam and a flourish of brass and strings carry the members of the Fellowship into Caras Galadhon, while cascading harps and female voices (singing 'Galadriel's Song') maintain the ambiguously impressive air. (Adams *AS:FotR* 11)

Concerning the choral singing of the Elves of Lothlórien, Howard Shore states: "This is Middle-earth of 5000 years ago. […] I started thinking about the history of music back hundreds of years, and of course you get to voices: Gregorian chants" (Adams *CR* 16). The songs are really reminiscent of the measured notes of Gregorian choirs and have a meditative, almost intoxicating effect in conjunction with the instruments. The theme opens on a grand and enchanting scale when the Fellowship sees Caras Galadhon for the first time and they are allowed to climb crystal steps into the trees. When Galadriel meets the Fellowship and looks into their souls, the music also seems to take a hypnotising turn and is interwoven with calm, comforting strings. The Fellowship is awestruck and has finally found another secure haven. Later at night, when the golden forest is lit only by blue Fëanorian lamps, the Elves mourn Gandalf with an elegy.

> Elizabeth Fraser and a female chorus trade phrases in a call-and-response texture with the monochord. In this despondent ceremonial music, the 'Lament For Gandalf', Shore explores his adapted Maqam Hijaz scale over drone-like open harmonies in the low strings. (Adams AS:FotR 11)

The choir can be heard in the background while Elisabeth Fraser performs her stanzas quite independently. After she stops singing, the choir starts up again till the song fades seamlessly into the melancholy Gondor theme.

Choir text for "Lament for Gandalf" (first stanza in Quenya):

A Olórin i yáresse	(Olórin whom long ago)
Mentaner i Númeherui	(Sent the Lords of the West)
Tírien i Rómenóri,	(To guard the Lands of the East,)
Maiaron i oiosaila	(Ever-wise of the Maiar)
Manan elye etevanne	(What drove you to leave [lit. "why you left"])
Nórie i malanelye?	(Land which you loved?)[4]

Gandalf's name Olórin is mentioned; his heritage and task are revealed. The solo verses two and three are written in Sindarin and contain further names.

In gwidh ristennin,	(The bonds cut),
I fae narchannen	(The spirit broken)
I Lach Anor ed ardhon gwannen	(The Flame of Anor has left this World)
Mithrandir, Mithrandir! A Randir Vithren!	(Mithrandir, Mithrandir, O Pilgrim Grey!)[5]

In the book, the Fellowship also hears the Elves' singing and the name they use for Gandalf: Mithrandir. But in this lament some more relevant themes for the Elves are conveyed via the choir.

Melmelma nóren sina	(Our love for this land)
Núra lá earo núri	(Is deeper than the deeps of the sea)
Ilfirin nairelma	(Our regret is undying)
Ananta ilyar eccatuvalme	(Yet we will cast all away)
Ar ullume nucuvalme:	(Rather than submit:)
Nauva i nauva.	(What should be shall be.)
(Adams *AS:FotR* 21)	

---

4 These lyrics are different from the ones performed on the CD. The whole text of the original English poem by Philippa Boyens can be heard in the *Fellowship of the Ring Extended Edition* on DVD.
5 Version published in the Warner Brothers sheet music.

In the last stanza, the text again refers to the Elves' love of Middle-earth and the sadness they bear because they have to leave it. They know that their farewell is inevitable. Their immortality compared to Gandalf's supposed death is also a topic. This stanza in Quenya is an interpretation of Galadriel's words in *The Fellowship of the Ring*: "The Love of the Elves for their land and their works is deeper than the deeps of the Sea, and their regret is undying and cannot ever wholly be assuaged" (*FotR* 479).

These words, which Galadriel speaks to Frodo in the book after he has taken a look into the mirror, are taken up by the choir and form a bridge to the mirror-sequence in the film as well.

> The music shifts from brass tones to vocal timbres as Galadriel arrives and regards Frodo. 'This scene was tricky because it's so iconic,' Shore remembers. 'This whole scene, everybody who's ever read Tolkien knows every moment of it. It had to be done perfectly.' Galadriel and Frodo glimpse the potential future of Middle-earth in the Elf's mirror and, for the only time in the scores, Shore interweaves the music of Lothlórien with grating melodies of Mordor. The composer even allows the crudest of the Mordor themes, the Evil of the Ring, to sound in muted trumpets. Afraid of what the future may hold, Frodo offers Galadriel the Ring. Her temptation is scored with an obscene orchestral crescendo of burbling low strings and heavy brass chords – and a hint of the Mordor Outline in the timpani. (Adams, *AS:FotR* 12)

A hint of the influence of evil on the pure world of the Elves seems to permeate this song; a glimmer of Middle-earth's history appears in the music.

Elvish melodies on the soundtrack are not only represented by the usual orchestral instruments but also by the more exotic ones. Examples here could be the monochord, an antique wooden instrument with mutable strings which could also be used for scientific purposes; the Ney flute from Egypt (3000 B.C.), which is still used today in the Middle East and Morocco; and the sarangi from classic Indian music (Adams *AS:FotR* 25).

Námarië

Shortly after that scene, the Fellowship says its farewell to the Elves of Lothlórien. The parting words of Galadriel are soon blended with grave words of Elendil, while the Fellowship can be seen travelling down the Anduin. The first verse in "The Great River" is a fragment of Galadriel's elegy (cf. *FotR* 496); verse two consists of Elendil's words when he enters Middle-earth after the destruction of Númenor. These words are later repeated by Aragorn who speaks, or rather sings, them at his coronation. The Quenya words sung by the choir have thus literally been taken from Tolkien.

> Ai! laurie lantar lassi súrinen   (Alas! golden leaves fall in the wind),
> yéni únotime ve ramar aldaron!   (long years numberless as [the] wings of trees!)
>
> yéni ve linte [...]   (long years like swift [...])
> (Adams *AS:FotR* 21f)

The Elves in the Soundtrack of *The Two Towers*

Evenstar

"Evenstar", which is sung by Isabel Bayrakdarian, can be heard alongside Éowyn's theme in the song "One of the Dúnedain" after the Gondor theme.

> Beneath the Gondor theme the Rivendell arpeggios begin to flow, warm but somber, devoid of the lucent orchestrations that colored the lines in *The Fellowship of the Ring*. Lyric soprano Isabel Bayrakdarian enters singing "Evenstar" over female chorus divided three ways. The line, which moves from voice to alto flute, combines the ambrosial vocal tone of the Elves with melodic contours directly out of The Heroics of Aragorn theme—including the crucial down-and-back-up figure. Can Aragorn lead the World of Men without abandoning his love for Arwen? (Adams *AS:TT* 16)

In the film, Arwen's words to Aragorn are repeated by Bayrakdarian in song, while a female choir completes the scene and uses a phrase from "Gilraen's Song". The soloist Bayrakdarian again represents an Elvish theme with her voice. In her own distinctive and enchanting way, she mixes "The Diminishment of the Elves" theme with the new "Evenstar". Alto flute and low strings transport not only Aragorn into a dreamlike state, recalling from afar Arwen's gracefulness, Rivendell, and the light of their love. Tolkien's words have been translated into Sindarin by Salo:

> Ú i vethed nâ i onnad.   (This is not the end, it is the beginning.)
> [...] Estelio han, estelio veleth   (Trust this, trust love) (ibid. 32)

> 'Isabel is a lyric soprano. A friend of mine gave me a CD of her singing, and I asked her about performing very early on,' Howard Shore recalls. 'I knew that

if I wanted to write anything in her range she would be wonderful. She has a beautiful voice that I felt was appropriate for "Evenstar".' (ibid. 36)

Arwen's Fate / The Grace of the Valar

A further soloist deals with Aragorn and Arwen's theme. The latter appears as a vision in Aragorn's mind while he is drifting down the river. Her memory brings him back to life. In a flashback he asks Arwen to leave Middle-earth.

> Aragorn's unconscious form floats downriver, as the soothing graze of the monochord hums beneath him, conjuring the music of the Elves. Four alto flutes ascend in their element, airy tones, dreamily hailing the arrival of a soprano voice. Sheila Chandra performs "The Grace of the Valar". (ibid. 19)

> Chandra was born to a family of South Indian immigrants living in South London. Shore encountered one of her Indipop records and immediately noticed her unique voice. "I thought this was a great voice—more of a mezzo-soprano sound." Sheila Chandra performs "The Grace of the Valar" text, coupled with four alto flutes, dilruba and monochord as Aragorn's unconscious form floats downriver. (ibid. 36)

Another reminiscence to the exotic, distant character of the Elves thus emerges. Aragorn's heroic theme stands out against the Elvish sounds while he is filled with new vigour and manages to climb onto Brego's back to ride to Helm's Deep. Fran Walsh wrote the Sindarin text for Aragorn's song ("Breath of Life"):

Boe naer gwannathach, annant uich ben-estel	(Sorrowing you must go, and yet you are not without hope)
An uich gwennen na ringyrn e-mbar han	(For you are not bound to the circles of this world) (ibid. 32)

> Meanwhile in Rivendell, Shore continues to turn the musical tables. Arwen is told by Elrond that it is time for her to board the ship to Valinor, but the Elves' signature vocal timbres are nowhere to be found. Alto flute, instead, solos over elegant string chords. And so, in this complicated love affair, Man is now momentarily represented by a female voice while Elf is represented by a solo instrumentalist. (ibid. 19)

Arwen's vision in Rivendell and her decision to leave Middle-earth are accompanied by all Elvish themes heard up until that point.

> Yet despite the female voices intoning "Hymn to Elbereth", the harp *glissandi* and robust arpeggio figures, the Rivendell theme moves slowly and softly, almost receding. After a single rhapsodic statement of the line it evolves into a sadder, more linearly expressive shape that draws the stylistic tendencies of

the "Evenstar" and "The Grace of the Valar" music closer to Rivendell. Over a lingering shot, the monochord reappears in clarification of its appearance in the music of Rivendell: Elrond has been in telepathic communication with Galadriel. The Eastern-tinted Lothlórien theme – sarangi doubled with female chorus singing "Footsteps of Doom" – makes its debut appearance in *The Two Towers* as Galadriel peers into the future of Middle-earth." (ibid.)

Arwen's fate is enmeshed with both the fates of the Elves and Men but her motif still revels in the magnificence of her Elvish heritage. As she leaves Rivendell with the Elves, bells ring a farewell; this can be heard especially clearly in the Live to Projection concert.

The Host of the Eldar / Haldir's Lament

The Elves are also warriors and Peter Jackson wanted to make that clear in his films. The perfection of the weapons and their fighting style is reflected in the accompanying music.

> The Lothlórien theme takes a heretofore unheard guise, its florid current solidified into a militant march. Voices and brass in Elf-like unison carry the theme over rhythmic percussion and strings. (ibid. 22)

When Haldir of Lórien is stabbed from behind by an Uruk-Hai blade, Elisabeth Fraser, who sang the "Lament for Gandalf" in *The Fellowship*, returns to create a uniquely Elvish sound to mourn his death.

> Shore's composition takes a similar shape, a call and response for solo soprano and female chorus, as Fraser performs "Haldir's Lament," set to excerpts of "Namárië". In death Haldir's music returns to the Elves' ethereal mysticism. (ibid. 24)

> Fraser came to the performing world as the lead singer and lyricist of the highly influential Cocteau Twins. In *The Fellowship of the Ring* and *The Two Towers*, her voice is associated with the mystical music of Lothlórien and can be heard in *The Two Towers* on "Haldir's Lament." (ibid. 36)

A fragment of "Galadriel's Lament" is again used for "Haldir's Lament".

| Ar sindarnóriello mornie caita, | (And grey-country-from lies darkness,) |
| Ar ilye tier unduláve lumbule | (And all roads down-licked [the] clouds)[6] |

---

6 www.theonering.net; cf. Tolkien *FotR* 496. The text seems to describe a way through the darkness – the transition from life to death.

The Elves in the Soundtrack of *The Return of the King*

Twilight and Shadow / The Grace of Undómiel

An altogether new voice is given to Arwen and the Elves on *The Return of the King* soundtrack. Renée Fleming presents a mournful version of the Evenstar theme and depicts the Elves leaving Middle-earth. "Renée Fleming is one of the most renowned and respected operatic sopranos of modern times" (Adams *AS:RotK* 44). Her voice is deep and full of grief. It can be heard not only in conjunction with the Elves but also later during the decisive moments of the story at Mount Doom. It is emotionally charged and seems to invoke shrouds that veil the souls of the protagonists.

> The music of *The Fellowship of the Ring* embraced the pure, almost folk-like tones of vocalists such as Enya and Isabel Fraser. The palette in *The Two Towers* became more varied and exotic. Vocal performances from Emilana Torrini, Sheila Chandra and Bayrakdarian underscored the emphasis on Northern European, Eastern Asian and European tones. *The Return of the King* represents the peak of this progression – *The Lord of the Rings*' vocal music at its most developed and resplendent. Renée Fleming's voice is that of a *coloratura soprano*, one of the most revered and complex tones in music. (ibid. 6f)

Boyen's text is called "Evening Star" and is sung by Fleming and a choir (just as "The Grace" which can already be heard in "Breath of Life" in *The Two Towers*).

Ngil cennin firiel vi	(I saw a star fade in the)
Enel aduial,	(Evening sky),
[...] A meleth, perónen.	(For a love half given). (ibid. 33)

The evening star fades away and the riddle of "a love half given" is presented. While the procession of the Elves from Rivendell is making its way through the forest, Arwen has a vision of her son. She immediately returns to Rivendell and confronts her father with what she has seen and her final decision against the security of Valinor, for love. The Evenstar melody is taken up by strings and interwoven with the Rivendell arpeggios. Soft woodwinds accompany the end of "Evenstar" when Arwen asks Elrond to forge the sword anew. The orchestra again mixes the already heard Rivendell arpeggios into the score. The Rivendell theme starts to blossom in rolling crescendo notes. The shards of Narsil are reforged by the Elves and are given back into the world of Men.

The Houses of Healing and Asëa Aranion

For the first and only time in the trilogy, an actress depicting an Elf sings a song herself. Liv Tyler as Arwen performs "Arwen's Song" during the scenes in the Houses of Healing. As the song was originally written by Fran Walsh for Arwen's vision, it contains references to the last conversation between Aragorn and Arwen.

> With a sigh you turn away
> With a deepening heart no more words to say
> You will find that the world has changed forever
> And the trees are now turning from green to gold
> And the sun is now fading
> I wish could hold you closer (ibid. 39)
>
> Under Aragorn's care, Éowyn recovers in the Houses of Healing. 'Arwen's Song' acts here as an elvish blessing – an ethereal prayer for the suffering. Arwen, too, is somewhere in Middle-earth, just as lovelorn. [...] Faramir has also recovered in the Houses of Healing. He smiles at Éowyn. 'Arwen's Song' continues, 'I wish could hold you closer'. (ibid. 24)

The lines can thus apply to Arwen and Aragorn as well as to Éowyn and Faramir. After the second scene with the latter two in the Houses of Healing (on the terrace), the song "The Last Debate" / "Asëa Aranion" is heard. It is performed by the Norwegian singer Sissel during the fan credits of "The Return of the King", though it was initially planned as a song to be heard in the Houses of Healing. The text refers to "Grace of the Valar" from "The Two Towers".

> Sissel took a circuitous route into the music of Middle-earth. She was originally engaged to perform the solo soprano part in select performances of *The Lord of the Rings Symphony: Six Movements for Orchestra and Chorus*, then was subsequently asked to perform "Asëa Aranion" for the Extended DVD Edition of *The Return of the King*. (ibid. 45)[7]

In "The Last Debate", *Asëa aranion* is the healing herb also known as *athelas* or kingsfoil. "[I]ts ancient name in Valinorean Quenya was remembered. That name, asëa aranion, seems to be a direct Elvish equivalent of the common name 'kingsfoil'."[8]

---

[7] Sissel later also toured the world with the *Lord of the Rings Symphony* and performed most solo-soprano parts during the live concerts.
[8] http://www.glyphweb.com/arda/a/aseaaranion.html

Coronation

"The Song to Tinúviel", which accompanies Arwen's first appearance and is sung by Aragorn by the fire now becomes Queen Arwen's song.

> Aragorn turns to Legolas, who stands with a group of Elves, including [...] Arwen. Aragorn's love steps out from behind a white Gondorian pennant. Renée Fleming sings Arwen Revealed, the same melodic strain that first brought her into the story back in *The Fellowship of the Ring*. Mixed chorus joins Fleming's solo voice as Arwen approaches. This is Elvish music, yet the addition of men's voices indicates something has changed. Arwen is shy, reluctant even. She has given up her immortality for this man, but does he still love her? Aragorn takes her chin in his hand and, as the strings reenter, kisses her passionately. She is to become his Queen. (Adams *AS:RotK* 50)

Almost all choral pieces and solos in *The Return of the King* (e. g., "Don't Let Go", "For Frodo", "The Eagles", "The Destruction of the Ring") have an Elvish text. The Elves have defined Middle-earth for a long time and during the time of the War of the Ring their influence is still strong. This influence is certainly felt in the film score; its texts are written in Sindarin and Quenya for the most part.

Tolkien's Elves in General Musical Interpretation

The Tolkien Ensemble

The ambition of the Danish Tolkien Ensemble was to compose the first complete musical interpretation of all the poems and songs in *The Lord of the Rings*. The ensemble was founded in 1995 by Caspar Reiff, and from 1997 to 2006 they managed to release numerous albums which include all the songs and poems from the book. The project was supported by the Tolkien Estate as well as by HarperCollins Publishers. Queen Margrethe II of Denmark gave permission to use her illustrations for the CD booklets.[9] They received further prominent encouragement by Christopher Lee, who plays Saruman in the films. At the Danish premiere of Peter Jackson's film *The Fellowship of the Ring*, the musicians of the ensemble met Christopher Lee. He subsequently acted as narrator and singer on their third CD "At Dawn in Rivendell" (2002).[10]

---

9 cf. de.wikipedia.org/wiki/Tolkien_Ensemble
10 cf. http://www.tolkien-ensemble.net

The works of the Tolkien Ensemble are partly classical and partly Irish folk in style. The songs of the Elves, for example, are reminiscent of opera arias but have a more ethereal sound. In a review, Christian Weichmann states that the members of the ensemble mostly have classical music training which is of course reflected in their works. One often finds solemn art and opera songs or recitatives, evocative of classical or romantic music, which are then given long instrumental introductions and conclusions. However, there are some songs (mainly those for the Hobbits) which tend more towards folk. The classical focus can also be seen in the selection of partners who support the ensemble in some of their recordings. There are, for example, the Danish Radio Sinfonietta, the national Danish chamber choir, the Copenhagen Young Strings, the chamber choir Hymnia, and the Copenhagen chamber choir Camerata (cf. Weichmann 28ff).

"A Elbereth Gilthoniel", the song in Sindarin that can be heard on *The Lord of the Rings* soundtrack in various versions, has also been set to music by the Tolkien Ensemble and recorded in different versions. Violin and guitar harmonise as in chamber music with the soloist, whose "Gilthoniel" version 1 is reminiscent of an ornate romantic ballad which seems to have sprung from the 19th century. Variation 2, however, is an *a capella* solo by an operatic female mezzo-soprano. It is artistically embellished and expansive, yet remains calm, full of grandeur and devotion. Version 3, another female solo with orchestra, appears to be most "Elven-strange". The spheric-melancholic singing is similar to that of the female soloists of the Sindarin songs on *The Lord of the Rings* soundtrack. A solemn mixed choir joins in later. Slowly and mournfully, like the yearning for the stars, and with the dignity of a real hymn, the Elbereth melody fades into the Eldamar motif of "Galadriel's Song of Eldamar" at the end. Number four is Samwise Gamgee's mystic and worshipful version of the song. It is accompanied by a folk guitar and a single female voice.

Aragorn's "The Fall of Gil Galad" could be the song of a lonesome guitar player at the campfire. Accompanied by the piano, the "Song of Beren and Lúthien" is an aria in the vein of those performed in Empire salons at the beginning of the 19th century. The character of a lay is supported by this form of delivery: A singer tells a story and possibly also plays an instrument to accompany the song. "The Song of Earendil" and the "Song of Nimrodel" (which is sung to the music of the Nimrodel waterfall in Lothlórien by Legolas in *The Fellowship of the Ring* (445f)) are similarly structured. In contrast, the previously mentioned "Galadriel's Song of Eldamar" displays a soundtrack quality. The main theme of the song is very catchy and appealing and is repeated by all the instruments. A woman's voice (performing as Galadriel), sings her lines to the same melody. In the middle part of the song, the motif changes, only to re-emerge, accompanied by strings, to a lyric grandeur. The second part of the song ("Song of the Elves beyond the Sea") begins with a rather exotic xylophone, an aria, and an unobstrusive male choir that almost sounds Gregorian. It uses a wholly different theme from that of Galadriel in the first part. The text about mysticism and far-off Valinor playfully merges with the melody, just as described in the citation above. In the translated version of Galadriel's song, narrator Christopher Lee speaks the Elvish text in English above the chant. This adds the aura of a long spell to the song, a magic chant, which allows the spoken words to appear in the minds' eyes of the listeners. This variation is Tolkienesque like no other. "Galadriel's Messages" is also performed by Christopher Lee, accompanied by an orchestra. This song also receives an enchanting and mysterious quality through Lee's voice and the soft melody in the background. "Gandalf's Song of Lórien" starts like a classical chamber piece but is then permeated by a faint echo of the Galadriel theme. Gandalf's and Galadriel's voices seem to sing along two distinct but intertwined lines and thus artfully combine the Gandalf and Lórien themes.

"Malbeth the Seer's Words" seems orchestral and soundtrack-like, while played in a fateful minor key, almost as if it was written for a film scene. Strings, which grow ever softer on the same note, sometimes dying down completely, sometimes dissonant, accompany what seems like a dark prophecy that becomes deeper and darker the longer the song progresses. Then Christopher Lee's momentous words can be heard. They lend the song force and instill it with the soul of Malbeth's words which the listener has been expecting since the beginning. "Legolas' Song of the Sea" starts on a more optimistic note again, but the arrangement is just as orchestral. Legolas' words from *The Lord of the Rings* are here embedded into merry song which brings a somewhat different, hopeful tone to the otherwise dark and melancholy tenor of the Tolkien Ensemble's Elvish melodies. Once more, the popular theme of the Elves' longing for the sea is thus taken up.

Battlelore

The Finnish metal band Battlelore is, just like the Tolkien Ensemble, recognized by most Tolkien fans. The band is almost exclusively (with the exception of one album) concerned with events and people from Tolkien's mythology. According to Jyri Vahvanen, the band's name is based on the main theme of Tolkien's work, i.e. the battles. This is then linked with the idea of folklore. The band calls its own music epic fantasy metal.[11]

Their album "Where the Shadows Lie" (2001) includes some tracks with an Elvish context. The title "Journey to the Undying Lands" already speaks of a voyage to Valinor, the promised land of the gods and immortals. The title seems to hint at a solemn, sad song, especially when one thinks of Howard Shore's "Passing of the Elves" or "Gray Havens". Battlelore, however, transform the wistfully glorified journey into the land behind the mists into an arduous and hidden way full of danger and transform the ocean into an insurmountable force that has to be weathered:

> Mystic path you sail
> To reach their presence[12]

The description of the land is reminiscent of Gandalf's words about a "far green country" in *The Return of the King*. The lyrical first person is an Elf in this case:

> There's a land beyond the great sea
> [...] Valinor home of the Valar
> Eldamar the elven domain.
> [...] Land of magic and fantasy
> Place for my final rest
> Farewell my mortal friends.[13]

The rough sea and paradisiac Valinor beyond are mentioned in almost all of Tolkien's works, even the unfinished manuscripts. One example can be found in the *Unfinished Tales*: "But the seas were wild and wide, and shadow and enchantment lay upon them; and Valinor was hidden." (*UT* 70); another in *The Book of Lost Tales*: "And these [Enchanted Isles] were strung as a net in

---

11 cf. http://de.wikipedia.org/wiki/Battlelore
12 http://www.songmeanings.net/songs/view/3530822107858503105/
13 http://www.songmeanings.net/songs/view/3530822107858503105/

the Shadowy Seas [...] before Tol Eressëa, the Lonely Isle" (*LT1* 253) or in *The Silmarillion*. Unconventional journeys, such as the one along the path of dreams on the back of a whale in *Roverandom*[14] are also a topic in Battlelore's "Elves of Luva" song.

"The Green Maid" describes an Elven or Human girl, but the fact that she is waiting for a "mortal" seems to hint at an Elvish lineage.

> Green shades of the elven wood
> Covers her face so pale
> Those eyes like a stars in the night
> Her hair like a golden flame
> [...] no earthly creature can ever reach
> A beauty like hers
> Young elven knights come to her
> There's so much love to share
> But still she's awaiting the one
> The one with a mortal way[15]

An all-consuming love stricken by fate is set to harsh music. The lovely poetic text seems to act as a counterpoint to the hard rhythms. Soon enough, though, it becomes clear where the musical journey leads: death and doom follow the lovers in text and melody. A black blade and victims are mentioned:

> His sorrow turns to hate
> By his blood he swears the oath (ibid.)

The song could be about Túrin Turambar and Finduilas or Niniel from the "Narn I Hín Húrin" (The Lay of the Children of Húrin). Kaisa Joukhi's high-pitched voice accompanies the setting and only a single guitar supports her and Patrik Mennander's singing. Mennander left the band shortly after his last performance at Ring*Con 2004 in Germany in order to focus on his work as lead singer of "Ruoska". Tomi Mykkänen joined in initially as guest singer but decided to stay on. He can be heard on their 2005 album "Third Age of the Sun", which starts with the mystical and mysterious song "Usvainen Rhûn". Rhûn is the country from whence the Easterlings hail in *The Lord of the Rings*. This song deliberately does without the instruments which are typical for

---

14 "It was the whale who took them to the Bay of Fairyland beyond the Magic Isles, and they saw far off in the West the Shores of Fairyland, and the Mountains of the Last Land and the light of Fairyland upon the waves." (*R* 111f.)
15 http://www.songmeanings.net/songs/view/3530822107858678379/

Battlelore. The rippling of water merges into flute and string music which is overlaid with a dark conjuring sprechgesang that seems like an elegy, part of a saga or a spell. Though Kaisa Jouhki does not intone an Elvish text but sings in Finnish, the song seems to have come directly from Middle-earth with a sound as nature-bound and enchanted as the Elves themselves.

Pinnan alla	(Under the surface)
varjoissa Rhûnin	(In the shadows of Rhûn)
[...] On kolmas aika auringon	(It's the third age of the sun)[16]

The album title is referred to again here: it is conceptually set in the Third Age as described in *The Lord of the Rings*. Since Tolkien was inspired by the Finnish *Kalevala*, this Finnish text seems to close the gap between the myths. Maybe Rhûn here actually refers to Finland itself and the enchanting song conjures the rune-songs of the ancestors in a Tolkienian cosmos.

In "Valier – Queens of the Valar", Battlelore convey their impression of the female Valar in a considerably more martial vein than Shore or the Tolkien Ensemble:

One with the light of the stars
[...] Masters of Menel
Almighty of Arda
Valier, Queens of the Valar
Loving hearts, joy and majesty
Varda, Yavanna, Nienna
Vana, Nesse, Este, Vaire[17]

The delicate image of the graceful goddesses becomes a mighty hymn in Battlelore's hands. The goddesses are described in terms of power and strength rather than those of beauty usually attributed to female characters.

Joukhi's clear voice describes the deeds of the Valier in English. Mykkänen's roaring voice joins hers, and basses accompany the whispered names of the Valar. Their power is thus represented by basses and guitars and only partly by the female singer's graceful voice. The song "Thousand Caves", in which the Elven grottoes of Menegroth are described, is similar. "It was the secret fortress-palace of the Sindar King Elu Thingol and his Queen Melian the Maia"

---

16 http://www.lyricsdownload.com/battlelore-usvainen-rhn-lyrics.html
17 http://www.songmeanings.net/songs/view/3530822107858678396/

(Day 98). A catchy melody and the typical guitars accompany the singing in a fluid tempo:

> Elven underworld
> Colours of the stars
> [...] Elven underworld
> So far from the stars
> [...] Thousand caves it's stalk
> Cursed by Sindar
> All the beauty's gone
> Under the waves[18]

The curse of the Sindar is mentioned. The hard riffs suit the faded realm, which was once great and magnificent. Thingol was murdered in Menegroth through the curse of the Silmaril, and Melian departed. Finally, Menegroth sank into the sea together with the rest of Beleriand.

The Elves themselves prove to be the blue print for their enemies, the Orcs. Melkor "captured many of the newly risen race of Elves [...] and with hideous acts of torture he made ruined and terrible forms of life. [...] These were the Orcs" (Day 214). Elves are thus related to the Orcs. Their differences as well as their kinship become especially clear in the song "Of Orcs and Elves". While Joukhi is singing sweetly, fast electric guitars and drums can be heard. The Orcs are represented by Mykkänen's voice:

> First borns noble crowd
> [...] Beast, filthy kind
> Sick soul, broken mind
> Light burns their blackened eyes
> Spoiled blood, impure heart[19]

The light that shines in Elves' bodies and souls is turned into darkness in Orcs and thus blackens blood and heart.

> Denote the total contrast of
> The race made by Morgoth
> [...] Dark side of the distant stars
> [...] From the one and the same awakening
> [...] Unaware folk of the stars
> Forced into wounds and dreadful scars

---

18 http://www.songmeanings.net/songs/view/3530822107858678397/
19 http://www.songmeanings.net/songs/view/3530822107858678399/

> To raid the lands under his summons
> Destroy the race that they once were (ibid.)

The text here directly refers to the dreadful irony that the Elves, as protectors of Middle-earth, are used as instruments to subdue the world and destroy their own people by Morgoth/Melkor. The Heavy Metal interpretation again suits the subject matter.

The song "Elves of Luna" is much calmer in contrast to Battlelore's usual sound. Accompanied initially by only one guitar, Joukhi sings of far-off coasts and enchanted songs, flutes and harps. Little by little, more instruments enrich the scenery but the song never becomes loud or hard.

> From a shore I have known for long
> I heard enchanting songs
> Meadow was dancing
> By the flute and the harp
> [...] I walked to the path across the sea
> I walked to the place ever unseen
> [...] Beyond the land of the dreams[20]

Again, as in "Journey to the Undying Land", the song vaguely refers to the manifold paths by which one can reach Valinor.

More "Elvish Musicians"

The album "Music Inspired by Middle Earth" by David Arkenstone, whose stage name itself is inspired by Tolkien[21], deals solely with that setting. He uses only computers for his "Cinematic New Age Rock", thus giving Elvish music a completely new electronic touch. "Technology has produced some wonderful tools for making music. The computer allows me to fully orchestrate my pieces and really fine tune them," says Arkenstone in an interview on his website.[22] His themes for Galadriel and Arwen, as well as his music for Lothlórien, though all Elvish in nature, are very different from each other. "Galadriel" unfolds mystical electronic sounds mixed with high-pitched female voices that seem to describe the expanse of space. Galadriel herself is musically

---

20 http://www.songmeanings.net/songs/view/3530822107858667765/
21 King Thorin's prized treasure, the Arkenstone from *The Hobbit*.
22 http://www.davidarkenstone.com/about.html

depicted as a star princess, as flower of her people, in whose eyes the universe glitters. Arkenstone uses triangles and metallic wind chimes in order to depict Galadriel's opaqueness. An undertone in minor by harp and bass depict her as a millennia-old being. Arwen's characteristic instruments, however, seem to be exuberant harps and flutes. Here too, the harp is the instrument that represents Elves. Arwen's melody is softer and more human. She is a half-elf who is at home in Rivendell, a house of knowledge and homeliness. Her melody, though lovely and beautiful, still has earthly roots; in contrast to Galadriel she stays tangible. The beauty of her surroundings seems to blend with her own grace in the melody, like a waterfall caressing the rock beneath. Chorals sung by women can be heard in the background and the notes in minor seem to speak of her inauspicious love. Towards the end, the theme dissolves into a merrier play of different instruments. Lothlórien is dominated by solemn harps and strings which later turn exhilarant, almost merry. Light percussions mark the undertone. The composition seems to have a courtly element and appears as a measured medieval dance. Arkenstone's interpretation is thus totally different from Shore's exotic Lothlórien.

Enya also interpreted the Lothlórien theme long before she worked on the soundtrack to Peter Jackson's films. Her "Lothlórien" is purely instrumental and dominated by a piano.

The German band Qntal mixes medieval and electronic sounds. In the music video to the operatic song "Von den Elben" (Of the Elves), alchemistic symbols and masked people appear and books are opened. Elves are here represented as a mysterious secret cult with black magical crystal balls. Words like enigma, luna, sol, aqua surround the "Elves" in their lavishly designed masks in the video.

> Von den elben wirt entsen vil manic man
> [...] Swenne ir lichten ougen so verkeren sich
> daz si mir aldureh min herze sen.[23]

---

23 http://www.magistrix.de/lyrics/Qntal/Von-Den-Elben-182650.html
 Many men are enchanted by the Elves
 When the light of their eyes falls on me
 such that they look through my heart.

The song does not speak of Tolkien's Elves, however, but of the Germanic fairy women who were feared for their arts of enchantment. They were certainly an inspiration for Tolkien.[24]

The popular Finnish band Nightwish could not avoid Tolkien's Elves either. "Elvenpath" is a rushed, chaotic song which does not only deal with Elves but a whole armada of different mythical creatures. The only link to Tolkien is a citation from the Bakshi *Lord of the Rings* film about the forging of the rings.[25]

The American artist Jessica Butler also treated Elves as a topic in her music. Butler studied music in California. Her great interest in linguistics led her to learn Sindarin and to write "Elven music". Inspired by Shore's ethereal music, Butler creates melodies that evoke church music. She calls on people to compose Sindarin or Quenya lyrics to her songs.[26] Her music is purely vocal, many-voiced and high-pitched, as if it came from Elves sitting amongst the dizzying heights of mallorn trees. Ethereal, as if floating in another sphere, the octaves of echoing voices unfold. The total renunciation of instruments makes Butler's songs sound more Elvish than most other interpretations.

With instruments, but without voices, Enam re-creates Middle-earth in a similar spheric vein. Irish harp and synthesizer dominate the meditative sounds. The instrumental "Sauron's Dream" refers to Middle-earth's dark side but the dark rumbling and floating tunes of the song, together with the panpipe-like sound, complete the picture of the Elves' magical world and show a glimpse of yet another mystery to which not even the Elves are immune: evil.

Another formation that deals with Tolkien is the band *The Fellowship* from New Zealand. It was founded in 1999 in order to reconstruct the music of the lost

---

24 The same song has been set to music by the Middle-Age band Faun.
25 The elf-folk is calling me | Tapio, Bear-king, Ruler of the forest | Mielikki, Bluecloak, Healer of [...] | The moonwitch took me to a ride on a broomstick | Introduced me to her old friend home gnome | Told me to keep the sauna warm for him | At the grove I met the rest – the folk of my fantasies | Bilbo, Sparhawk, goblins and pixies | Snowman, Willow, trolls and the seven dwarves
http://www.musicsonglyrics.com/N/nightwishlyrics/nightwishelvenpathlyrics.htm
26 As seen in the Quenya song "Ninqueldan" by Arandil Elenion. "Arandil was the first prize winner in the Third Elvish Language Poetry Prize in 1999. The two poems are about a Vanyarin elf who fought in the War of Wrath and after the battle ended guarding the Silmarils and was killed by Maedhros. [...] Arinya losse or lord 'aire (In the morning – snow over the sleeping sea) [...] Eresse Tol-Eresseasse. (Loneliness at the Lone Island.)"
http://www.elvish.org/gwaith/arandil.htm

civilisations of Tolkien's mythology. Their album "In Elven Lands" contains texts in English, Elvish, and Anglo-Saxon. They have also produced a version of "A Elbereth Gilthoniel". Their "hymn" sounds like folk music and could be a traditional song from British/Celtic lands. The same goes for the rest of their songs which are intoned with medieval instruments (e.g. bagpipes) and female voices. The texts directly refer to *The Silmarillion* and deal with different legends, one of them the "Ainulindalë" (music of the Ainur) in "Creation Hymn".

Conclusion

Elvish music is often represented by sacral and meditative elements. Antique instruments allude to the Elves' old age, mystic sounds refer to their nature, complicated soundscapes to their craftsmanship. Women's voices, delicate motifs and harps express the Elvish perfection of which they sing. What especially forms and affects the Elves is also reflected in their musical interpretation: beauty. In spite of all the different interpretations, the motifs share a basic similarity and musical tone: they are all spherical, transcendental, and mystical. They seem to long for countries far away and appear as a deeply moving story. The music thus always underlines the character and the history of the Elves in equal measure.

But the topic "Music of Tolkien's Elves" has not nearly reached its final discussion. Not all bands and solo artists who deal with the topic have been mentioned. The section on "More 'Elvish Musicians'" is much too short to go into the musicians in detail and only serves to give an idea of what has been done. I would also like to mention the field of "medieval music", which is especially lively in Germany. Guillermo del Toro's screen adpatation of *The Hobbit* will create new Elvish themes as well. New compositions about the Elves of Mirkwood are currently being worked on in Germany: In the independent film, *REDBOOK – das Vermächtnis des roten Buches*[27] (working title), the Mirkwod-Elves will play some sort of role. We can look forward to encountering Elves musically in the future.

---

27 Legacy of the Red Book.

About the Author

Mira Sommer has studied German, journalism, sinology and English and is now working as a journalist in print and online media. She has been involved with several film projects (shorts, documentations, feature film). Apart from her studies, she also works artistically as a painter and in applied arts. In 2006, she published her first works (lyric, fiction, technical literature). Her passion for Tolkien includes visits and workshop at Ring*Con, regular visits to the LOTR symphony, work on various Tolkien projects, and roleplay and manufacturing costumes from *The Lord of the Rings* films. She also translated the *Annotated Scores* to the film soundtracks.

Tolkien References

TOLKIEN, J.R.R., *The Book of Lost Tales 1*, (ed. by Christopher Tolkien), New York: Ballantine Books, 1992a.

The Book of Lost Tales 2, (ed. by Christopher Tolkien), New York: Ballantine Books, 1992b.

The Fellowship of the Ring, London: HarperCollins, 1999.

The Hobbit, London: Grafton, 1991.

Roverandom, (ed. by Christina Scull and Wayne G. Hammond), London: HarperCollins, 2002.

Unfinished Tales, (ed. by Christopher Tolkien), London: HarperCollins, 1998.

References

ADAMS, Doug, *Annotated Scores: The Fellowship of the Ring*, PDF New Line Productions Inc., 2005a.

Annotated Scores: The Two Towers, PDF New Line Productions Inc., 2006.

Annotated Scores: The Return of the King, PDF New Line Productions Inc., 2007.

The Complete Recordings, Fellowship of the Ring (booklet), 2005b.

ARDAPEDIA, "Leithian Lied", http://ardapedia.herr-der-ringe-film.de/index.php/Lay_of_Leithian, 27.03.2009.

ARKENSTONE, David, "About David Arkenstone", On: Arkensounds, http://www.davidarkenstone.com/about.html, 22.02.2009.

ASK LYRICS, "Enya – Lothlorien Lyrics", http://www.asklyrics.com/display/Enya/Lothlorien_Lyrics/117692.html, 22.02.2009.

BATTLELORE INTERVIEW Jyri Vahvanen, http://www.morrigans.pit.org/mp/int_battlelore0703.php, 22.02.2009.

BATTLELORE, Homepage, www.battlelore.net, 22.02.2009.

BUTLER, Jessica, http://www.elvish.org/gwaith/j_butler.htm, 27.03.2009.

DAY, David, *Tolkien: The Illustrated Encyclopædia,* New York: Macmillan, 1992.

ENAM, Homepage, http://www.enam.nl/, 27.03.2009.

THE ENCYCLOPEDIA of Arda, "Asëa Aranion", http://www.glyphweb.com/arda/a/aseaaranion.html, 27.03.2009.

GWAITH-i-Phethdain, "Quenya Poems", http://www.elvish.org/gwaith/arandil.htm

LYRICS Download, "Battlelore – Usvainen Rhûn", http://www.lyricsdownload.com/battlelore-usvainen-rhn-lyrics.html, 27.03.2009.

MAGISTRIX, "Qntal – Von den Elben", http://www.magistrix.de/lyrics/Qntal/Von-Den-Elben-182650.html, 27.03.2009.

MUSIC Song Lyrics, "Nightwish Elvenpath lyrics", http://www.musicsonglyrics.com/N/nightwishlyrics/nightwishelvenpathlyrics.htm, 27.03.2009.

SONGMEANINGS, "Elves of Luna", http://www.songmeanings.net/songs/view/3530822107858667765/, 22.02.2009.

"Journey to the Undying Lands Lyrics", http://www.songmeanings.net/songs/view/3530822107858503105/, 22.02.2009.

"Of Orcs and Elves", http://www.songmeanings.net/songs/view/3530822107858678399/, 22.02.2009.

"The Green Maid", http://www.songmeanings.net/songs/view/3530822107858678379/, 22.02.2009.

"Thousand Caves", http://www.songmeanings.net/songs/view/3530822107858678397/, 22.02.2009.

"Valier – Queens of the Valar", http://www.songmeanings.net/songs/view/3530822107858678396/, 22.02.2009.

THEONERING.net, "Soundtrack Analysis, Language in the Lord of the Rings Movie – The Two Towers", www.theonering.net

THE TOLKIEN ENSEMBLE, http://www.tolkien-ensemble.net

WEICHMANN, Christian, "The Lord of the Rings: Complete Songs and Poems", In: *Der Flammifer von Westernis,* no. 27, (2006) 28-30.

WIKIPEDIA, "A Elbereth Gilthoniel", http://en.wikipedia.org/wiki/A_Elbereth_Gilthoniel, 14.06.2009.

"Battlelore", http://de.wikipedia.org/wiki/Battlelore, 22.02.2009.

"Tolkien Ensemble", http://www.wikipedia.de/Tolkien_ensemble, 23.03.2009.

Fabian Geier

Making Texts Audible:
A Workshop Report on Setting Tolkien to Music

Introduction

Two years ago, I was fortunate to be able to devote myself to Tolkien. I therefore decided to read *The Lord of the Rings* in the original again. In doing so, I noticed that I had not previously taken much notice of the poems included in it. As a youthful reader, I had usually skimmed them, and even when I read them *in extenso*, they were hardly accessible to me. For that reason I decided to go about it differently this time, and not to read on from those passages until I had set the poems to music – with the result that I haven't yet finished reading the book. However, the plan was successful up to the chase of the hunters Aragorn, Gimli and Legolas across the plains of Rohan: the music compelled me to read the verses over and over again, to let each word melt in my mouth. Soon I found myself in a thicket of questions and inclinations that expanded into still more basic reflections. The concrete attempts to strike the right note interacted with the general thoughts about the connection of word and sound, the nature of Tolkien's world, and the music it could contain, both possible and impossible. These reflections are the subject of this essay.[1]

The questions that were raised are complex, and not all can be handled briefly. The overriding theme is of course the attribution of styles, sound colour and motifs to peoples, musical keys and individuals. Upon that, such questions are established as the use of tonality and periodic, keys and instruments and the style elements of western musical forms (the only ones I know). I would also like to defend the thesis that it is good that some things are not set to music. Finally, I would like to look at and compare a few other attempts to set Tolkien to music. However, following the line of Aristotele's argument that one should move from the concrete to the general when conveying thoughts, I would like to begin with concrete questions concerning settings.

---

1 Paper is, of course, conceivably unsuitable for the reproduction of musical ideas. I have therefore provided audio files to supplement the musical examples in this essay at the following website: www.vulturis.de/musica_tolkieniana

Peoples

Those who speak of races today, even connoting their intellectual characteristics, quickly find themselves in the pillory. That may be unnecessary as long as it is fiction being considered and only styles and cultural forms, not judgements, are concerned; however, Tolkien's ethnic classifications are indeed associated with intellectual gifts.[2] But however we may judge this morally, for the given purpose it seems to be sensible to delineate the musical boundaries between Dwarves, Men, and Elves more strongly than between the Noldor and Sindar, Gondor and Dale, or Erebor and Moria.

It was perhaps easiest for me to determine a style for the Dwarves, though the development of the music was more time-consuming. A rhythm along the lines of steady hammering seemed ideal to me, which would capture both endurance and stubbornness. Dwarven music should have something relentless, driving, yet not fast, and yet stable as clockwork to it. Drums are therefore appropriate, but no offbeat, rather evenly distributed accentuation, even bordering on monotony. Every beat counts – and this thought should characterise the melodies as well, which meander in notes of equal length beyond the boundaries of measures. This could by all means be complex, i.e. not repetitive, but through-composed[3], and by all means conservative, i.e. tonal and periodic. Dwarvish songs should be quite classical works of art – as if carved in stone. Every note should be exactly fixed. Practice would be complex (time-consuming) and every mistake at a performance would be difficult to pardon. On the other hand, the Elves could then be allowed a certain measure of improvisational scope: every performance of a song would be slightly different, thereby more organic and alive than the fixed constructions of the Dwarves.

---

[2] I am, however, not of the opinion that Tolkien can in any way be described as a protofascist. On this problem see Curry's well-balanced article. As a counter-example compare Guido Schwarz' *Jungfrauen im Nachthemd – Blonde Krieger aus dem Westen*. I have commented on this issue in Geier, *J.R.R. Tolkien*. Incidentally, not blonde but dark hair belongs to Tolkien's ideal of beauty.

[3] With this in mind, the band *Blind Guardian* does come close to my perception of Dwarves. It is likely that they, or heavy metal in general, have influenced my Dwarves. Besides, we can see here why the relationship between certain forms of fantasy and certain forms of heavy metal exists: both have a proximity to the martial and archaic, and both require an unbroken pathos free from irony.

Making Texts Audible

Second Melody of Gimli's Song

The Hobbits – and this is so obvious that the rule should be broken sometime – seem to have an affinity for simple, cheerful melodies. One should be able to learn them without great effort and they should have "hookline" characteristics to stimulate people to sing along. The task, therefore, is to write quasi-folksongs. However, several of them turned out triolic, though I had not planned them that way. Since it happened[4], it seemed good to me – a conceivable possibility that gave the Hobbits a special touch, that no longer sounded too much like German folk songs, yet not more English than I could plausibly claim to be[5].

Melody of the Bath Song

---

4 See the passage "Idea and Realisation" below.
5 At any rate it should be clear that such assignations can at best claim the status of plausibility, not of necessity. Except for a few central issues, one cannot deduce what the music for one or the other people should have been like.

Now for the humans: I can hardly go wrong here – whatever I write is human music. Of course it isn't that simple, if Tolkien's Men are to be distinguished from other peoples. Tolkien says of the humans that their cardinal flaw is pride. They are shorter-lived, less sensitive, but strong and knowledgeable in their own short-sighted way. How does appropriate music sound? Certainly brisk and martial, but lacking the difficult standards of the Dwarves; and certainly homebound, but without the small-mindedness of Hobbits. In this way at least Aragorn's Gondor song was captured, which can be imagined best sung by a small group of guards at sunrise on the pinnacles of Minas Tirith.

Gondor Song

And the Elves? How can a human set a style to music, of which it is explicitly said that it is superior to all that humans can make in aesthetic regard?

Music Beyond the Sound

With this we come to one of the most crucial problems: namely the things that cannot be heard. Music appears in Tolkien's works in the only form in which it is possible for it to occur in a book: as a described sensation. We can only read a depiction of how a character experiences music which cannot be heard by the reader. However, precisely this provides literature with possibilities that go beyond real music. How can sensations be described which the reader could never experience with music heard by himself, or even sensations that are absolutely impossible when listening? For example, how could music be written that is described as follows?

> At first the beauty of the melodies and of the interwoven words in elven-tongues, even though he understood them little, held him in a spell, as soon as he began

to attend to them. Almost it seemed that the words took shape, and visions of far lands and bright things that he had never yet imagined opened out before him; and the firelit hall became like a golden mist above seas of foam that sighed upon the margins of the world. Then the enchantment became more and more dreamlike, until he felt that an endless river of swelling gold and silver was flowing over him, too multitudinous for its pattern to be comprehended; it became part of the throbbing air about him, and it drenched and drowned him. Swiftly he sank under its shining weight into a deep realm of sleep. There he wandered long in a dream of music that turned into running water, and then suddenly into a voice. It seemed to be the voice of Bilbo chanting verses. Faint at first and then clearer ran the words. (*LotR* 306)[6]

In reality the same music can evoke various impressions, depending on the listener and the occasion. With music described in literature it is opposite: the impression is fixed, but not the music that produces it. In this way a kind of music can be described and divined that is greater and more lofty than any real music. It is, by definition, moving or induces one mood or another – and it cannot be disenchanted by music criticism or boredom, for it is not *in concreto* at hand.

This trick of description of literary sensation is not limited to listening, but includes all sensory perceptions and all emotions that can be described with words. Not only can something that is by definition moving be created in this way, but also things that are *per se* impalpable and that stretch the grandeur of the object into infinity. It is this very element of leaving things open that Tolkien uses intensively; he writes of it in a letter to his son Christopher:

> It is the untold stories that are most moving. I think you are moved by Celebrimbor because it conveys a sudden sense of endless untold stories: mountains seen far away, never to be climbed, distant trees (like Niggle's) never to be approached – or if so only to become 'near trees' (unless in Paradise or N[iggle]'s Parish). (*L* 110f)[7]

Freely interpreted: It is the unheard music which is most moving. For exactly this reason I would never set the Music of the Ainur to music and never want to hear it set to music. For the same reason I do not wish to see *The Silmarillion*, which is much more remote and mythic than *The Lord of the Rings*, filmed.

---

6 In my opinion, Hans Bemmann goes too far in *Stein und Flöte* (2008), where he lets characters communicate in the language of music as if it could achieve the informational content of a symblolic, intersubjective language.
7 Tolkien here refers to the story *Leaf by Niggle*, in which he describes an artistic vision that becomes reality, yet despite that reality does not lose the magic of enchantment.

Admittedly, I realise that this is a very idiosyncratic approach. However, it is driven by the fear of objective destruction of the fragile element of the individual imagination by the visual implementation in the film: real pictures engrave themselves into the mind much more deeply than the vague images one has in reading about Elrond, Bilbo or Aragorn. Honestly, who did not see the faces of Peter Jackson's actors when reading the names just now? Whether or not their appearance is appropriate for the roles is not decisive. The point is that mental images achieved by pure reading can give the feeling that any concrete depiction is wrong – because the depiction takes away the magic of vagueness from these mental images. One can have a notion of certain contours when reading, but many further characteristics, all of the surfaces between the contours, remain indefinite. No visualisation is such a comprehensive picture as a genuine perception. One can say that the gaps in a sensual perception are filled with both the predefined impressions by the author and the idiosyncratic associations added by the reader – and out of this comes the impossibility of actually depicting them. It seems that one can find an ally for these thoughts in Tolkien:

> I have not seen anything that immediately recalls niphredil or elanor or alfirin: but that I think is because those imagined flowers are lit by a light that would not be seen ever in a growing plant and cannot be recaptured by paint. Lit by that light, niphredil would be simply a delicate kin of a snowdrop; and elanor a pimpernel (perhaps a little enlarged) growing sun-golden flowers and star-silver ones on the same plant, and sometimes the two combined. (*L* 402)

The same effect is applicable for music, perhaps even more so, since it is usually imagined even more vaguely: almost everyone has a sufficiently clear idea of Elrond's appearance and could perhaps attempt to sketch it. But few have even the vaguest melody in mind when we read, "They began to hum softly" (*LotR* 112).

Still, we must not give up all attempts to set this to music, for the light spoken of by Tolkien is interwoven above all in the realm of the Elves, and more so in the high Elves coming from the blessed realm than in the green Elves. As long as we remain with Middle-earth, Tolkien's world is concrete enough to enable us to think about concrete notes. Yet we must still consider an uncapturable magic to have been in the music of the Elves, and possibly that of the Númenóreans as well. However, this is impossible: either one composes the song or one does not. There is a further possibility though, one frequently used by Tolkien: one declares the concrete realisation as a subsequent transcription. If the attempt to present something that is moving succeeds and one can simultaneously imply that it is only a shallow reflection of the original sublimity (as the sun is said to be only a single fruit of the much more glorious tree of light Laurelin), then something can be sketched that is on the one hand sensual, yet surpasses all of our sensual experience.[8]

The idea of imagining the songs as a transcription came to me for two of the greatest poems in *The Fellowship of the Ring*: the ballad of Gil-Galad (*LotR* 249) and Aragorn's song of Beren and Lúthien (*LotR* 257). The basic idea for both songs originated very quickly – so quickly that I no longer paid much attention to my stylistic guidelines. In this way, something emerged that would definitely not fit into the basic idea for Elven music, as described below. (This is probably what happens, in contrast, to good composers: they achieve an "inner consistency" (*OFS* 138ff), as Tolkien calls it, writing all parts of a cycle in one spirit.) Of course, I could rewrite the songs until they fit. But first of all I would have to part with my primary ideas (which also Tolkien seldom did) and secondly, I was pleased with the results the way they were – so I had to make them plausible in the context of the cycle.

Fortunately this worked out fairly well. Tolkien does not say from whom the songs originate. They cover themes of the First Age, yet could come from the pen of a Human just as well as an Elf. At any rate they are performed here by a Man and that in the common speech of Middle-earth, not an Elvish language. Should they be of Elvish origin, then we can not clearly know just what it is that is Elvish in the present performance.[9] This is something one could only know if familiar with the original.

In this way the song of Beren and Lúthien has become a classical human art song (I imagine that a separation between art and folk music makes little

---

8 Concerning such tricks for producing mysterious inconceivability see the paper "The Magic of Magic", which I wrote for the Tolkien Seminar 2008 in Jena. A preview can be found here: www.vulturis.de/doctrina/libraria
9 Compare Tolkien's comments on the text of Gildor's song: "The singing drew nearer. One clear voice rose now above the others. It was singing in the fair elven-tongue, of which Frodo knew only a little, and the others knew nothing. Yet the sound blending with the melody seemed to shape itself in their thought into words which they only partly understood. This was the song as Frodo heard it." (Tolkien 1981: 114).

sense for Elves[10]). It is without a doubt, the song about which I thought the longest and in most detail (excepting perhaps Gimli's song in Moria, which is, however, less complex), about how to put which melody to which words. There is a Lúthien melody and a Beren melody but otherwise few repetitive parts. At the end the clarity and simplicity of Lúthien's melody is broken harmonically, adjusting to the Human, earthly tragedy of Beren. Could this mirror the sorrow of an Elf over Lúthien's farewell from her people? I do not know.

The situation is similar for the ballad of Gil-Galad: this too could be considered a half-remembered version made by a Human with knowledge of the Elvish song – having the feeling of not being able to quite capture the magic in doing so. Perhaps it is the reproduction of a great Elvish song by Aragorn, who was raised in Rivendell? It is better to leave even this explanation obscure; the fictional music history which one weaves together in such thoughts is no end in itself, but intended to help create a musical conception.

Elven Music

All of these tricks cannot prevent the direct confrontation with Elvish songs that appear in *The Lord of the Rings*. These are not only songs of the Moriquendi who remained in Middle-earth, but also songs of those who have seen the blessed realm Valinor and have been influenced by its light, even though it is lessened after many years in Middle-earth.

It would be legitimate to refuse to set these to music – but then, Tolkien himself did set a High Elven song to music[11]. Moreover this music takes place in Middle-earth. What is real enough to be documented by Hobbits can be set to music. I would not want to make a song of the Vanyar or songs of Valinor audible, but certainly could compose the last sounds of the remaining Noldor, Sindar and Nandor.

---

10 For a long time I doubted that these categories could actually be differentiated. However, it cannot be denied that there is a conscious and rough handling of the many-layered levels of meaning and impression of the musical material. This does not mean that the mixture cannot be very complex at times, and it does not always follow the lines of milieu.
11 Compare Swann/Tolkien, *The Road Goes Ever On*.

Due to the fact that the last two groups had merged by the time of the events of *The Lord of the Rings*, the existing poems can be separated into basically two Elvish styles. Since music usually follows language and the majority of the Nandor adopted Sindarin, we can see Sindarin as the strongest cultural influence in the musical tradition of Lothlórien, the location at which we read most of the Elvish songs.

In comparison with the Sindar, the Noldor are more scientific, therefore more analytically inclined, which gives them a certain spiritual kinship to the Dwarves. The music of the Noldor should then be more like a building, not a river. Speaking without metaphors: the music of the Noldor should have a clearly ordered construction that makes a complex cooperation (interplay) possible, while the music of the Sindar is simpler, yet livelier and more organic. This could be the reason why the Sindar are said to be the better singers, more sensitive and original, since they have never simply reproduced an established piece. Nevertheless, the music of the Noldor should not have the cold sternness of Dwarven quasi-symphonic music and their music should be less different from that of the Sindar than that of the Dwarves. Both Elven music styles should have in common that they do not exhaust themselves in the simple periodics and harmonics and rhythm of Dwarven music. They should not be formally limited and for the same reason both should remain open for improvisation and change. More so than for other peoples, Elven music should be convincing even as solo song without accompaniment.

What difference should there be between the music of the Sindar and the Noldor? One could attempt to connect Tolkien's linguistic aesthetics directly with music. Tolkien emphasised the fact that the assignment of phonetics and meaning did not happen arbitrarily when his languages were created, but had to feel consistent to him[12]. On this basis, it sounds sensible to have the feeling that every word must be sung in a certain way. The idea would be a system in which every root word would have a musical characteristic. This would not need to be so narrow as to assign a certain motif to a word. A certain tendency would suffice, for example, singing diatonically upwards, always being dominant, or including a certain interval or one of two complementary intervals (thirds

---

12 Compare Tolkien, "A Secret Vice".

or sixths, for example). Such tendencies occur almost involuntarily with the rhythm of words and yet they are not as concrete as true motifs, so why not try the same with melodies?

A Elbereth, Gilthoniel

These specified attributions could have developed historically, would live and grow like a language: what was sung as a scale upwards in one century was later perhaps a single leap. In this way a form of music would develop that would be very cognitive and complex and would have the complicated character necessary for the Noldor, yet would be more dynamic than the Dwarves' stone-carved musical monuments. In the meantime, the music of the Sindar could be quite similar stylistically, much freer without the predefined assignments, yet also more indiscriminate. Sindarin song would then sound more beautiful and natural without the constraints, yet also less historically conscious. Tolkien's statement, that the Elves of Valinor consciously continued to develop their languages, whereas that happened unconsciously and uncontrolledly with the Sindar, fits in with this stylistic definition.

In practice, the system has not prospered far as of yet – not to the point where difficulties could arise. This is because there is only one longer Elvish passage[13] in the songs I have so far set to music – and the system can only be assigned to one Elven language, since it is inevitably lost in translation, or can be utilised only in part. Even then I fear that it would soon become too narrow for the meaningful composition of songs that do not simply originate according to a construction kit principle. This leads to a further fundamental problem.

Idea and Realisation

One of the fundamental observations I have made in composing music is that it cannot simply be written according to a guideline, for one cannot reason from the abstract to the concrete. An abstract concept does not tell us how we are to implement it.[14] I want to compose a sad song – but must it be in a minor key? If so, in which key, if in any at all? In 5/4 or 3/4 time? On which note shall I begin? How to continue? All of this and a hundred things more must be decided, yet the guideline that something should sound sad or be complicated, or should characterise the idea of a Dwarven people, does not produce a melody by deduction. More precisely: every melody is as good as another, if it only fulfills the guideline; every single note would be arbitrary and could be a different one as well. Good music, however, gives the feeling that it could not possibly be different.[15]

If specific music is to be more than a random conglomerate sequence of elements, it needs more than an abstract guideline. If only this is fulfilled, like, for example, the described scheme of musical characteristics of single words or the monotonous rhythm of a Dwarven melody, the effect can be very artificial. It is like absolutely wanting to write a song in 5/4 time and then arbitrarily filling the measures just for the sake of filling them. The result of this is usually that any part can be replaced with a different one without affecting the rest of the song.[16] On the contrary, while composing the feeling must ensue that

---

13 One can easily imagine that the Noldor applied their principle in Beleriand to the Sindarin which they had adopted and then declined it for both Elven languages.
14 Compare Geier, *Die Irrelevanz des Wirklichen*.
15 Compare Adorno, *Philosophie der Neuen Musik*.
16 This can be done tendentially. Individual parts of larger works can be challenged. I would advocate a regulative rather than an absolute holism.

one thing results in another (even when the continuation is perhaps a rigorous break). Sometimes one note demands a certain continuation, so that one has the feeling that the song writes itself. This again conforms with Tolkien's idea of the primacy of the immanent fascination of the message of a work of art[17] as well as his aesthetic objectivism: "I have long ceased to invent [...]: I wait till I seem to know what really happened. Or till it writes itself" (*L* 231). It should never appear as if a scheme was only filled with effects.[18]

Of course there are guidelines that can be more easily fulfilled than others. A guideline of mood, for example, that something should be martial or melancholic, leaves many things open, thereby making it easier to simultaneously give the music a harmonious (consistent) independent existence. Guidelines that determine the material strongly are much more difficult, as in the musical characteristic for each word as mentioned above or another idea, with which I experimented for a while: giving each race a preference for a certain interval: Dwarves the pure fifth, Men the fanfare-type fourth, Hobbits melodies that move in seconds, and Elves thirds and sixths. Such mechanical ideas can quickly become obstacles and it would take a better composer than me to create music that still makes sense within such a tight corset.

Individuals

After speaking so much about the general problems of guidelines I would like to return to concrete questions of execution: the setting of individual differences.[19] In the lyrics of *The Lord of the Rings* we repeatedly find passages that are directly associated with one person. This applies especially to Bilbo, who liked to draw attention to himself by reciting his own poetry. This necessitates a particular Bilbo-style, for example in order to differentiate it from that of Aragorn, when they write a song together in Rivendell:

---

17 Tolkien, "On Fairy Stories", 120; compare Geier, "Leaf by Tolkien".
18 Compare "Die Formel ersetzt das Werk. Die übergreifende Idee stiftet Ordnung, nicht Zusammenhang." Adorno/Horkheimer, *Dialektik der Aufklärung*, 134.
19 In the above context these have their place between the concrete and the abstract. As far as the attribution of thoughts and music is concerned, the connection is involuntary or originates in concrete work on the musical material. Inasmuch as the attribution shows up as a permanently assigned motive in other contexts, it becomes an abstract, external guideline for these and must be harmoniously integrated into them.

> 'Well, my dear feallow,' said Bilbo, 'now you've heard the news, can't you spare me a moment? I want your help in something urgent. Elrond says this song of mine is to be finished before the end of the evening, and I am stuck. Let's go off into a corner and polish it up!' Strider smiled. 'Come then!' he said. 'Let me hear it!' (*LotR* 233)

Concerning the result of this cooperation, we read:

> 'What!' cried Bilbo 'You can't tell which parts were mine, and which were the Dúnadan's?' 'It is not easy for us to tell the difference between two mortals,' said the Elf. 'Nonsense, Lindir,' snorted Bilbo. 'If you can't distinguish between a Man and a Hobbit, your judgement is poorer than I imagined. They're as different as peas and apples.' 'Maybe. To sheep other sheep no doubt appear different,' laughed Lindir. (*LotR* 309f)

What could Bilbo's style look like? We need a touch of naivete – something which shows that Bilbo could not quite imagine how crucial Eärendil's deed was. For Bilbo it is perhaps a nice story, like that of St. Nicholas or of St. Martin, though less for children. Then we need Aragorn's careful efforts to improve it. So far I was able to achieve only the first of these influences successfully.

It is generally advisable to differentiate between the styles of individual Hobbits, since they are most frequently also the composers of their own songs. Besides Bilbo's tunes we also have Sam's troll song, for example, and Frodo's elegy on Gandalf. The first of these examples should be set to music in a way that it is typically Hobbitish on the one hand, and yet specifically mirrors Sam's simple and yet somehow gifted nature on the other. The song should have something slightly inappropriate, perhaps an improper enthusiasm for a rhythm or a melody that would not produce such enthusiasm in others. This appears to me to be more difficult than finding a melody for Frodo.

Frodo is certainly one of the most complex characters in *The Lord of the Rings*, especially since he develops so much in the course of the story. He is knowledgeable, sensitive and thoughtful without being one who speaks much about his thoughts. He is not inclined to monologues or the scurrilous, academic personality of Bilbo with its little vanities. On the other hand he is not one of the Wise or a perfect Hobbit – and he knows that. His music should be unassuming, without affectations, without complicated melody lines, without particular ambition. In the case of this particular song, it is especially important because it concerns the loss of his mentor. For one who has a feeling for composition without having much experience, who was also in a melancholy mood after intensive mourning, it seemed right to me to set some long notes at the beginning – as if hesitantly feeling his way into the music, or for the first time raising his voice after a long silence.

Frodo's Lament

Then we even have one case in which the song mirrors the connection with the listener rather than with the composer: when Gimli finishes his song about Durin in Moria, Sam is so impressed that he says: "'I like that! […] I should like to learn it. In Moria, in Khazad-dûm!'" (*LotR* 412). What Sam cites is not, as could be expected, the last line, but the fifth to last. Thus, the song must be composed so that that line is more memorable than the last four lines. It is not by chance that it is the line which includes the name of Moria in Dwarven language, so that it seems to make sense to imagine that Gimli would sing this line more vigorously. This part could be something like this:

Last Stanza Moria Song

Other Paths

These examples should suffice to give some insight into my attempt to read *The Lord of the Rings* by way of setting its poetry to music. My own unsteady steps are not the first and certainly not the last attempt of this kind. The first was Donald Swann's song cycle[20], and the perhaps most ambitious project of this kind was the composition of music for the complete *Lord of the Rings* trilogy by the Tolkien Ensemble over a period of ten years. I made an effort not to listen to any of it while I was working on my own project. Yet afterwards it was fascinating to see which similarities and which differences there are in the settings of the songs. The general question that is interesting here is whether a certain text itself prompts us to set it in a certain way. I would like to remark on that briefly:

Since Swann composed very subtle art songs with piano accompaniment, and there are few overlapping elements with the songs I have set to music, the comparison concerns mostly the settings of the Tolkien Ensemble[21]. I find general similarities in rhythm and dynamics or instrumentation. The former is developed from the rhythm of the words, the latter from their meaning. In this way the Tolkien Ensemble, too, had the idea to construct the middle part of Gimli's songs in Moria after a change of mood more formally and majestically and they, too, used a fiddling violin for "The Man in the Moon". The violin is of course mentioned in the lyrics, but as a matter of fact, for the "The Man in the Moon" we also used an almost identical melody rhythm. This seems natural, since there is less leeway for a fast song suitable for an inn than for a ballad or elegy; it is necessary to stick closely to the rhythm that is given by the text and its emphases.

And the differences? They can be found foremostly in the arrangements, which are generally more fully instrumented than my attempts, which often have to make do with one or no accompanying instrument. In contrast to Swann and

---

20 Swann / Tolkien, *The Road Goes Ever On*.
21 Furthermore there are the film sound tracks of Rosenberg and of Shore, which would merit a discussion of their own, but are not relevant here, since they do not specifically take up the book's lyrics. Additionally there are the song settings in the context of the BBC radio play of *The Lord of the Rings*, to which I did not at this time have access but which are dealt with in the article "Microphones in Middle-earth: Music in the BBC Radio Play" on pages 241-54 of this book.

the Tolkien Ensemble, I did not use long notes for the "Old Walking Song", finding my solution more appropriate for walking, where long notes are difficult to sing steadily. Additionally, I found it important to emphasise certain passages that, in the Tolkien Ensemble, stick with the flow of stanzas and refrain more strongly: the call of Tinúviel in Aragorn's song as well as the line concerning Khazad-Dûm.

On the other hand, the songs of the Ensemble are freer harmonically and often more interesting than mine. In fact, the question of harmonics is important: I tended to use tonality and classic schemata for most songs, employing more daring chords and modulations sparingly. Perhaps that is not entirely inappropriate for Tolkien, since he also utilised archaic stylistic devices and unbroken structures of meaning and he did that during an era of broken subjectivity and avantgardistic art forms. However, this does not mean that one should completely renounce the rich stylistic devices that have been discovered since the Romantic Age. One should only ensure that even dissonance is used in the service of grandeur: it should contribute to the structure of the building and not break it. Also, a simple system of harmony based on cadences may be good for Hobbits, Dwarves and Men, but the Elves should not be limited by such patterns. They should be distinguishable from other peoples in that they can go beyond the simple formalisms of Human art without relinquishing beauty in doing so. However, the possibility of abandoning all harmony at least once and being released from the call of beauty is given in the appearance of the Barrow Wight.

Instrumental Motif Barrow Music. To be played on a piano with distortion pedal

Conclusion

The considerations described above are certainly very idiosyncratic. Though they refer to Tolkien's opinions, they do not mirror them; they cannot even be considered Tolkien scholarship. It would therefore be not entirely wrong to call this project "musical fan fiction". However, the focus was just the opposite of that of many fan projects: I do not want to develop new ideas randomly or as I think best, but to stay as close to the text as possible with my music and to think about it more intensively in order to understand Tolkien's world better. It is also, as I described at the beginning, simply one way to read Tolkien – and hermeneutics teach us that reading has always included a creative element.

About the Author

Fabian Geier studied philosophy, English Linguistics and Literature, Theory of Music, and Education in Heidelberg, Warwick and Würzburg, where he received his Ph.D. in 2006. Currently he is assistant professor (Wissenschaftlicher Assistent) for philosophy at the University of Bamberg, Germany.

Tolkien References

TOLKIEN, J.R.R., "A Secret Vice", In: *The Monsters and the Critics and Other Essays*, (ed. by Christopher Tolkien), London: George Allen & Unwin, 1983.

"Leaf by Niggle", In: *Tales from the Perilous Realm,* London: HarperCollins, 2002.

*The Letters of J.R.R. Tolkien, (*ed. by Humphrey Carpenter with the assistance of Christopher Tolkien), London: HarperCollins, 1995.

The Lord of the Rings, London: Allen & Unwin, 1981.

"On Fairy-Stories", In: *The Monsters and the Critics and Other Essays*, (ed. by Christopher Tolkien), London: George Allen & Unwin, 1983.

The Silmarillion, (ed. by Christopher Tolkien), New York: Houghton Mifflin, 2004.

References

ADORNO, Theodor W., *Philosophie der neuen Musik,* Darmstadt: WBG, 1998.

und Max Horkheimer, *Dialektik der Aufklärung,* Frankfurt a.M.: Fischer, 1988.

BEMMANN, Hans, *Stein und Flöte,* München: Piper, 2008.

CURRY, Patrick, "Tolkien and his Critics: A Critique", In: Thomas Honegger (ed.), *Root and Branch. Approaches towards Understanding Tolkien,* 2nd ed., Zurich and Berne: Walking Tree Publishers, 2005.

GEIER, Fabian, *Die Irrelevanz des Wirklichen,* Freiburg: Alber, 2007.

J.R.R. Tolkien, Hamburg: Rowohlt, 2009.

"Leaf by Tolkien. Annäherungen an Tolkiens Umgang mit Allegorie und Biographie", In: *Hither Shore 4* (2007).

SCHWARZ, Guido: *Jungfrauen im Nachthemd – Blonde Krieger aus dem Westen,* Würzburg: Königshausen & Neumann, 2003.

SWANN, Donald und J.R.R.Tolkien, *The Road Goes Ever On,* rev. ed., London: Allen & Unwin, 1978.

THE TOLKIEN ENSEMBLE and Christopher Lee, *The Lord of the Rings. Complete Songs and Poems,* 4-CD-Set, Membran Music, 2006.

Appendix

Friedhelm Schneidewind

Embodying the Voices: Documentation of a Failure

This brief contribution was originally intended as a complete chapter for this book. Unfortunately I was not able to put together enough material to justify that.

I had set myself an ambitious goal: I wanted to find out if it is possible to deduce the vocal ranges of the various humanoids in Tolkien's works on the basis of their descriptions. I intended to set up a kind of catalogue which would show whether Bilbo should be a tenor, Galadriel a soprano, and Durin or Thorin a deep bass when they sing.

Most people who have composed music for Tolkien's poems have probably considered this question. This applies to the official, legally published compositions[1] as well as to those which originate "in the closet" and are heard only by a close circle of family or friends.[2]

First of all, I found out that there is no uniform opinion on the subject of which vocal range should be assigned to which creature. The spectrum of a Hobbit goes from a deep bass to a boy soprano. The Elves are often sung by tenors or even countertenors, as well as by female voices, yet there are also pieces for low male voices. The Dwarves are frequently given deep parts, but tenors are heard as well. It is this variety that gave me the idea (aside from considerations for my own compositions) that it could be possible to allocate

---

1 I refer here especially to the movies by Peter Jackson, the two radio plays of *The Lord of the Rings* by the BBC (1981) and SWR/WDR (Germany 1991/92), the German radio play of *The Hobbit* (WDR 1980), and the well-known compositions by Donald Swann (1965 ff), the Tolkien Ensemble (1997-2006), and the group "The Starlit Jewels" with Marion Zimmer Bradley (1996).
2 It is permitted to set Tolkien's texts and poems to music. However, it is not permitted to publish those, including public performance, without the permission of those who hold the rights to his works. I know of numerous musicians and groups who have set Tolkien's poems to music without being allowed to perform their works in public. It would be an interesting project to exchange ideas about musical forms and the choice of vocal ranges. Fabian Geier's chapter in this book may provide an impulse for such a discussion.

voice ranges to the various singers according to the conclusions derived from their biology.[3]

My working hypothesis was the idea that it could be possible to classify groups[4] in Middle-earth according to their physical attributes, especially size and weight, and to assign them a vocal range – for example, a deep voice for Dwarves.

However, my attempt was doomed to failure right from the start, due above all to one important factor: it is not easy to extrapolate the voice range of a person from her/his physical constitution. There are too many different parameters involved. For one, there are the simple physical attributes. We can expect the humans of Middle-earth, including Hobbits[5], to resemble us, since Middle-earth is our world. This could be plausible for Elves and Dwarves as well, though not necessarily so in detail.

The human voice is produced by the cooperation of both vocal chords in the larynx and the upper end of the windpipe with the vocal tract, which consists of the open spaces above the vocal folds: throat, mouth, and nose.

The pitch of the fundamental vocal tone is approximately 125 Hz for men, 250 Hz for women, and 440 Hz for children (before voice break) in our western culture. This is due to the different size of the larynx and the length of the vocal tract, which is dependent on the first. These become thicker and longer during voice break so that the average speaking pitch drops approximately an octave for boys and a third for girls.

The vocal range then comprises an average of two octaves and can reach up to three octaves[6]; however, most people cannot utilise the whole range for singing.

---

3 Concerning the biology of the various groups cf. Schneidewind 2005b and Schneidewind 2007.
4 I have previously written about the designation of the different groups as races or species, as well as their degrees of relationship, biological similarities and differences in Schneidewind 2005a and in Schneidewind 2005b; the accusation of racism in Tolkien's works is refuted in Schneidewind 2005a and in Schneidewind 2006a.
5 Hobbits are humans, cf. Schneidewind 2005b and Schneidewind 2007, practically identical to us, for "Middle-earth is our world" ("Mittelerde ist unsere Welt" – Schneidewind 2006b).
6 The complete vocal range, from the lowest still reachable note ("phonic zero", Fischer 114) usually comprises 2½ to 3 octaves for professional singers (ibid. 73). The range of the normal human singing voice goes from C (profound bass – Russian singers are said to achieve an octave lower) to c^3 (soprano). Typical ranges (this can vary up or down, depending on voice type): bass $C-d^1/E-f^1$, baritone $G-F\#^1/Bb-a^1$, tenor $A-b^1/c-d^2$, countertenor/alto $e-e^2/g-g^2$, alto $f-a^2/g-bb^2$, mezzo-soprano $g-b^2$, soprano $c1-c^3$

The range in which a human can produce pleasing tones in the necessary volume, without suffering physiological damage, is called *tessitura*[7] and usually reaches from a fifth above the deepest physiologically possible pitch to approximately a fifth below the highest possible pitch. There are also cultural or technical aberrations as well as voices which are trained to be especially high or low, like the flageolet or the profound bass.[8]

Above all, both cultural and personal idiosyncracies can change the vocal range permanently or temporarily. Polish and German men have a higher average speaking voice than Americans.[9] Average American female voices are lower than those of Japanese women, Swedish female voices are lower than those of American women, and Dutch women have an even lower speaking voice. They reach almost the same vocal range that men have, while Japanese women affect a very high vocal range in order to distinguish themselves acoustically from men. In very polite communication, Japanese women can reach up to 450 Hz, while English women were never recorded at more than 320 Hz. Conversely, British men often speak almost as high as British women, while Japanese men usually speak lower than British men and never reach the vocal range of women.

In the course of time, the perception of vocal quality and the tastes of society change. In the 1940s actresses often spoke with a low voice; Lauren Bacall had to practise a deep timbre for months; Barbara Stanwyck, Katharine Hepburn and many others were allowed to sound brisk, quick-witted, and intelligent, for which a deeper voice was necessary.[10] In the 1950s, women's movie voices became higher again. Overall, women's voices have become lower in the past 50 years, by an average of 23 Hz in Europe from 1945 to 1993.

Personal voice range can change according to a person's general well-being: the more relaxed the vocal folds are, the slower they vibrate and the lower the

---

7 Italian: to tie, to weave, to braid
8 flageolet: the highest register of the human voice, normally used for notes above e^3, usually by women. The highest note ever sung by a man is recorded in the Guiness Book of Records; Adam Lopez sang a $C\#^5$ (4435 Hz), a half-tone above the highest note of a piano.
9 This and the following observations can be read in detail in Karpf's book, which allots this topic a complete chapter. Extensive literary references and sources can also be found there.
10 Interestingly, Liv Tyler, who played Arwen in Peter Jackson's *Lord of the Rings* movies, relates in the Appendices to the *LotR EE DVD* that she affected a lower speaking voice for the role in order to sound like an ageless Elf. Her father, Steven Tyler, did not even recognise her voice when he saw the film, thinking that it had been dubbed by another actress.

fundamental pitch becomes. Tension causes the vocal folds to vibrate more quickly, and the pitch becomes higher. Since persons who are aroused usually speak up to an octave higher, this becomes obvious; we can distinguish between an informational voice and an emotional voice in most persons, sometimes even in the middle of a sentence.[11] There are now management courses in which women learn to speak with a lower voice; some studies have shown that this is considered less emotional, more mature, and more confidence-inspiring. "Serious" newscasters are often trained to use deeper voices, not only in Europe: the best-known female Japanese TV newscaster, Etsuko Komiya, lowered her voice from an average of 223.4 Hz to 202.5 Hz from 1992 to 1995.

Finally there are cultural constraints: white American men, for example, usually utilise a relatively narrow spectrum of their voice range in order not to sound too emotional, or to avoid raising questions concerning their masculinity or sexual preference. This produces a relatively expressionless and emotionless speech pattern. In other subcultures, a much wider voice range is used.[12]

One factor does not affect the voice: the weight class! There are slender and stout singers in all vocal ranges. Size plays no important role either; consider the superb bass-baritone Thomas Quasthoff, who is 132 cm (52") tall!

All of these variables and peculiarities make it clear that it is not possible to determine which vocal range a particular group of people utilised on the basis of their physical characteristics. The great physical and cultural variables make anything possible, from a Hobbit with a profound bass to a Dwarf with a high tenor, from a diminutive Elf with a vigorous alto to a River-daughter with a jubilant soprano.

For that reason my attempt was doomed to failure.

Additionally, the limitations of our knowledge of the biology of beings in Middle-earth made my intention impossible to realise. Though I can extrapolate

---

11 During a guided tour of Sanssouci Palace in Potsdam the guide spoke in a low, relaxed voice, suddenly saw a colleague and called out with a girlish voice, "Hallo Susanne", then carried on in the original pitch.
12 Some known techniques are overtone and undertone singing. In the area of speaking many cultures have a considerable change of pitch in their speech melody. Sometimes the pitch height or word melody even plays an important part in communication, as in Chinese, where it is instrumental in determining the meaning of a word.

that humans of that time, including Dúnedain, Hobbits, and Drúedain, had a biology similar to ours, this would be sheer hypothesis for Elves and Dwarves, considering the history of their origin.[13]

It therefore seemed best to me to abandon the attempt to catalogue voice ranges or determine which should be attributed to groups or persons in Middle-earth.

Still, the attempt was not in vain. Now, on the basis of my investigation, I can justifiably claim: All of us who attempt to compose music to Tolkien's lyrics, to give them what we consider an appropriate musical form, or to interpret them musically, are completely free in our decision concerning their vocal range and pitch.

About the Author

Friedhelm Schneidewind studied biology and informatics and is now a free-lance lecturer, author, publisher and musician living near Heidelberg. He is an expert for mythology and fantastic literature who has published 15 books, among them *Mythologie und phantastische Literatur* ("Mythology and Fantastic Literature" – 2008) and *Das große Tolkien-Lexikon* ("The Big Tolkien Encyclopedia" – 2001), encyclopedias on Harry Potter, dragons, vampires, blood, and religious afterlife experiences, as well as two volumes of stories, two songbooks, and a vampire stage play. He is the founder and leader of the Medieval group "Conventus Tandaradey", with whom he performs Tolkien songs, conducted a Baroque ensemble for 5 years, and served as a flute teacher, organist and choir leader. His earliest compositions for Tolkien's poems are over 20 years old.

References

EGENOLF, Heinrich, *Die menschliche Stimme*, Stuttgart: Paracelsus, 1974.

FISCHER, Peter Michael, *Die Stimme des Sängers,* Stuttgart: Metzler, 1998.

HAEFLINGER, Ernst, *Die Kunst des Gesangs: Geschichte, Technik, Repertoire,* Mainz: Schott, 2000.

KARPF, Anne, *The Human Voice: The Story of a Remarkable Talent,* London: Bloomsbury, 2006.

SCHNEIDEWIND, Friedhelm, "Biologie, Abstammung und Moral", In: Thomas Honegger, Andrew James Johnston, Friedhelm Schneidewind, Frank Weinreich

---

13 cf. Schneidewind 2005b and Schneidewind 2007.

(eds.), *Eine Grammatik der Ethik. Die Aktualität der moralischen Dimension in J.R.R. Tolkiens literarischem Werk*, Saarbrücken: Verlag der Villa Fledermaus, 2005a.

"Biologie, Genetik und Evolution in Mittelerde", In: *Hither Shore 2* (2005b).

"Rassismus bei Tolkien?", In: *Der Flammifer von Westernis*, Nr. 26, Bonn: Deutsche Tolkien-Gesellschaft, 2006a.

"Mittelerde ist unsere Welt", In: Friedhelm Schneidewind, Frank Weinreich (eds.), *Mittelerde ist unsere Welt*, Saarbrücken: Verlag der Villa Fledermaus, 2006b.

"The Biology of Middle-earth", In: Michael D. C. Drout (ed.), *J.R.R. Tolkien Encyclopedia: Scholarship and Critical Assessment,* Oxford: Routledge, 2007.

Afterword

Greater Music Still Shall be Made

This book addresses many different aspects of music in Middle-earth, explored from varying points of view by international authors, whose interests and knowledge give them wide-ranging insights. Like the *Music of the Ainur*, however, it is only a beginning. It is our wish and hope that many readers will be inspired to bring their own specific thoughts and opinions to the topic, adding their variations to this theme.

For those who are interested in supplemental reading we are including a list of those books and internet links of which we know at present.

"The Development of Music for Middle-earth", an essay by David J. Finnamore, http://www.elvenminstrel.com/tolkien/memusic.htm

"Music in Middle-earth", an essay by Gene Hargrove, http://www.phil.unt.edu/~hargrove/music.html

"The Magic of the Minstrels", an essay by Michael Martinez, http://www.merp.com/essays/MichaelMartinez/michaelmartinezsuite101essay45

"The Tolkien Music List", by Chris Seeman, an exhaustive discography which provides an invaluable resource for all who are interested in hearing interpretations of Tolkien's lyrics and themes by musicians of our day, http://www.tolkien-music.com

Matthew Young, *Projecting Tolkien's Musical Worlds: A Study of Musical Affect in Howard Shore's Soundtrack to Lord of the Rings,* Saarbrücken: VDM Verlag Dr. Müller, 2007, ISBN 978-3-8364-2496-7
This published thesis by Matthew Young deals with music as used in Peter Jackson's films. He compares the basic elements of musical meaning to those of other compositions and gives numerous notated examples; there is also a chapter which deals with the music and culture of Middle-earth in general. The slim volume is interesting to read, though its price could discourage some potential readers from purchasing it.

Brad Eden, *The Scholar as Minstrel: Music as a conscious/subconscious element in the works of J.R.R. Tolkien*, will be published by McFarland Press in 2010.

Those who would like to contact the editors, publishers, and/or authors may do so by way of the e-mail addresses provided below. We will be happy to answer questions, discuss controversial points, and learn from others.

Kristine Larsen	Larsen@ccsu.edu
Reuven Naveh	rnaveh@gmail.com
Jonathan McIntosh	jmcintosh@nsa.edu
Steven Linden	steven.linden@yale.edu
Heidi Steimel	heidisteimel@web.de
Norbert Maier	harplantis@gmx.net
Gregory Martin	gjmart@gmail.com
Bradford Lee Eden	eden@library.ucsb.edu
Julian Eilmann	julianeilmann@web.de
Murray Smith	mjsmith@tcd.ie
Michael Cunningham	vargeisa@ntlworld.com
Paul Smith	countertenor@gmail.com
Mira Sommer	mirasommer@yahoo.de
Fabian Geier	fabian.geier@uni-bamberg.de
Friedhelm Schneidewind	autor@friedhelm-schneidewind.de
Walking Tree Publishers	info@walking-tree.org

Afterword

Would you like to exchange opinions, thoughts and ideas on this topic with other readers and fans of Tolkien's works? You're welcome to read about and discuss Music in Middle-earth on the Barrow-Downs forum, where there is an area devoted especially to this book.

http://forum.barrowdowns.com/forumdisplay.php?f=44

Though we realize that compositions based on copyrighted material are problematic when it comes to publishing (see page 291, footnote 2 in this volume for general information concerning copyright), we hope that many of Tolkien's readers are inspired to their own musical subcreation.

We look forward to discovering new melodies, both literally and figuratively, in the Great Music.

EDITION STEIN UND BAUM

Fach-, Sach- und belletristische Publikationen
zu Tolkien und phantastischer Literatur
VERLAG DER VILLA FLEDERMAUS
Lektorat und Herausgeber: Dr. Frank Weinreich,
Prof. Dr. Thomas Honegger · ISSN 1860-9252

This book is simultaneously released in German as *Musik in Mittelerde* by "STEIN UND BAUM EDITION", a branch of the VILLA FLEDERMAUS PUBLISHERS.

Dieses Buch ist zeitgleich erschienen als *Musik in Mittelerde* in der EDITION STEIN UND BAUM.

ISBN 978-3-932683-14-5 · 2010 · 20 Euro

Thomas Honegger, Andrew James Johnston, Friedhelm Schneidewind, Frank Weinreich: *Eine Grammatik der Ethik. Die Aktualität der moralischen Dimension in J. R. R. Tolkiens literarischem Werk*

160 Seiten · 2005 · ISBN 978-3-932683-11-4 · 20 Euro

Vier ausgewiesene Tolkienfachleute zeigen, dass in Tolkiens Werk weltanschaulich weitgehend neutrale, sehr moderne ethische Überzeugungen vertreten werden. Ergänzend finden sich ein Überblick über die Sekundärliteratur und Beispiele der Instrumentalisierung von Mittelerde.

»... durchaus überzeugend ... Bei der weiteren Diskussion wird man an diesem Buch nicht vorbeigehen dürfen.« Prof. Dieter Petzold

»... überzeugenden Entwurf zur Ethik in Mittelerde vorgelegt ... kann so das Thema auf sehr unterschiedliche Weise erhellen.« Thomas Fornet-Ponse

Friedhelm Schneidewind, Frank Weinreich (Hrsg.):

Mittelerde ist unsere Welt. Wie es »wirklich« war.
Anthologie mit 18 Texten von 7 Autorinnen und 3 Autoren
224 S. · 2006 · ISBN 978-3-932683-12-1 · 20 Euro

Von den kleinen Leuten.
Über Halblinge, Zwerge und andere (zu) kurz Gekommene
Anthologie mit 15 Texten von 7 Autorinnen und 2 Autoren
188 S. · 2008 · ISBN 978-3-932683-13-8 · 20 Euro

VERLAG UND PRODUKTIONSGESELLSCHAFT
HELGA SCHNEIDEWIND – VILLA FLEDERMAUS
Schlossgasse 51 · 69502 Hemsbach (Germany) · info@villa-fledermaus.de
WWW.VILLA-FLEDERMAUS.DE · WWW.STEIN-UND-BAUM.DE

Walking Tree Publishers

Walking Tree Publishers was founded in 1997 as a forum for publication of material (books, videos, CDs, etc.) related to Tolkien and Middle-earth studies. Manuscripts and project proposals can be submitted to the board of editors (please include an SAE):

Walking Tree Publishers
CH-3052 Zollikofen
Switzerland
e-mail: info@walking-tree.org
http://www.walking-tree.org

Cormarë Series

The *Cormarë Series* has been the first series of studies dedicated exclusively to the exploration of Tolkien's work. Its focus is on papers and studies from a wide range of scholarly approaches. The series comprises monographs, thematic collections of essays, conference volumes, and reprints of important yet no longer (easily) accessible papers by leading scholars in the field. Manuscripts and project proposals are evaluated by members of an independent board of advisors who support the series editors in their endeavour to provide the readers with qualitatively superior yet accessible studies on Tolkien and his work.

News from the Shire and Beyond. Studies on Tolkien
Peter Buchs and Thomas Honegger (eds.), Zurich and Berne 2004, Reprint, First edition 1997 (Cormarë Series 1), ISBN 978-3-9521424-0-0

Root and Branch. Approaches Towards Understanding Tolkien
Thomas Honegger (ed.), Zurich and Berne 2005, Reprint, First edition 1999 (Cormarë Series 2), ISBN 978-3-905703-01-6

Richard Sturch, *Four Christian Fantasists. A Study of the Fantastic Writings of George MacDonald, Charles Williams, C. S. Lewis and J.R.R. Tolkien*
Zurich and Berne 2007, Reprint, First edition 2001 (Cormarë Series 3), ISBN 978-3-905703-04-7

Tolkien in Translation
Thomas Honegger (ed.), Zurich and Berne 2003 (Cormarë Series 4), ISBN 978-3-9521424-6-2

Mark T. Hooker, *Tolkien Through Russian Eyes*
Zurich and Berne 2003 (Cormarë Series 5), ISBN 978-3-9521424-7-9

Translating Tolkien: Text and Film
Thomas Honegger (ed.), Zurich and Jena, Reprint forthcoming, First edition 2004 (Cormarë Series 6), ISBN 978-3-905703-16-0

Christopher Garbowski, *Recovery and Transcendence for the Contemporary Mythmaker. The Spiritual Dimension in the Works of J.R.R. Tolkien*
Zurich and Berne 2004, Reprint, First Edition by Marie Curie Sklodowska, University Press, Lublin 2000, (Cormarë Series 7), ISBN 978-3-9521424-8-6

Reconsidering Tolkien
Thomas Honegger (ed.), Zurich and Berne 2005 (Cormarë Series 8),
ISBN 978-3-905703-00-9

Tolkien and Modernity 1
Frank Weinreich and Thomas Honegger (eds.), Zurich and Berne 2006 (Cormarë Series 9), ISBN 978-3-905703-02-3

Tolkien and Modernity 2
Thomas Honegger and Frank Weinreich (eds.), Zurich and Berne 2006 (Cormarë Series 10), ISBN 978-3-905703-03-0

Tom Shippey, *Roots and Branches. Selected Papers on Tolkien by Tom Shippey*
Zurich and Berne 2007 (Cormarë Series 11), ISBN 978-3-905703-05-4

Ross Smith, *Inside Language. Linguistic and Aesthetic Theory in Tolkien*
Zurich and Berne 2007 (Cormarë Series 12), ISBN 978-3-905703-06-1

How We Became Middle-earth. A Collection of Essays on The Lord of the Rings
Adam Lam and Nataliya Oryshchuk (eds.), Zurich and Berne 2007 (Cormarë Series 13), ISBN 978-3-905703-07-8

Myth and Magic. Art According to the Inklings
Eduardo Segura and Thomas Honegger (eds.), Zurich and Berne 2007 (Cormarë Series 14), ISBN 978-3-905703-08-5

The Silmarillion - Thirty Years On
Allan Turner (ed.), Zurich and Berne 2007 (Cormarë Series 15),
ISBN 978-3-905703-10-8

Martin Simonson, *The Lord of the Rings and the Western Narrative Tradition*
Zurich and Jena 2008 (Cormarë Series 16), ISBN 978-3-905703-09-2

Tolkien's Shorter Works. Proceedings of the 4th Seminar of the Deutsche Tolkien Gesellschaft & Walking Tree Publishers Decennial Conference
Margaret Hiley and Frank Weinreich (eds.), Zurich and Jena 2008 (Cormarë Series 17), ISBN 978-3-905703-11-5

Tolkien's The Lord of the Rings: Sources of Inspiration
Stratford Caldecott and Thomas Honegger (eds.), Zurich and Jena 2008 (Cormarë Series 18), ISBN 978-3-905703-12-2

J.S. Ryan, *Tolkien's View: Windows into his World*
Zurich and Jena 2009 (Cormarë Series 19), ISBN 978-3-905703-13-9

Music in Middle-earth
Heidi Steimel and Friedhelm Schneidewind (eds.), Zurich and Jena 2010 (Cormarë Series 20), ISBN 978-3-905703-14-6

Liam Campbell, *The Ecological Augury in the Works of J.R.R. Tolkien*
Zurich and Jena, forthcoming

Constructions of Authorship in and around the Works of J.R.R. Tolkien
Judith Klinger (ed.), Zurich and Jena, forthcoming

Rainer Nagel, *Hobbit Place-names. A Linguistic Excursion through the Shire*
Zurich and Jena, forthcoming

Collector's Edition

Beowulf and the Dragon
Old English text with translation, illustrated by Anke Eissmann, introduction by Tom Shippey, Zurich and Jena 2009, ISBN 978-3-905703-17-7

Tales of Yore Series

The *Tales of Yore Series* grew out of the desire to share Kay Woollard's whimsical stories and drawings with a wider audience. The series aims at providing a platform for qualitatively superior fiction with a clear link to Tolkien's world.

Kay Woollard, *The Terror of Tatty Walk. A Frightener*
CD and Booklet, Zurich and Berne 2000 (Tales of Yore Series 1)
ISBN 978-3-9521424-2-4

Kay Woollard, *Wilmot's Very Strange Stone or What came of building "snobbits"*
CD and booklet, Zurich and Berne 2001 (Tales of Yore Series 2)
ISBN 978-3-9521424-4-8

www.ingramcontent.com/pod-product-compliance
Lightning Source LLC
Chambersburg PA
CBHW070722160426
43192CB00009B/1283